# The Concept of World
# from Kant to Derrida

# The Concept of World from Kant to Derrida

Sean Gaston

ROWMAN &
LITTLEFIELD
INTERNATIONAL
London • New York

Published by Rowman & Littlefield International, Ltd.
16 Carlisle Street, London, W1D 3BT
www.rowmaninternational.com

Rowman & Littlefield International, Ltd. is an affiliate of Rowman & Littlefield
4501 Forbes Boulevard, Suite 200, Lanham, Maryland 20706, USA
With additional offices in Boulder, New York, Toronto (Canada), and Plymouth (UK)
www.rowman.com

**British Library Cataloguing in Publication Information Available**
A catalogue record for this book is available from the British Library

ISBN: HB 978-1-7834-8000-5
 PB 978-1-7834-8001-2

**Library of Congress Cataloging-in-Publication Data**
Gaston, Sean.
 The concept of world from Kant to Derrida / Sean Gaston.
  pages cm
 Includes bibliographical references and index.
 ISBN 978-1-78348-000-5 (cloth : alk. paper)—ISBN 978-1-78348-001-2 (pbk. : alk.
paper)—ISBN 978-1-78348-002-9 (electronic)  1. Metaphysics.  I. Title.
 BD111.G38 2013
 110—dc23                                      2013015821

∞™ The paper used in this publication meets the minimum requirements of
American National Standard for Information Sciences—Permanence of Paper
for Printed Library Materials, ANSI/NISO Z39.48-1992.

Printed in the United States of America

# Contents

# Acknowledgements

This project began in earnest in 2009 and I am grateful to William Leahy, Head of the School of Arts at Brunel University (London), for supporting my application for research leave in 2010. I have also received constant encouragement from my colleague William Watkin at Brunel. I am grateful to the staff of the Upper Reading Room of the Bodleian Library and of the Taylorian Institute at the University of Oxford for their ready assistance and would like to pay tribute to the late and much lamented Vera Ryhaljo who worked for many years in the Upper Reading Room. I also owe a great debt to Sarah Campbell for seeing this work through the press. Jane Brown has graciously allowed me to use one of her exquisite photographs for the front cover. For those who are interested in the work of this remarkable photographer, see www.janebrownphotography.com.

An earlier version of "Derrida and the End of the World" first appeared in *New Literary History* 42, no. 3 (2011). I would like to thank Rita Felski and Johns Hopkins University Press for allowing me to include this material. A slightly longer version of "Derrida and the Eco-Polemicists" was also published in *Paragraph* 36, no. 3 (2013). Kevin Hart of the University of Virginia kindly offered very constructive comments on earlier drafts of this work. I am also grateful to Peter Otto of the University of Melbourne for his judicious advice and for his own remarkable work *Multiplying Worlds* (2011), which encouraged me to address the problem of world. My old friend Stephen Farrow was an early and much appreciated reader.

This work is dedicated to my friend Tony Birch from Melbourne, ex-fireman, historian, poet, photographer, museum curator, political agitator, academic, short story writer and novelist. Everything else is for Carmella Elan-Gaston.

# Preface

## Writing on the World

**I**

In the mid-eighteenth century metaphysics was broadly understood as the study of three areas of philosophical thought: theology, cosmology and psychology. It is commonly recognized that throughout the nineteenth and twentieth century philosophy first challenged the place of God as the centre of all things and then turned to the status and claims of the self. This book is concerned with the fortunes of the third of these formidable metaphysical concepts, the world. Its aim is to provide a clear and concise account of this field of philosophical investigation from the middle of the eighteenth century to the end of the twentieth century and to explore the possibilities and limitations of the concept of world.

Obviously the scope of such an enterprise would far exceed this book without some selections and exclusions. I have chosen to concentrate on the history of Western, Continental philosophy and have limited myself as far as possible to five principal thinkers noted for their distinctive concepts of world: Immanuel Kant (1724–1804), G. W. F. Hegel (1770–1831), Edmund Husserl (1859–1938), Martin Heidegger (1889–1976) and Jacques Derrida (1930–2004). If the scope of this project were to provide a comprehensive examination of world, I would have included whole chapters on Arthur Schopenhauer (1788–1860), Friedrich Nietzsche (1844–1900) and Maurice Merleau-Ponty (1908–1961) as well as an extended discussion of the more recent work of Jean-Luc Nancy (1904–).[1] However, the five philosophers that I have focused on work within a shared tradition of problems which begin with Kant's reaction to traditional metaphysics and culminate with Derrida addressing the problem of world in the wake of Husserl and Heidegger. Clearly a book could be written on how each of these five philosophers treats the concept of world and I have had to make some judicious if rather severe choices. At the same time, there is an evident tradition of common gestures, motifs and problems that arise from Kant to Derrida in writing on the world.

The concept of world raises the problem of how one deals with what is always already there—the world—and to what extent one gives the subject the power to shape or to constitute a world or many worlds of its own. The concept of world also brings attention to the possibility of a discrete domain, realm or sphere. Since Plato, philosophy has relied on the assertion of such world-like concepts that do not describe the world or my world but a distinct conceptual domain. As will soon become apparent, these three types of world—the world, my world and a contained world-like domain—are often difficult to distinguish.

Beyond the broader issues that concepts of world raise in relation to the object and the subject and the attempts in the twentieth century to move beyond these traditional designations, world also presents the need to establish an essential difference between what is merely *in* the world and the assertion of a unique vantage point or wider perspective of the world *as a whole*. The five philosophers that I look at all attempt to establish new grounds for seeing the world as a whole. Nonetheless, from Kant to Derrida philosophy has been driven by the familiar but difficult imperative to be truly and authentically *in* the world while also searching for the most reliable vantage point above and beyond the world *as a whole*. The history of philosophy shows us that philosophy not only requires world-like discrete concepts or clear structures of containment but that it also needs the secular equivalent of a god-like vantage point from which one can sufficiently stand back from the world itself and judge it as a whole.

Though concepts of world have been a part of Western philosophy since the biblical and classical period—there are countless references to *haolam*, *kósmos*, *mundus*, *orbis*, *universitas*—there has been relatively little scholarly attention to the concept of world itself.[2] Not least at a time when the concept of world has been given a new scope in recent ideas of globalization and when the earth itself has become the focus of an urgent ecological imperative, there is need for a more comprehensive account of the history of the concept of world.[3] While this book is not directly concerned with the politics of globalization or with the various forms of environmental, geographical and ecological writings on the present perilous state of the planet, it is hoped that it will be of use in challenging the often seemingly self-evident and ahistorical use of concepts of world.

Finally, this account of the concept of world can also be called a *critique* in the sense that on occasion—and particularly in the fifth and sixth chapters—it questions the self-evident use of the concept of world in philosophy. A critique of the concept of world tests and challenges the implicit designation of some kind of perfectly discrete realm, sphere or domain and the all-too-ready acceptance of a seemingly unavoidable logic of containment that has its origins in the classical tradition. A critique also draws attention to the often very limited grounds upon which a world-like perspective of the world as a whole claims to oversee a highly determined concept of world. The tradition of necessary distinctions and containments may not be dispensed with, but it can be complicated. This book also asks whether one can indeed move beyond the need for a world-like vantage point to maintain a concept of world. From Kant to the present day this concept has been a problem for philosophy, and it remains to be seen if we need a new Copernican revolution when it comes to the concept of world.

## II

While the opening section of the first chapter offers an introduction to the terms and frameworks that will be used throughout the book, a brief overview of the following chapters will be of some help. Chapter 1 starts by examining the history of the concept of the metaphysical world from Plato and Aristotle to Kant's pre-critical writings. The metaphysical world assumes that there is a timeless essence and ordered whole that supports all concepts of world, from the physical universe to the designation of discrete realms such as the sensible world and the intelligible world. In the *Critique of Pure Reason*, Kant challenged the presumption of treating the concept of world as something that is self-evident on either traditional empirical or rational grounds. In forming the regulative world as an instance of reason providing a systematic and unified *idea* for what remains beyond our possible experience—the experience of the world *as a whole*—Kant removes the concept of world from its metaphysical and ontological foundations. At the same time, rather than leaving us with the rather fragile but quite revolutionary possibility that we can do no more than act *as if* there is a world as whole for us, Kant asserts that there is a moral or categorical world that has the same objective authority—if not different epistemological grounds—as the metaphysical world.

Chapter 2 is concerned with Hegel's attempts to establish a more secure concept of a categorical world without recourse to the Kantian regulative world, which he sees as overly subjective. However, like Kant, in his principal works—the *Phenomenology of Spirit* and the *Science of Logic*—Hegel is unable to start with a concept or idea of world. The world as a mere appearance can only be countered when consciousness takes itself as its own object and rises to a sufficient level of objectivity that it can recognize the world *as* spirit. For Hegel, it is only when the world is taken as spirit that one can grasp the *actual* world. This allows Hegel to treat world as the retrospective possibility of all the discrete shapes and developmental stages of the *Phenomenology*. However, as the *Philosophy of Nature* and the *Philosophy of Mind* suggest, this also creates the problem of a concept of world that is least apparent in nature and for animals and most apparent in the difference between the human soul and the spirit. Hegel attempted to counteract this narrowing of the concept of world through his later emphasis on world-history, which should allow us to grasp the teleology of the world as a whole. The reading of Hegel in the twentieth century is also addressed in some detail at the start of chapter 6.

Chapter 3 turns to Husserl's remarkable attempts to reconstitute the traditional relation between subject and object through the phenomenological world. While arguing in *Ideas Pertaining to a Pure Phenomenology and to a Phenomenological Philosophy: First Book* for a suspension of the "natural attitude" to the world in the name of discerning a more refined notion of the shifting mobility, varied contexts and ontological realities of perception, in *Ideas Pertaining to a Pure Phenomenology and to a Phenomenological Philosophy: Second Book* Husserl attempts to establish the primacy of the spiritual world through demarcating the phenomenological differences between the body, the soul and spirit. In his later work, Husserl elaborates the dynamic connection between coexisting phenomenological worlds and the life-world, which provides a larger scope and common ground of possibility for the self, the world and the human sciences. In contrast to Kant and Hegel, Husserl explicitly starts with the world but he also begins with a transcendental subject that already constitutes the phenomenological world.

Chapter 4 begins with an examination of Heidegger's very influential account of being-in-the-world in *Being and Time*. Being-in-the-world is concerned with the world not as a concept but as a phenomenon, which Heidegger places beyond the traditional relation of the subject and object as well as the seemingly self-evident boundaries of the internal and external. He also situates the phenomenon of world within a series of contextual or immersive structures that ultimately give Dasein a world-like perspective of the world as a whole. While Heidegger insists that world cannot simply be understood by what is merely in the world, he also argues that the traditional search for a vantage point above and beyond the world is a source of profound anxiety.

Heidegger's acknowledgement that world is still a problem after *Being and Time* is apparent in the extraordinarily condensed treatment of the conceptual or historical world in "On the Essence of Ground." Heidegger's later analysis of the comparative world in *The Fundamental Concepts of Metaphysics* highlights his difficulties in securing a vantage point of the world as a whole through distinguishing the unique claims of human Dasein on the world from those of the animal and the stone.

Chapter 5 addresses the importance of the concept of world in Derrida's thought. In his early work, Derrida criticizes the use of language in the idealization of the spatio-temporal world in Husserlian phenomenology. At the same time, throughout his work Derrida also relies on a Husserlian perspective of the world as a whole, first articulated by Eugen Fink (1905–1975), to register the ethical relation to the other *as* other and to the death of the other as the "origin" or "end" of the world. On the other hand, in his readings of the Kantian regulative world, Derrida addresses both the distinct political status of the concept of world that is not the earth or the globe and the unavoidable fictions that arise from the assertion of opening or closing discrete, world-like spheres, domains or realms. Derrida's reading of the unconditioned in Kant also allows us to think of the possibilities—and the limitations—of a concept of world beyond the logic of containment. While it may be possible to think of world without a unifying or overarching horizon, Derrida's work suggests that the celebration of the world as absolutely uncontained gives it an idealized and limited status. With his notion of the play of the world—inspired chiefly by Nietzsche—and an extended reading of Heidegger's comparative world, which excludes animals from world, Derrida suggests the possibility of a cohabitation of the world that is *uncontained without being absolutely uncontained*.

Having examined various philosophical attempts in the twentieth century to rethink the concept of world beyond its limitations as a mere subject-oriented object or an idealized structure of containment, I turn in chapter 6 to some related and more contemporary problems. The chapter is divided into three sections: the first section examines the relation between the philosophical concept of world and the status of world in literary fictions; the second section turns to the recent ecological interest in the earth and its effect on the concept of world; and the final section addresses the attempts to construct a philosophy without world.

The first section of chapter 6 returns to Hegel and the celebrated readings of the *Phenomenology of Spirit* by Alexandre Kojève (1902–1968) and Jean Hyppolite (1907–1968), which display the interpolation of both an apparently self-evident concept of world and a pointed critique of literature. One can contrast this to Maurice Blanchot's remarkable 1949 essay "Literature and the Right to Death," which offers a rereading of Hegel to chart the relation between language and literature. Blanchot (1907–2003) suggests that the elusive search for a hermetic fictional world can be used to challenge the philosophical concept of world. At the same time, Blanchot's critique of the world as a sustained discrete sphere or a secure vantage point of the whole does not offer an alternative concept of world: it merely registers its impossibility.

The second section of chapter 6 examines recent readings of Derrida's work in relation to climate change. Faced with the impasse of the philosophical world, with all its conventions, limitations and problems, there is always the temptation to find a radical alternative, to search for a non-world. I argue that this earth-centred criticism of Derrida's work is in danger of generating both a very limited concept of world and of treating the earth as the idealized other of philosophy.

The third section of chapter 6 brings the book to a close with a brief account of the lure of the *sans monde* or the temptation to construct a philosophy *without world*. As much as it is tempting to treat the concept of world as no more than a metaphysical conceit or a heuristic fiction, attempts to construct a philosophy without world are always reliant on preexisting concepts of world. The search for a philosophy without world is the irrepressible dream of a transcendental immersion beyond words.

February 2013

CHAPTER ONE

# The Kantian World

## 1. The Metaphysical World

On April 12, 1961, the Russian cosmonaut Yuri Gagarin became the first human being to orbit the earth. Seven years later, the Apollo 8 mission in December 1968 was the first manned spaceflight to produce an image of the earth from the lunar orbit. In this striking photograph, the upper half of the earth is visible surrounded by black space. This would be followed during the Apollo 11 mission in July 1969 by the first images of the earth taken from the surface of the moon. The famous so-called blue marble photo of the earth, when it was seen for the first time as a complete sphere, appeared in 1972 during the Apollo 17 mission. It is perhaps surprising to recall that it is only in the last forty years that we have been able to see the earth as a whole. From Gagarin to Apollo 17, the earth became a visible object that could be encircled. To use William Blake's phrase from the late eighteenth century, which he attributes to the labour of a god-like reason, after Gagarin we became "englob'd."[1] Even without the recent emphasis on globalization or global climate change, which were no doubt given a tangible authority by these famous images from the 1960s and early 1970s, one could treat this visualization of the earth from afar as the Copernican revolution of the twentieth century. Today we can all encircle the globe.

In 1781, 180 years before Yuri Gagarin's flight, Immanuel Kant had argued in the *Critique of Pure Reason* for his own Copernican revolution. For Kant, the significance of the hypothesis that the earth rotates around the sun was that Copernicus formulated it "in a manner contradictory to the senses

1

yet true" by seeking "for the observed movements not in the objects of the heavens but in their observer."[2] Kant compared the project of critical philosophy to a Copernican revolution, insisting that we should not start with the object as given but with how it is possible that we can experience and understand the object.[3] This displacement of the priority of the object in philosophy was not simply a rejection of empiricism, which had become a recognized philosophical tradition since the publication of John Locke's *Essay Concerning Human Understanding* in 1690. Kant's work was primarily focused on challenging the assumptions and impasses of metaphysics "as a wholly isolated speculative cognition of reason that elevates itself above all instruction from experience."[4] Kant's critical philosophy was devoted to challenging the excessive claims of both empiricism and rationalism. He would attempt to find a new middle way between these competing philosophical perspectives.

As much as Gagarin's circumvention of the earth ushered in a new era—the significance of which is still being formulated today—Kant's critical philosophy would profoundly change the understanding of the concept of world in the history of philosophy. In the nineteenth century, Hegel, Schopenhauer and Nietzsche would all argue for a new concept of world in reaction to critical philosophy. Indeed, Schopenhauer described the works of Kant as "the most important phenomenon to emerge in philosophy over the past two thousand years" and then devoted over a hundred pages to a sustained critique of Kantian philosophy at the end of the first volume of *The World as Will and Representation* (1818).[5]

The refutation of the Kantian concept of a world that is confined and regulated by transcendental idealism would prompt the search throughout the nineteenth century for the concept of world itself, whether this was in the name of the world as spirit (Hegel), of the world as will and representation (Schopenhauer), or of the play of the world (Nietzsche).[6] The reaction against Kant would continue into the first half of the twentieth century, most strikingly in the work of Husserl and Heidegger. In making the case for a more original life-world, Husserl argued that Kant had "never penetrated" the enigma of the world.[7] Heidegger's criticisms of Kant as he formulated the influential notion of being-in-the-world were clear and emphatic. He argued that Kant had failed "to recognize the phenomenon of world and to clarify the concept of world."[8] In this opening chapter, I will explore in detail three very different formulations of world in Kant's work: the metaphysical world, the regulative world and the categorical world.

We all broadly know what the concepts of planet, earth and world mean: the planet is a celestial, rocky or gaseous body; the earth is the name for our planet as well as its ground, surface, sea and soil; and world is used to describe, variously, a planet, the earth or a part of the earth, human existence, human action and human thought. Not least from its ability to stand at times for both the earth itself and for what is on the earth or indeed in the purview of one individual, the concept of world has always had a great deal of latitude: it can be at once geographical and intellectual. This latitude is part of what makes world an integral but elusive concept in the history of philosophy. World is clearly something more than a planet and the earth. This is why Kant also includes world in the trinity of transcendental ideas (the soul, the world and God) that have led pure reason into its own metaphysical delusions and dogmas.[9] Perhaps somewhat too easily, Gilles Deleuze attempted to signal the end of this metaphysical tradition in the *Logic of Sense* (1969)—published in the year of the moon landing—by describing the trinity of these "great terminal ideas" as "the Grand Canyon of the world, the 'crack' of the self, and the dismembering of God."[10]

## An Ordered Whole

We are fortunate to have extensive student notes from nearly thirty years of Kant's lectures on metaphysics, which gives us an insight into the concept of world that he was questioning in the *Critique of Pure Reason*.[11] In these lectures, Kant is concerned with the philosophy of cosmology (*Weltwissenschaft*), and his most likely source is Alexander Baumgarten's *Metaphysica* (1738), which was influenced by the ideas of Christian Wolff, who had in turn formed his own philosophy through reading the then available works of Gottfried Leibniz.[12] Both Baumgarten and Wolff rely on the very traditional metaphysical distinction between the sensible world (*mundus sensibilis*) and the intelligible world (*mundus intelligibilis*).[13] One can trace this metaphysical treatment of world back to Plato and Aristotle.

In classical Greece, *kósmos* had a number of varied meanings, including ornament or decoration, but was broadly defined as an ordering or arranging that referred at times to the universe and at other times to the world. We might say that *kósmos* is an *ordered whole* or a world that is ordered and contained by the universe. Plato gives us one of the most orthodox accounts of *kósmos* in the *Gorgias*, when Socrates remarks,

> In fact, Callicles, the experts' opinion is that co-operation, love, order, discipline, and justice bind heaven and earth, gods and men. That's why they call the universe an ordered whole [*kósmos*], my friend, rather than a disorderly [*akosmosían*] mass or an unruly shambles.[14]

The notion of *kósmos* as an ordered whole is still retained in the sense of cosmology as a rational account (*lógos*) of the world (*kósmos*). Diogenes Laertius reports that Pythagoras was most likely "the first to call the heaven the universe [*kósmon*]."[15]

The *Metaphysics*, Aristotle's collection of drafts and students' notes on first philosophy, was devoted in part to trying to find an accurate definition of substance or *ousia*.[16] Aristotelian substance is a general essence that is found to be first or prior to anything else.[17] Substance precedes any combination of form and matter and indicates that which is entirely "in itself."[18] If the universe as a whole has a primary substance, this substance must be eternal and actual.[19] There must also be an eternal form "that moves without being moved" and which in turn gives rise to the spatial and material movements of the heavens and nature.[20] This first or Prime Mover allows us to treat the universe as an eternal and ordered whole (*kósmos*).[21] The *Metaphysics* would create the framework for the later medieval scholastic tradition of placing theology at the heart of metaphysical cosmology. As David Hume dryly observed in his *Dialogues Concerning Natural Religion* (1779), "Whatever cavils may be urged, an orderly world, as well as a coherent, articulate speech, will still be received as an incontestable proof of design and intention."[22]

The *Metaphysics* also reinforced the need to think of the world within what we can call a pervasive *logic of containment*. While the essence of a form is that which cannot be created or produced by something else, the essence of a material entity is found at the level of a species placed in relation to its genus.[23] This latter definition is significant because it suggests a framework or *logic of containment*: there is the genus (the container that contains), the species (the contained that contains) and the individual (the contained). This structure of containment is also found in Aristotle's *Physics* when it comes to defining the world: there is the universe (the uncontained that contains), the world (the contained that contains) and beings and things (the contained).[24] Plato had already alluded to a similar structure in the *Timaeus*, where the form of *kósmos* is defined as that which is contained and contains. As he observes,

> But we shall affirm that the Cosmos, more than aught else, resembles most closely that Living Creature of which all other living creatures, severally and generically, are portions. For that Living Creature embraces and contains within itself all the intelligible Living Creatures, just as this Universe contains us and all the other visible living creatures that have been fashioned.[25]

For our purposes, we will call this influential classical logic of containment the foundations of *the metaphysical world*.

According to Johann Gottfried Herder's notes from Kant's 1762 lectures on metaphysics, cosmology begins with the assertion that "the world is a *real whole*." The world is whole because it is "not part of another."[26] Twenty years later, in the notes taken in 1782–1783 by Christoph Coelestin Mrongovius, Kant still begins his lectures with this basic proposition. "The world," he observes, "is a substantial whole which is not part of another."[27] The metaphysical world is real because it is a substantial whole. In other words, the metaphysical world has an essential and objective reality that transcends the material world. This real whole must also be distinguished from an ideal whole, which is formed by my subjective representations. The metaphysical cosmos is a concept of reason and its reality should not be confused with the world as an empirical object.[28]

This easy dismissal of the empirical world is founded on the Aristotelian distinction of treating the world as a substance that is constituted not by bodily matter but through form working on matter and generating a "connection of substances." For Aristotle, form gives matter unity. "The form of the world is a real connection," Kant remarks in his lectures, "because it is a real whole."[29] From the point of view of metaphysics, the world is an absolute and not relative whole and it is only when world is treated relatively and in the physical sense that it can be described as the earth or a globe.[30] As notes from Kant's 1790–1791 lectures succinctly state, this metaphysical world is an intelligible world and its real connections or unity are founded on God.[31]

Kant's critical philosophy, which begins with the publication of the first edition of the *Critique of Pure Reason* in 1781, does not by any means reject metaphysics but it does test and challenge the traditional foundations of metaphysics. Kant's attempts to construct a new critical metaphysics will include a sustained reconstitution of the metaphysical world on epistemological grounds. This project will begin with questioning any concept of world that is presented as being purely rationalist or entirely empirical. In his 1790–1791 lectures, Kant argues that the intelligible world should not be called an intellectual world because this assumes that the world can be fully grasped by our intellectual faculties alone.[32] At the same time, in his 1781 lectures Kant warns against the traditional designation of the sensible world as an observable world that can give us real knowledge of things in themselves.[33] The sensible world, he argues, "lies merely in my head and is given not in itself, but rather in the progress of my experience of things."[34]

Kant's critical philosophy will introduce a new caution around using terms like "the intelligible world" and "the sensible world." Though Kant himself often has recourse to phrases like "the world of sense" (*Sinnenwelt*) in the *Critique of Pure Reason*, he treats these terms with care and only refers to "the intelligible world" (*intelligible Welt*) on a few specific occasions. By arguing that these concepts have been broadly misused in the past, Kant will transform the epistemological status of the concept of world in philosophy.

As Kant noted in his correspondence, his 1770 work *On the Form and Principle of the Sensible and Intelligible World* marks the beginning of his critique of the traditional metaphysical concepts of the intelligible and sensible world.[35] As he later described it in a letter from 1781, in drawing the traditional distinction between the sensible and intelligible world he was confronted with the problem of "the *source of the intellectual* elements."[36] In his 1770 dissertation, Kant is preoccupied with establishing various degrees of unity for both the sensible and intelligible world. A complete synthesis, he argues, produces "a whole which is not a part, that is to say a world."[37] Kant is searching here for the right conditions to establish the most secure concept of world. This will in turn allow him to grasp the sensible and the intelligible *as* worlds.

Addressing the problem of "how it is possible for several substances to coalesce into one thing," Kant still relies in 1770 on a broadly Aristotelian terminology.[38] A world is constituted by a synthesis of essential and not accidental properties, and this is why Kant's title refers to the *form* of the sensible and intelligible worlds. It is not matter but form alone or an immutable essence that ensures a world remains the same "throughout all its successive states."[39] Having established the form of a world, Kant then turns to what he calls "the principle of the form." He writes, "The principle of the form of the universe is that which contains the ground of the universal connection, in virtue of which all substances and their states belong to the same whole which is called *a world*."[40] This is a very orthodox articulation of the metaphysical world.

It is this assumption of "the principle of the form" or primary essence of world that allows Kant to draw an absolute distinction between the sensible and the intelligible worlds. The sensible world "contains the ground of the universal connection of all things, in so far as they are *phenomena*." In contrast, the intelligible world is not concerned with the subjective unity of phenomena but with an "objective principle" that oversees the "combining together of the things which exist in themselves."[41] Kant is rather vague about the origins of this second level of synthesis and, as he says, this is what eventually prompted him to write the *Critique of Pure Reason*.

### Starting without the World

One of the most striking aspects of the opening of the *Critique of Pure Reason* is the almost complete absence of any reference to a concept of world. Kant will hold back his account of world until the last section of his work, the Transcendental Dialectic. If we follow the sequence of the first section, the Transcendental Aesthetic, first there are bodies and objects, and then we learn that it is the *a priori* form of space that provides the framework for our representations of objects that are outside us. These objects are in space but space is not an empirical concept and only gives rise to our representations (not to objects themselves). It is only through this *a priori* form of space that we can register different places.[42] There are bodies, there are objects outside us and there are different places, but there is no concept of world. There is space as our outer sense but there is no world.

The sensible is certainly apparent in the *Critique of Pure Reason* as the necessary content that arises from the experience of objects but, tellingly, Kant only refers once to "the world of sense" in the Transcendental Aesthetic.[43] As the *a priori* form of the outer and inner sense of appearances in general, space and time are the most universal and involuntary structures of intuition that arise from sensations. However, these basic and ubiquitous intuitions do not explicitly give rise to the *world* of sensibility or the *world* of intuitions. The problem of the exact relation between world and the *a priori* ideas of space and time will preoccupy Kant until his last writings.

The concept of world also hardly seems to play any role in the next section of the *Critique of Pure Reason*, the Transcendental Analytic. The pure concepts or categories that provide a framework for the concepts that have arisen from intuitions do not provide the *world* of the understanding. Nor does Kant explicitly refer to world when he briefly touches on the laws or unity of nature in the Transcendental Analytic.[44] It is only when he comes to the ideas of reason in the Transcendental Dialectic that he devotes significant attention to the status of the world. This caution in using the concept of world as a participating or coordinating term in an account of the senses and of the understanding is one of the more revolutionary aspects of Kant's work.

One could argue that Kant's project displaces the concept of world because it is only concerned with appearances arising from our experience and with setting limits on the claims of our reason to know things in themselves. But it is quite remarkable that Kant does not use a concept of world to indicate the *a priori* objective formal frameworks of space and time and the pure categories in his account of sensibility and the understanding. Nor is the relative absence of world simply a result of an idealism that refutes the existence of reality. In a footnote added to the preface to the second edition of 1787, Kant could not be more emphatic that critical philosophy does not lead to "psychological idealism." On the contrary, he insists, it is "a scandal of philosophy and universal human reason that the existence of things outside of us . . . should have to be assumed merely *on faith*."[45] Kant does not need a concept of world to justify that his philosophy has a clear relation to "objective reality," "external things," "outer intuition" and "outer sense."

Kant uses the "outer sense" that is structured through the *a priori* form of space to reinforce the reality of phenomenal experience. As he observes in the first edition, "Of course space itself with all its appearances, as representations, is only in me; but in this space the real, or the material of all objects of outer intuition is nevertheless really given, independently of all invention."[46] One could therefore say that space as the *a priori* outer sense has replaced or reconfigured the metaphysical concept of the sensible world. However, Kant insists that space only gives us "the form of all appearances" and not "the sum total of all appearances."[47] Outer sense and inner sense alone cannot give us a *world* of sense. Kant also suggests that the understanding alone cannot establish a world. The concepts of the understanding are contained by the twelve categories—which include unity, plurality and totality—and unified by the schemata and synthesis of the imagination and consciousness. Strictly speaking, there is no *concept* of world.[48] Mechanisms of boundary, containment and unity are already at work in the understanding and there appears to be no need for an additional or overarching category of world. It is only with the *ideas* of reason, which do not refer directly to or rely on objects of experience, that world becomes an explicit problem for the *Critique of Pure Reason*. World is an *idea* and not a concept for Kant.

On the threshold of the Transcendental Dialectic, Kant briefly returns to the terminology of his 1770 dissertation and the status of a "*mundus sensibilis & intelligibilis*" as he examines the possibility and limitations of drawing a distinction between *phenomena* and *noumena* or appearances and pure thought.[49] He rejects a positive notion of the *noumenon* as the erroneous assumption of a pure form without content or the assertion of an intellectual domain that bypasses sensibility.[50] According to Kant, this is Leibniz's chief failing. As he observes, "deceived by the amphiboly of the concepts of reflection, the famous Leibniz constructed an *intellectual system of the world*, or rather believed himself able to cognize the inner construction of things by comparing all objects only with the understanding and the abstract formal concepts of its thinking."[51] The critique of traditional metaphysics, he concludes, should "not allow us . . . to indulge in intelligible worlds, or even in the concept of them."[52] Kant's critique of an intellectual world could not be clearer. Leibniz himself had argued in the *Discourse on Metaphysics* (1686) that each substantial form "is like a whole world, and like a mirror of God, or indeed of the whole universe."[53] According to Leibniz, a substantial form or monad is a soul-like force or action that is found in all corporeal and incorporeal entities and should give us a secure insight into the fundamental unity of both vast multiplicities and indivisible particulars.[54]

Kant goes on to argue that the *noumenon* is a necessary but empty "*boundary concept*" which keeps sensibility away from presuming to know things as they truly are as opposed to how they appear in our representations.[55] Kant also uses the commonplace division of "*mundus sensibilis & intelligibilis*" to criticize what he calls the "empty trafficking of words" in contemporary philosophy.[56] The metaphysical world—or at least Wolffian-Leibnizian metaphysics according to Kant—has become no more than an empty word. Kant suggests that there has been a tradition of using the concept of world to create erroneous domains, divisions and distinctions.[57] He concludes, "The division of objects into *phenomena* and *noumena*, and of the world into a world of sense and a world of understanding, can therefore not be permitted at all in a positive sense, although concepts certainly permit of division into sensible and intellectual ones."[58] It is in this context that we can begin to speak of a concept of world in critical philosophy.

## The World as Idea

Kant's criticisms of the misuse of the concept of world primarily concern the failure to recognize the transcendental idea of a *container* for "the sum total of all appearances."[59] In other words, from the perspective of critical philosophy one cannot describe "the world of sense" as "the sum total of all appearances." Nor can one call "the world of understanding" the unity of "the sum total of all appearances."[60] The problem of world arises when one begins to think about the world *as a whole*. For Kant, we cannot have any actual experience of the world *as a whole,* and without this experience we cannot have a true concept of world. Critical philosophy requires that we recognize that the world as a whole for us is only an idea.

Gagarin's flight in 1961 might have changed everything for Kant. It is only because we can have no possible experience of the world *as a whole* that Kant can argue that the concept of world belongs exclusively to the province of the pure ideas of reason. As he observes, from the perspective of a critique of pure reason "we can say nothing about the magnitude of the world in itself."[61] The question of the world can only deliver us to the possibilities and the limitations of ideas. Without experience, Kant argues, "every concept is only an idea."[62]

Kant begins the Transcendental Dialectic and his critique of the ideas of pure reason by confirming what we have long suspected. Reason promises "the highest unity" for concepts of the understanding because it is founded on principles that have no direct relation to objects of experience.[63] However, as a transcendental idea—since it cannot be an object of possible experience—the world is also prey to the unavoidable illusions that arise from judgements founded on pure reason alone.[64] A transcendental illusion is a subjective view that takes itself as an objective summation of things as they really are.[65] For critical philosophy, world is then at once an idea that needs to be demarcated and an illusion that needs to be corrected.

Kant's treatment of world is made more complex by the fact that when reason addresses the problem of world it is also directed to find the *unconditioned* possibility of any conditioned series. To reach the vantage point of the unconditioned is to see the conditioned series as a totality.[66] While the search for the unconditioned offers the "highest possible unity of reason," it also reinforces the errors of pure reason as it readily assumes that a complete picture is given.[67] In addition to being an idea without a direct connection to an object and an illusory insight into things as they really are, world is part of the project of reason to claim that which is whole, complete, universal, total and absolute.[68] Pure reason, Kant comments, "reserves for itself only the absolute totality in the use of concepts."[69] If it were possible, the unique *vantage point* gained from the movement of a conditioned synthesis to the unconditioned should allow us to grasp *the world as a whole*.

The problem with the world as an idea of pure reason is then apparent: it is as an idea that can produce illusions when it is taken as a whole by treating the unconditioned as a means of experiencing the totality of a conditioned series. "No experience is unconditioned," Kant insists, and we therefore cannot experience the world as a whole. If we use the idea of reason to give us the world *itself*, we will only fall into a metaphysical cul-de-sac.[70]

To start to address the possibilities and limitations of the world as a transcendental idea or what he calls *cosmologia rationalis*, Kant places the world between the transcendental ideas of the soul and God.[71] The Kantian world will always be part of this trinity of ideas. *Cosmologia rationalis* may not have direct access to an object but it is concerned with a distinct area which Kant calls "the manifold of the object in appearance" or the "*unity* of the *series of conditions of appearance*."[72] In contrast to the unity of the subject and the soul (psychology) and unity of all things (theology), the world denotes "the sum total of all appearances."[73] As Kant observes, one must not confuse the cosmological world with the physical world.[74] The physical world is concerned with particular experience, the cosmological world with experience in general or "the sum total of all experiences." The cosmological can never be satisfied with the sensible even if it always starts with the sensible, since it is searching for "the object of all possible experience."[75] In this context, the Kantian world can be treated as the idea of reason acting as a *container* for the empirical as a whole. As a cosmology, there is no phenomenon of world *as a whole*. We do not see the world as a whole. The idea of world is only a principle of reason that enables us to formulate "the sum total of all appearances."

In the antinomy or dialectic of pure reason Kant explores the inherent contradictions in traditional cosmology. He does this in part to reinforce a fundamental boundary: the *idea* of world "cannot be made to agree with appearances."[76] For Kant, all of the ideas that he examines in the antinomy can be described as erroneous world-concepts (*Weltbegriffen*).[77] World-concepts account for the search for "absolute totality in the synthesis of appearances"—the "sum total"—and its problematic relation to "the unconditioned totality on which the concept of the world-whole also rests."[78] The essential boundary between idea and appearance is founded on the elusive connection between an absolute totality and the unconditioned. As he remarks, world-concepts confront us with a synthesis that is always set beyond experience.[79]

Kant's focus here is very much on the interests and demands of reason.[80] When it comes to the *idea* of the world as the sum total of appearances, reason requires that time, space and matter can all be thought as a conditioned series that is driven toward an absolute completion or synthesis (the unconditioned).[81] At the same time, Kant establishes "a special limitation" on the projects of reason: the idea of the world will always entail the idea of "the successive synthesis of the manifold of intuitions."[82] In other words, the idea of world as a whole cannot find its absolute synthesis merely in the imagination or in concepts of the understanding alone. It must have a mechanism for some kind of reference to possible experience. It is the absence of this mechanism to link the interests of reason directly to a possible experience of the soul, the world and God that Kant will chart at some length in the antimony of pure reason. In this sense, world describes a profound disjunction between reason and experience.

The question of how to grasp the world as a whole becomes most acute when Kant starts to address the traditional question of a cause of the world that is *outside* the world.[83] Kant makes it clear that we are not yet in the province of theology, and that cosmology, as the formal relation of a conditioned series to an unconditioned point of origin, end or totality, simply cannot answer this question without falling into a circle of contradictions. What is striking about this discussion in the third and fourth antimony is the proliferation of terms to describe the world. This is in part due to the fact that in the antinomies Kant is not employing his own views as much as advancing a "*sceptical method*" by juxtaposing conflicting "dogmatic cognitions."[84] But it is also a sign of the more general constrictions in finding an alternative language beyond the traditional metaphysical terminology for the world. For example, though Kant has referred once or twice in the previous five hundred pages to something being "in the world"—without offering any clear explanation of this phrase—we are now confronted with a clear difference between what is "in the world" and what is "outside the world."[85]

Within the limits of a cosmological idea, Kant remarks that it is "a bold presumption" to assert that there is an object or faculty that is *outside* the world in an attempt to reach the unconditioned possibility of the world when world is defined as an ongoing series of alterations.[86] However, this in itself is quite a remarkable definition of the world. The "world of sense"—a term that is now used quite freely—describes the operations of a temporal series that is no more than an "empirical contingency."[87] If one were taking the world of sense here as nature this might describe the sum total of all the changes in the natural world over thousands of years. Kant's point is that mere empirical contingency could not provide a comprehensive or secure vantage point to take in all these manifold changes in "the world of sense" as a whole.

Within the confines of cosmology, even the claims for "a necessary being" as the origin or possibility of the world cannot provide a causal link between what is "in the world" and what is "outside the world."[88] The contingency of the empirical cannot lead to the necessity of the intelligible.[89] The world cannot be thought as a whole from what is *in* the world, which is all that a cosmology can offer.[90] The seemingly unavoidable seriality of the world—the "world-series" (*Weltreibe*) as Kant calls it—cannot be encapsulated either inside itself or outside itself.[91] Taking it merely as a series of interrelated changes, one could say that there is no world—no world as a whole—in Kant's critical philosophy.

## 2. The Regulative World

For Kant, there is a "critical solution" to this impasse in the regulative ideas of reason.[92] He will argue that to resolve the traditional difficulty with the world "we must seek the cause in our idea itself."[93] He states bluntly that when it comes to the world, "your object is merely in your brain and cannot be given at all outside it."[94] In this sense, the concept of world in the *Critique of Pure Reason* operates primarily to clarify and to systematize our ideas of reason. One could say that the Kantian concept of world illustrates the efficacy of reason.[95]

Before we turn to Kant's account of the regulative ideas of reason, it is worth emphasizing two key issues: the necessity to treat the world *as a whole* and the importance of a clear distinction between what is *in* the world and a wider perspective or vantage point of the world as a whole. All of Kant's labour in this section of his work is premised on the impossibility of seeing the world as a whole (*Weltganze*). "The object can never come before you," he insists.[96] However, it is by treating the *idea* of the world as a whole that Kant himself can mark out the failure of previous philosophical systems in relation to the world. Pure empiricism can only produce a "comparative" whole, while dogmatic rationalism can only assume an "*absolute whole*" that can never be verified in perception.[97]

## The World as a Whole

As we have seen, Kant argues that the world as a whole cannot be found *in* the world as an intuition of sensibility or as a concept of the understanding. If the world as a whole is only apparent as our idea of a container for "the sum total of all appearances," it must be formulated from a vantage point beyond or above what is merely *in* the world. For Kant, we cannot use what is in the world to understand the world itself as a whole. This is not a matter simply of the difference between the particularity of what is found "in the present world" and the generality of a cosmology in search of the sum total of all appearances.[98] As Kant insists, one must never confuse "the explanation of appearances in the world" with "the transcendental ideas of the world-whole itself."[99] As an idea of reason the world is not *in* the world. This is an essential difference that informs Kant's critique of cosmological ideas and underwrites his attempt to establish new grounds for securing a vantage point of the world as a whole.

It is in this context that we can examine the regulative ideas of reason and treat the regulative world as an alternative to the traditional metaphysical world. According to Kant, when pure reason attempts to grasp the world as whole it takes an interminable successive temporal series, in which each term conditions the next term, as a *simultaneously* given unconditioned sum total.[100] The persistent error of traditional metaphysics is that it thinks it can be given everything at once. For Kant, on the contrary, the world is "never wholly given."[101] Kant's answer to this all-too-common error is for reason to be guided by a *regulative* rather than a constitutive principle.[102] Regulative ideas do not create concepts but order concepts when they can be taken only as ideas.[103] Regulative ideas offer a viable alternative to the errors of pre-Kantian metaphysics because they provide the rule for a schema that always looks toward the greatest unity without assuming a self-evident totality.[104] The unconditioned can now be taken as a rule and not an object. In this sense, the idea of world registers "the unconditioned condition" of the sum total of all appearances.[105]

Regulative ideas of reason suggest both new possibilities and new limitations for the transcendental idea of the world.[106] We must accept that the world can never be taken as the basis for an assured judgement of either the infinite or the finite: the world as an empirical object can only be indefinite and indeterminate.[107] However, Kant does not leave us with only the interminable conditioning of a sensible series. If he does not refer to an intelligible world, he still wants the intelligible or what is "outside the series" to play a critical role in recasting world as a regulative idea of reason.[108] From its origins in the differences between the sensible and the intelligible worlds, rational cosmology has now become a question of nature (what is inside the series) and freedom (what is outside the series). Kant's solution to the conflict between the natural necessity and the freedom of choice or the will is to *interweave* the sensible and the intelligible. The intelligible is outside the sensible series but "its effects . . . are encountered in the series."[109] The regulative ideas of reason allow for the demands of both nature and freedom. We are at once in the world (inside the series) and have a vantage point above and beyond the world (outside the series).[110]

The fact that we are now not talking about the world as an object as much as the subject in relation to nature and freedom is made explicit by Kant using the example of a human being to illustrate his point: "The human being is one of the appearances in the world. . . . Yet the human being . . . is [also] a merely intelligible object."[111] For Kant, the world as a regulative idea does not delineate the form and substance of the sensible and intelligible world. Rather it reveals something that operates without the world as an object: the operation of the faculties of understanding and reason.[112] The regulative world is truly an idea.

Aristotle noted that when Socrates "started to think about ethics" he stopped thinking "about the whole of nature."[113] In his own way, by turning the metaphysical speculations about the world as an object that could be known entirely and in its innermost workings into an interaction between nature and freedom through the workings of human understanding and reason, Kant stopped thinking "about the whole of nature." However, contrary to the views of P. F. Strawson, Kant does not simply say there is no world as a physical object or indeed no natural world as natural necessity, order and empirical manifold, but that *for us* there is no world *as a whole*, no absolute container for the empirical that is given all at once in its entirety.[114] It is not the reality of the world that is being denied—or the "immeasurable showplace of manifoldness" that so often renders us speechless—but that our mere *concepts* of the world can give us immediate and full access to this reality.[115]

## The Limits of the World

In the revised edition of *Kant's Transcendental Idealism* (2004), Henry E. Allison offers an acute defence of Kant's insistence on the fundamental distinction between our reliance on appearances and our inability to grasp things in themselves. Allison argues that Kant's project cannot be confused with Berkeley's pure idealism because Kantian epistemology breaks with the inherent *ontology* in both rationalism and empiricism.[116] Rather than discrete ontological designations (things in themselves), Allison argues, there are *a priori* epistemic conditions and discursive distinctions (appearances) that arise from relying on both concepts and sensible intuitions.[117] These discursive conditions are neither simply ontological nor merely psychological or logical.[118] When it comes to discursive knowledge, we are always dealing with concepts in relation to *a priori* intuitions. There are no immediate or intellectual intuitions.[119] As Allison suggests, critical philosophy deals not with *given* ontological states but with the discursive conditions of epistemology.

Transcendental philosophy, Kant argues, considers "a system of all concepts and principles that are related to objects in general, without assuming objects that *would be given* (*Ontologia*)."[120] "The proud name" of ontology, he remarks earlier, "must give way" to the modest claims of a "mere analytic of the pure understanding."[121] For Allison, this shift from the ontological to the discursive marks the great difference between Kant's 1770 dissertation on the form of the sensible and intelligible worlds and the *Critique of Pure Reason*.[122] Allison's reading of Kant has profound implications for how we understand the transformation of the concept of world in critical philosophy.

If we were to take the world only as a *concept*, it would not be known ontologically but discursively. It would then be a question not of the world as it is given in either immediate or intellectual intuition, but of our knowledge of the world through concepts that arise from sensible intuitions. In this sense, the world for us would truly be a *concept* of the world. However, for Kant the regulative world is not a concept. We can then no longer simply equate the world with nature. The regulative world is concerned with the "the sum total of all appearances," not with "the sum total of *given* objects" or "nature."[123] At the same time, Kant does not stop here: he takes things a step further. Beyond Allison's possibility of the discursive world is Kant's insistence that *the world is only an idea*. In the Transcendental Dialectic we are not dealing with a discursive world but with a regulative world.

For Kant, the world is not a concept arising from *a priori* intuitions. The world is an idea; it is not ontologically given nor is it discursively known. There are no sensible intuitions or concepts for the world *as a whole*. The world is only a regulative idea of reason. This may explain why Kant does not include the world as an explicit presence in the Transcendental Aesthetic. The world cannot be known through an immediate or intellectual intuition, nor can it be described as an *a priori* intuition. We do not receive *the world* as an involuntary and necessary framework for all our external representations (space). The regulative world is not space. Again, this is a revolutionary change in the traditional thinking of world. The regulative world is a world that is not already given. It is not *always already there*, always already at the start of things. The regulative world is not presupposed. Only the *a priori* forms of space and time as outer and inner sense have this function. However, this does not mean that we simply make the world. As a regulative idea, we give the world form but we do not create it. We gain the world as a regulative idea and systematic unity through the progress of our reasoning.

## As If There Is a World

The shift of the concept of world from cosmology to transcendental ideas— from an ontological state to a regulative function—is most apparent in a remarkable addition to Kant's argument in the last sections of the Transcendental Dialectic, which is concerned with the idea of God. Kant has already contrasted the relation of nature as a conditioning series of natural causes and of freedom as the possibility of "unconditionally necessary being" that stands "outside the series" and points to a "transcendental and unknown" intelligible ground for the sum total of all appearances.[124] As he challenges what he calls *cosmotheology*, or the attempt to deduce this unconditionally necessary being *from* the contingency of an interminably conditioning series, Kant introduces a new aspect to the regulative ideas of reason.[125] Within the limited framework of this approach, necessity and contingency must be taken as subjective ideas of reason that can then "coexist" as regulative ideas of reason. In their coexistence, necessity must act "*as if*" there is a world and contingency "*as if*" there is God.[126]

It is only when Kant finally turns to the relation between the transcendental idea of the world and the transcendental idea of God that he evokes the regulative principle of acting *as if* (*als ob*) we can take the world and God in a certain way. The *als ob* allows Kant to evoke a "systematic unity" at the farthest point from possible experience. If we can act *as if* the idea of the world were created by the idea of God, reason can finally grasp the regulative world *as a whole* through evoking "the greatest systematic unity in the empirical use of our reason" without falling back on traditional ontological designations and metaphysical distinctions.[127] From this vantage point, we can still think of the world as a whole without losing sight of what is in the world. For example, rather than take the sensible as simply an indefinite series of interrelated modifications, we can now speak in proper terms of the *world* of sense and act "*as if* nature were infinite in itself."[128] This is possible because we can now also think of the idea of God in relation to the world as a whole, acting "*as if* the sum total of all appearances (the world of sense itself) had a single supreme and all-sufficient ground outside its range."[129] In the Transcendental Dialectic, Kant takes the world *itself* away from us but he also gives it back as a highly effective and wide-ranging regulative function of reason.

The *Critique of Pure Reason* changes the status of the world in philosophy. Before Kant, the concept of world was commonly used to describe the absolute division and easy containment of the sensible and the intellectual. Critical philosophy suggests that we can hardly use the former with any confidence and that the latter must be thought not as a possibility of sense or understanding but only as a regulative idea of reason. After Kant, one must be far more attentive to the use of the concept of world to separate and distinguish seemingly distinct concepts. Before critical philosophy it was easier to speak of the world as something ontologically given. It was also easier to speak of a concept of world in general on this basis. Kant implies that there can be no concept of world in these terms and that we must use the idea of world in general with the epistemological limitations and possibilities of reasoning.

For Kant, to act *as if* there is a world—a container that contains—is to register the harmonious agreement of a reason that contains itself by recognizing the greatest possible formal systematic unity, without presuming to circumnavigate the earth. But the *Critique of Pure Reason* also leaves us with a more radical proposition. At best, it is far harder than we thought to use the concept of world as a container that contains since we now understand that the concept of world itself must also be contained. In the labour of critical philosophy, we are also encouraged to be far more cautious about using the concept of world as an index for what is total, whole and complete. The world cannot simply be conflated with the planet, the earth or the globe. We are also challenged not to take it for granted that the world is always already there, always preceding us as a fully given totality. Traditional metaphysics, we are led to infer, mistakenly presumes a ready-made world.

At the same time, because we are guided by the infinite promise or goal of the greatest unity, the Kantian idea of the world as a regulative function leaves us relying on a necessary fiction as an immovable boundary marker: one must always act *as if* there is a world. Beyond a theological gesture that embraces this newly chastised concept, there is no total, whole or complete world. We must always act as if there is a world, but Kant's great work also raises the possibility that there is *no world*. This is a possibility not of the nonexistence of the world itself as an object—of the earth or globe—but of the radical insufficiency of a concept of world. The concept of world may be the most profound example of what Friedrich Schiller called in his own reading of Kant the "dubious principle of perfection."[130]

## 3. The Categorical World

When Kant turns from theoretical to practical critical philosophy, his treatment of the concept of world changes. If anything, the terminology used for world in the Kantian analysis of morality, politics and anthropology is more conventional. In these disciplines, there is seemingly always *a given world ready at hand*. This is already apparent in the last section of the *Critique of Pure Reason* when Kant discusses the "moral world," without giving a clear indication of how such a discrete domain is possible. The "moral world" is not the sensible world as a whole that we can only treat as a schematic and regulative idea of reason. The "moral world" is more akin to the traditional metaphysical distinction between the sensible and the intelligible world that uses "world" as a self-evident means of securing a timeless, unshakable division and absolute designation. One might call this a *categorical* use of the world, following both the Aristotelian and Kantian use of primary substances or *a priori* pure categories to discriminate and divide a series of absolute predicates into discrete functions. One of our persistent questions in this book is how these types of philosophical functions become *world-like realms, domains, spheres, regions and places*.[131] We can describe this as the problem of *the categorical world*.

To put this in broader classical terms, this takes us from the problem of the world as *kósmos* to that of world as *tópos* or *khōra*. In the opening of his 1942 lectures on Friedrich Hölderlin's poem "The Ister," Heidegger accounts for the dominant history of metaphysics by linking Kant's 1770 dissertation *On the Form and Principle of the Sensible and Intelligible World* to Plato's distinction between the senses and the understanding.[132] However, contrary to what one may have thought, Plato does not actually refer to the world (*kósmos*) when he distinguishes the visible and the intelligible in his famous allegory of the cave and analogy of the sun in the *Republic*. He writes, "What the good itself is in the intelligible realm [*tópō*], in relation to the understanding and intelligible things, the sun is in the visible realm, in relation to sight and visible things."[133] Plato uses the word *tópos* here, which is generally translated as "place" and often linked with *khōra* or "region." In the *Metaphysics*, Aristotle carries on this tradition by speaking of "the realm of sense" (*aisthē tou tópos*).[134] Plotinus would later treat the intelligible realm as a key aspect of Neo-Platonism.[135]

In the *Categories*, Aristotle does not describe his ten distinct functions as worlds. *Kósmos* only appears in the midst of the discussion about place and region within the category of quantity.[136] Kant also, of course, does not describe the *a priori* pure concepts or categories as worlds in the *Critique of Pure Reason*, even if like Aristotle before him he uses some of these categories to address the idea of the world *as a whole*.[137] The Kantian categories are functions that give unity to our representations. The pure concepts of the understanding that arise from our faculty of thinking indicate the presence of a "transcendental content" in response to the synthetic unity of our intuitions.[138] From the point of view of Kant's theoretical philosophy, the claim for a "moral world" (which can be distinguished from an amoral world) may not be a category but it does imply what I am calling a *categorical use* of the world.

### The Moral World

Kant turns to the moral world (*moralische Welt*) in the *Critique of Pure Reason* to illustrate that pure reason can be of use in a practical philosophy and that practical philosophy can extend or "guarantee" the possibilities of reason beyond its theoretical parameters.[139] The question of one's own happiness as a moral law replicates the relation between nature and freedom as an interweaving of what is at once inside the world as a conditioned series and outside the world as an unconditioned totality.[140] However, the difference with the moral law is that it invites the possibility of "a special kind of systematic unity." This is a moral unity based on "free actions" that can be considered complete and total in contrast to the limitations set on knowing the world "as the whole of nature."[141] Allison argues that we should read these gestures in "axiological rather than ontological terms." It is a question of a "higher set of values," he observes, not "membership in some higher order of being."[142] However, I am not persuaded by Allison's reading of Kant when it comes to the status of world in practical philosophy.

As the analysis of freedom in relation to the moral law, practical philosophy gives us the moral world *as a whole*. As Kant observes, "I call the world as it would be if it were in conformity with all moral law (as it *can* be in accordance with the *freedom* of rational beings and *should* be in accordance with the necessary laws of morality) a *moral world*."[143] As we would expect, Kant then goes on to distinguish this "idea of a moral world" from a morally ideal "intelligible world" and places it firmly in relation to "the sensible world." He ends, nonetheless, by reaffirming that the moral world cannot be "grounded merely in nature" and must always keep in view "the ideal of the highest good."[144] The moral world then gives us a "special" *vantage point* of the world as a whole. This is not an ontological world with its God-like perspective, nor is it simply a psychological projection—it is a regulative world with an elevated or expanded perspective that gives it the authority to address moral imperatives and theological possibilities.[145] It is a *categorical* world.[146]

It is worth quoting Kant at some length here. In the name of a necessary ideal, he articulates a quite conventional relation between morality and religion that relies once again on a clear distinction between the sensible and intelligible worlds:

> Thus only in the ideal of the highest *original* good can pure reason find the ground of the practically necessary connection of both elements of the highest derived good, namely of an intelligible, i.e., *moral* world. Now since we must necessarily represent ourselves through reason as belonging to such a world, although the senses do not present us with anything except a world of appearances, we must assume the moral world to be a consequence of our conduct in the sensible world; and since the latter does not offer such a connection to us, we must assume the former to be a world that is future for us.[147]

The assumption of a moral world that cannot be found merely in *the* world leads reason to the possibility of a future world, of *a* world that is beyond nature. As Kant goes on to suggest, he is quite close to Leibniz here who drew a distinction between "the realm of grace" and the "realm of nature."[148] It is not the physical world as a whole that is at stake but rather the world as a *discrete realm* (*Reich*).[149] This is the categorical world. It is in the name of this ideal and regulative goal of theologically contained morality that Kant returns to the intelligible world.[150]

**Spheres, Realms and Domains**
Kant's later moral philosophy will rely on this designation of discrete realms of sense and understanding.[151] The freedom and the obligation to be moral are grounded on the independence of reason from pathological determinations. Moral laws, Kant argues in the *Groundwork of the Metaphysics of Morals* (1785), require that a human being not intuit or feel but think of itself in a "twofold way": "belonging to the world of sense" and "belonging to the world of understanding."[152] Even if it only treats the world of the understanding as a limited "*formal* condition" or a mere "*standpoint*" for reason, Kant's practical philosophy reinstates the relation between *mundus sensibilis* and *mundus intelligibilis* as a discursive condition if not an ontological distinction.[153] For Kant,

it is imperative that these designated realms can be taken as entirely discrete. As he suggests in his discussion of good and evil in *Religion within the Bounds of Mere Reason* (1793), we must avoid thinking of these "two realms" as "bordering on each other and losing themselves into one another by gradual steps." For this very reason, the traditional designations of heaven and hell are "philosophically correct" because they reinforce the need to represent good and evil as "separated by an immeasurable gap."[154]

In the *Critique of Practical Reason* (1788), Kant generates new terms to account for the new duties of the concept of world. In relation to freedom as a moral faculty, the sensible world and the world of understanding give rise to the different regions of the sensible and supersensible, which in turn are described respectively as "the *ectypal world*" and "the *archetypal world*."[155] As Kant explicitly states, the moral world resolves the problem of the necessary suspension of the world as a cosmological idea. The framework for the freedom of the will, the moral law gives an "objective reality" to the intelligible world but only as a discursive condition of pure practical reason. The moral law "determines that which speculative philosophy had to leave undetermined."[156] Practical reason then alone facilitates "the grand disclosure . . . of an intelligible world through the otherwise transcendent concept of freedom."[157] Practical reason makes the intelligible world immanent.[158] One might say that Kantian moral philosophy returns us to a traditional world-based philosophy.

This use of the categorical world as a distinct realm, domain or sphere that can be taken as a whole—which can operate on the scale of a world-concept without falling into the contradictions of taking the world as its object—can also be found in Kant's discussion of science in the *Critique of Pure Reason* as "the system of pure reason."[159] The great labours of critical philosophy have produced a *new metaphysics* founded on a systematic unity arising from pure *a priori* cognition.[160] As Kant observes in the last pages of his work, "we will always return to metaphysics as to a beloved from whom we have been estranged."[161] Pure reason can be described as a science when our cognitions are treated as a system. This systemisation requires that the "unity of manifold cognitions" be placed under "one idea." This is produced by "the scientific rational concept" of "the form of the whole" and "the unity of the end." Guided by the ends of reason "as a single supreme and inner end," this *world-like* whole in turn enables "the domain of the manifold" to be taken in its entirety as determined *a priori*.[162]

There is an echo of this gesture in the introduction to the *Critique of the Power of Judgement* (1790, 1793). Having described understanding and reason as "two different domains," Kant goes on to use the term *domain* to indicate the "incalculable gulf" between the concept of nature and the concept of freedom. This suggests that understanding and reason can be treated as distinct domains (*Gebiet*) in relation to the distinct domains of nature and freedom. The concept of nature and freedom, Kant notes, should be treated respectively "as the sensible" and "as the supersensible." As he remarks, the need to keep each of these domains quite distinct leads us to think "just as if there were so many different worlds."[163] The "as if" of the regulative ideas of reason is at work here, but in this case it is used not to counteract the ontological treatment of the world as much as to make possible the clear distinction between a series of world-like domains.

## Political and Anthropological Worlds

This categorical use of world is apparent in Kant's other practical works written after the *Critique of Pure Reason*. In *Toward Perpetual Peace* (1795), in contrast to both the theoretical and moral philosophy that takes such care with claims to grasp the world *as a whole*, Kant recognizes that "the whole world" itself can be at stake when it comes to political philosophy and to the common practices of states and nations. It is in Kant's political philosophy that the world as a whole is treated, uniquely perhaps, as a given. As Elisabeth Ellis remarks in linking Kant's theoretical work to his political writings, "Just because Kant claims that human beings cannot grasp the world in its totality does not mean that Kant denies that the world itself is whole."[164] The implication here is that for Kant, as for many others, politics becomes a discipline that requires taking the world *as a whole*. This is both a political reality and a political ideal.

The "craving of every state," Kant notes, is to achieve a permanent peace "by ruling the whole world where possible."[165] "World" and "earth" become almost interchangeable terms in Kant's political writings, denoting states and continents on the planet.[166] In the name of his call for a federalist league of nations and a cosmopolitan right, Kant speaks both of "the *right of citizens of the world*" and of "the right to the *earth's surface*, which belongs to the human race in common."[167] As Pauline Kleingeld has pointed out, these ideals of world citizenship on the earth were quite common in the late eighteenth century.[168] At the same time, one could argue that the analogy in the *Critique of Pure Reason* between circumventing the earth and the regulative ideas of reason is still very much at work here: the earth remains a *sphere* of reason, as does the world. As Kant argued in 1784, the "*public* use of one's reason" is measured by "the entire public of the *world of readers*."[169]

*Toward Perpetual Peace* relies on a commonplace distinction that we did not encounter in the theoretical philosophy: one is always *on* the earth and always *in* the world.[170] What Kant means by this distinction is more apparent in *Anthropology from a Pragmatic Point of View* (1798). In contrast to his critical and political philosophy, in his pragmatic philosophy Kant explicitly addresses the subject as "an earthly being."[171] However, he also introduces a now familiar distinction between what is merely *in* the world and the need for a wider perspective or comprehensive vantage point of the world *as a whole*. Pragmatic anthropology is based not on "*things* in the world" but on "knowledge of the human being as a *citizen of the world*." For Kant, in anthropological and political terms, human beings are uniquely on the earth *and* have a unique vantage point of the world as a whole.

This configuration of the human as an earthly being who is also a citizen of the world allows for a dual gesture in the *Anthropology*. On the one hand, the human being recognizes that he or she "constitutes only one part of the creatures of the earth," and it has recently been argued that Kant's anthropology cannot avoid the nonhuman in his attempt to give a complete account of the *anthropos*.[172] However, Kant's use of the world here is, if anything, more traditionally metaphysical. The world has already been removed from the nonhuman, in particular from "irrational animals," which are considered only as things.[173] It is in this sense that Kant concludes his work by speaking once again of "the citizens of the earth."[174]

At the same time, this use of the nonhuman to demarcate the difference between *earth* and *world* gives the concept of world a new political and ethical force. As Kant observes, "The opposite of egoism can only be *pluralism*, that is, the way of thinking in which one is not concerned with oneself as the whole world, but rather regards and conducts oneself as a mere citizen of the world."[175] Nonetheless, the ethics of this displacement of the self-regarding subject, which includes a recognition of the earth beyond the sphere of reason and of the nonhuman, still entails a very metaphysical projection or extension of the self *as* the world, whether it is cast as "the whole world" or as "a mere citizen of the world."

Michel Foucault noted in his 1961 introduction to Kant's *Anthropology* that Kant's work places a particular emphasis at the outset on the "*knowledge of the world*."[176] As we have seen, for Kant this knowledge is found not merely in the world: it requires a knowledge of the world as a whole that can be secured only by taking a perspective above and beyond what is in the world. In the *Anthropology*, this knowledge of the world is entirely focused on the human being. Foucault points out an early announcement of this project at the end of a short lecture by Kant on physical geography, first published in 1777. Kant suggests in this lecture that the knowledge of the world, as a form of anthropology, should be taken, ultimately, as a form of *cosmology*. In other words, it is "not with respect to the noteworthy details that their objects [nature and the human being] contain . . . but with respect to what we can note of the relation as a whole."[177] As Foucault remarks, Kant's *Anthropology* of 1798 changes the emphasis from cosmology to cosmopolitanism. It is now more a question of the world "as a republic to be built than [of] a cosmos given in advance."[178] However, this republic is still concerned with the human being as a "citizen of the world" and with securing the vantage point of the world as a whole.[179] Kant's pragmatic anthropology may recognize the earth as a shared political domain in which the human can only claim to be one among others, but its definition of world reinforces the classical logic of containment and returns us to the metaphysical world or the evocation of *a world* as a whole. In rethinking the concept of world, Kant's most radical work still remains the *Critique of Pure Reason*.

## Kant and Gagarin

We've not forgotten Gagarin's flight in 1961. It is worth noting that having described at some length the dangers of using "world-concepts," Kant nonetheless suggests toward the end of the *Critique of Pure Reason* that reason can in fact circumvent the earth.[180] Critical philosophy should lead to science or inquiries that take account of the "*a priori* grounds" that establish the necessary boundaries of reason.[181] In contrast to an empirical knowledge that is always reminded of its limitations but can still conclude that the earth is flat, Kant argues that once I know that the earth is a sphere, "I can cognize its diameter and, by means of this, the complete boundary, i.e., surface of the earth, determinately and in accordance with *a priori* principles."[182] He goes on to compare reason itself and its own proper boundaries to a *sphere*. Rationally circumvented, the earth serves as a perfect analogy for Kantian reason within the sphere of critical philosophy.

It is perhaps no more than a fortuitous concurrence of events, but two key figures who challenged Kant's critical philosophy of world in the twentieth century, Martin Heidegger and Jacques Derrida, were both busy at work in the spring of 1961. In a late lecture given a month after Gagarin's journey in May 1961, Heidegger would criticize, as he had often done in the past, what he called Kant's pervasive "onto-theo-ology."[183] Some months later in July 1961, Derrida completed his first publication, a translation of and introduction to Edmund Husserl's *The Origin of Geometry*, where he charts Husserl's attempts to redefine the idea in the Kantian sense.[184]

There were also two short but quite remarkable pieces written in this period directly in response to Gagarin's flight: Emmanuel Lévinas's "Heidegger, Gagarin and Us" (1961) and Maurice Blanchot's "The Conquest of

Space" (1964). For Lévinas, Gagarin's journey marked an opportunity to challenge what he saw as Heidegger's hostility to modern technology and his reactionary celebration of the world as *place*. "What counts most of all" about Gagarin's flight, Lévinas insists, "is that he left the Place."[185] "For one hour," Lévinas goes on to say, "man existed beyond any horizon—everything around him was sky or, more exactly, everything was geometrical space. A man existed in the absolute of homogenous space." For Blanchot, we must also treat Gagarin's trip as a rupture of the traditional relation to place and the announcement of a new understanding of space: "Man broke with place. . . . There was someone, not even in the sky, but in space, space without being and without nature which is nothing but the reality of a measurable quasi-void. Man, but man without horizon."[186] Despite the attempts to gain political capital from the flight, Blanchot notes, Gagarin's journey put the notion of "place itself" into question. Blanchot concludes by warning against making too much of "a momentary utopia of some non-place."[187] One could say that Kant's critique of metaphysical cosmology also "broke with place," though this rupture very much remained within the horizon of man.

One might broadly say that due to technological, scientific innovations today we can take the world as an object of the senses and have used singular events such as Gagarin's flight to establish our mastery of the world as a whole. However, I have suggested that Gagarin's flight around the earth would have made no difference to the Aristotelian metaphysical tradition that Kant reacted against in his critical philosophy. The world as a general essence would be unchanged by such an extraordinary event. Nonetheless, if we take Gagarin's trip as a slightly exaggerated way of thinking of Kant's critique of traditional metaphysical cosmology, it does seem that the transcendental use of reason would need to respond to an event where the earth as a whole had been registered under empirical conditions. Beyond the systematic unity of regulative ideas, cosmology would then also become a problem of the empirical use of reason.[188]

From the perspective of the *Critique of Pure Reason*, Kant would still insist on the unavoidable contradictions that arise from taking the world as an idea of pure reason, and this change in status would only alter part of the first antinomy of reason—the question of the world in space. He would also maintain the necessity to distinguish between appearances and things in themselves and the need to treat the world as a regulative function rather than as an ontological distinction. Nonetheless, if one can take the world *as a whole* as a possible experience, it would no longer be on the same level as the ideas of the soul or God. The world will still be caught between the tensions of the understanding and reason, but there will be a new and compelling case for treating the world as both a concept and an idea.

## The Highest Standpoint

Kant himself gestured to some of these challenges in the wonderfully entitled late fragment "The Highest Standpoint of Transcendental Philosophy in the System of Ideas: God, the *World*, and *Man* in the World. Restricting Himself through Laws of Duty" (1800–1803). This unfinished work is a testament to Kant's ongoing attempt to extend the transcendental project from the natural sciences to physics, while affirming the moral and theological imperatives of practical philosophy.[189] He treats the world here not only as a regulative and categorical world but also as an *a priori* intuition of space. In other words, Kant has finally linked the concept of world that is taken as an object *in space* to a regulative idea of the world.

Now he can think of the world as both a material and empirical object. As he observes, "The concept of world is the complex of the existence of everything which *is* in space and time, insofar as empirical knowledge of it is possible."[190] Eckart Förster has argued that Kant reached this position through seeing the limitations of his earlier work on metaphysics and on the question of matter in general. In the *Critique of the Power of Judgement*, he had also formulated the relation between reflective judgements and the purposiveness of nature, thus providing "an *a priori* justification to think of nature as itself systematic in its empirical laws."[191] One might say that Kant had finally found a way to place the world at the start of the *Critique of Pure Reason*.

While in other fragments from *Opus Postumum* (1786–1803) Kant also sketches out his ideas for moving forces of matter that one can link to the world as "the totality of sense-objects," his primary aim in this late work is to reaffirm what I have called the *categorical* world.[192] For Kant, the natural world must be thought with the moral world. It is the ability to think these two forms of world systematically that distinguishes man as a "rational world-being."[193] Man is in the world, a sensible being and an "inhabitant of the world." But man can also think of God and of the world as a whole in relation to this sensible being that finds itself in the world. This means that man has freedom of will and must recognize moral duty and the priority of God.[194] This ability to think of nature and freedom, of what both is in the world and has a wider perspective of the world as a whole, ultimately enables "the thinking subject" to create "a world" for itself.[195] In its final articulation in Kantian philosophy, the concept of world allows the subject to become a self-creator.[196]

Kantian philosophy presents us with two new and compelling approaches to the world. One might describe this as the difference between *die Welt* and *ein Welt*, between *the* world and *a* world. The limitations of the regulative idea of the world mark a break with a longstanding theological and metaphysical tradition of knowing the world—as both an object and a concept—as an unchanging and essential whole. As evidence of an assured logic of containment, the metaphysical world is then reconfigured by critical philosophy as a world founded on the necessary discursive and regulative conditions for human cognition. This presents us with the new possibilities of the regulative world, of treating world as the idea of a systematic unity.

However, while Kant challenges the traditional ontological use of world to indicate the given differences between the sensible and intelligible, he also generates new duties for using world as a function of the cognitive faculties of the subject. In critical philosophy, this categorical world makes no claims on an empirical use of reason to know the world as a whole, but it does use the imperative of the moral law as an affirmation of free will to construct an analogous concept of world that can be both taken as a whole and divided into the distinct realms of nature and freedom. As Kant remarks in *Opus Postumum*, "Transcendental idealism is the mode of representation which makes concepts, as elements of knowledge, into a whole."[197] After Kant, *the* world may have new limitations, but the concept of *a* world that is discerned by the subject has vast new possibilities and responsibilities. The ability of the subject to apprehend, suspend or objectify a post-ontological world—a world that will either *enhance* or *displace* the subject—dominates philosophy well into the twentieth century. Kant's philosophy marks the beginning of the end of treating the world as a self-evident theological and ontological concept. It also announces the start of a great labour in the aftermath of Kant: the need for each philosopher to create a distinctive concept of world.[198]

Kant's *Critique of Pure Reason* may have generated a regulative world in place of the traditional ontological world, but a *critique* of the concept of world itself must also address the valorisation of a world that is both purely regulative and entirely categorical. The philosophical world no longer automatically registers an immutable being, which invariably had placed it among the ideas of the soul and of God. At the same time, the regulative world withholds *the world itself* as both a secure object of experience and a platform for some form of internal objectivity for the self. Reason can find its own unity through the idea of the world as a whole, but the self cannot use the world for its own projects of unity, morality or the claim for an authority beyond the interests of the self. This reticence around the concept of world, this refusal *to give the world* to the self, is perhaps Kant's finest achievement.

Nonetheless, one can also argue that the regulative world is an idea that is always vulnerable to changes in the possibilities of experience. After Gagarin, the regulative world has taken on a new and unexpected contingency. It remains a domain of ideas, but the focus of these ideas must alter in light of historical changes or the regulative world will revert back to the metaphysical world. As Husserl will later suggest, nonempirical ideas or idealities must also have a *history* or what he calls a "historicity" (*Geschichtlichkeit*).[199] Today, in our acting *as if* one can experience the world as a whole, the range of possibilities must be even more extravagant. Now that we have a photograph of the earth as a whole, I might be prompted to act *as if* I can see the earth at a great distance from some new and extraordinary vantage point in our solar system (for example, the image of the earth as a "blue dot" taken from the edge of the solar system by the Voyager spacecraft in 1990). Nonetheless, the world as an object of human experience may have changed but the world *as a whole* remains a regulative idea. The Kantian regulative idea of the world, which suspends any claim to the world itself as a given or self-evident concept, is still the most radical concept of world in the history of philosophy. In insisting that one must act *as if* there is a given world, it invites the possibility of a philosophy without world.

CHAPTER TWO

# Hegel and the World as Spirit

## 1. From Appearance to Actuality

In his two principal works, the *Phenomenology of Spirit* (1807) and the *Science of Logic* (1812–1816), Hegel has relatively little to say about the world. This caution or reticence may in part be due to the influence of Kant. This is not to say that Hegel's formulation of a concept of world in the *Phenomenology of Spirit* and the *Science of Logic* is not innovative, influential and critical to his philosophical project. However, like Kant, Hegel does not begin with the world. The world is not already given. It comes late in both works and only gains its true status in the final stages. As one would expect, for a dialectical philosophy of progressive becoming, the world in its final form is not given as a simple or immediate being. It is constructed rather through a determined series of discrete and dynamic dialectic stages. In the *Phenomenology*, Hegel's philosophy declares a process of becoming and the achievement of a final goal: the world *as* spirit.

What is most distinctive about the Hegelian concepts of the world as spirit in the *Phenomenology* and the objective world as idea in the *Science of Logic* is the evident reaction against the limitations of the Kantian regulative world without turning back to the traditional positions of the metaphysical or ontological world. As the distinguished Hegelian commentator Jean Hyppolite observed, "The *Phenomenology* is not a noumenology or an ontology, but it remains, nonetheless, a knowledge of the absolute."[1] In Kantian terms, the Hegelian world is primarily a categorical world, a constructed domain or realm that is given an absolute authority when it is defined as the culmination of spirit and the idea.[2]

## Self-Consciousness and the World

The near complete absence of reference to the world in its initial stages is still one of the more striking aspects of the *Phenomenology of Spirit*. Charting the progressive experience of consciousness through sense, perception, understanding, reason and spirit, there is no world *for* consciousness when it is reliant on the mere sensation and perception of external objects to define its own consciousness. As in the *Critique of Pure Reason*, at this initial stage there are bodies and things, but there is no world. The world becomes an issue for consciousness only in the third and final stage of consciousness before it develops into self-consciousness. This section, entitled "Force and Understanding: Appearance and the Supersensible World," is devoted to consciousness moving from defining itself through external objects to taking itself as its own object and gaining self-consciousness. In this sense, the concept of world is marked at the very moment in the *Phenomenology* when consciousness turns from the external to the internal.

In perception, consciousness is both limited and stretched by its relation to objects. Becoming aware of itself in the shifting dynamics of the pull between the one and the many, consciousness still remains tied to the basic conceit that it can expand its own horizons only through the perception of external objects. The world may not be formulated, but the external plays a critical part in establishing the first, inadequate stages of self-consciousness in the *Phenomenology*, which Hyppolite aptly describes as "a knowledge of the knowledge of consciousness insofar as this knowledge is only for consciousness."[3] In the stage of "Force and Understanding," consciousness will no longer define its possibilities only through the perception of external objects. The distinction that Hegel introduces here between the world of appearances and the supersensible world enables the critical advancement from consciousness to self-consciousness. As is often the case after Kant, the concept of world primarily enhances the spheres or domain of the subject.

For Hegel, the dynamic operations of force (*Kraft*) facilitate this process. Force "supersedes its expression" as either the one or the many and is "driven back into itself."[4] Returning to itself, force eventually acquires the status of a universal medium and moves beyond the framework of a consciousness that measures itself in relation to external objects.[5] Force directs consciousness toward the concept, to a thought that does not define its possibilities through reference to the external.[6] It is only after this critical step that we can even begin to think of a *concept* of world. Indeed, it is at this moment that the world first appears in the *Phenomenology*. With the concept in view, the understanding now "*looks through*" the appearance-based stages of sense, perception and limited understanding. The "*play of Forces*" coalesces into "a *totality* of show" which gives rise to the world of appearance.[7] This new concept of world *as a whole* provides a necessary point of summation for all the previous stages of the *Phenomenology* and facilitates the advance from consciousness to self-consciousness.

Consciousness now looks through the whole of appearance and has its first intimation of "*the true background of Things.*"[8] It "distinguishes this reflection of Things from its own reflection into itself" and begins to form "the inner" as the future source of self-consciousness. It is at this moment that Hegel explicitly introduces the concept of world. "There now opens up," he observes, "above the *sensuous* world which is the world of *appearance*, a *supersensible* world which henceforth is the *true* world."[9] This true world promises a new *vantage point* for the science of consciousness. As Hegel remarks, "Above the vanishing *present* world there opens up a permanent *beyond*." This intimation of world beyond a mere response to immediate objects also provides the first glimpse of reason, which will follow the development of self-consciousness. At the same time, as Terry Pinkard has noted, Hegel is not claiming here that consciousness has complete access to the supersensible world at this early stage in its development. Consciousness is using this traditional framework of worlds to establish its *own* "structure for describing the world."[10]

It should also be noted here that Hegel is far more reticent in his use of the world in the *Phenomenology* than A. V. Miller, his best-known English translator. There is, for example, no "*sensuous* world," "*supersensible* world" or "*present* world" in the German text for the passages quoted above. Hegel actually says, "There now opens up above the *sensuous* which is the *world of appearance*, a *supersensible* which henceforth is the *true* world, above the vanishing *present* there opens up a permanent *beyond*."[11] The important point that can be gleaned from this revised translation is that the sensuous is only the sensuous—it does not have the status of a discrete world—but it can be taken now *as* "the world of *appearance*" (als der *erscheinenden* Welt). The supersensible can also now be taken *as* "the *true* world" (als die *wahre* Welt). At the very least, after Kant's critique of self-evident sensible and intelligible worlds, this suggests that Hegel must provide a carefully calibrated account of the possibility of each domain, sphere or realm that is given the authority of a world.

The Hegelian concept of world here does not simply generate an opposition between discrete domains (the vanishing present and a permanent beyond). World now becomes part of the dialectical process that creates a highly complex and ever expanding realm: the inner truth (*inneren Wahren*) of self-consciousness. A. V. Miller erroneously translates the inner (*das Innere*) here as "the inner world," when Hegel's intention *at this stage* in his argument is to demonstrate that the inner is far larger and far more developed than the concept of world as a mere container.[12]

Hegel goes on to refine this initial configuration of the world of appearance and the supersensible as "the *true* world." The latter, having been defined by its relation to the former, must now move beyond appearance in general.[13] The vantage point of the permanent beyond is limited by and should exceed the vanishing present.[14] At the same time, it is worth noting that Hegel does not address the question of the world itself here. The concept of "world" at this stage in the *Phenomenology* accounts at once for the sum total of the perceived world (*wahrgenommenen Welt*) *and* for placing the supersensible world (*übersinnliche Welt*) entirely beyond the world of sense and perception. Hegel argues that these distinctions are maintained by the labour of the *Aufhebung*, of the progressive differences—simple, mediated and absolute—that are at once negated and lifted up or preserved as one stage dissolves into the next stage of development in the *Phenomenology*. For Hegel, this fluidity of evolving differences is indicative of the "restlessness" and "pure activity" of thought as *spirit* (*Geist*) "and the negating or the ideality of every fixed determination of the intellect."[15]

It appears at this stage in the *Phenomenology* that the concept of world still only maintains discrete strategic configurations, aggregations or shapes but has no force or dynamics *in itself*. There is, as yet, *no world* in and for itself, to use Hegel's terms. Hegel gestures to the possibilities of this dialectical concept of world when he outlines the final stages of the separation of the world of appearance and the supersensible world. Initially, the supersensible world is tied to the perceptual world, and this relation can only produce a simple difference, or an "antitheses of inner and outer" that returns consciousness to its perceptual origins.[16] In contrast, the "second supersensible world" is constituted by the logic of "inversion" (*der Verkehrung*), or a mediating "inner difference" in which "it is itself and its opposite in one unity."[17]

This dynamic difference in turn produces a new kind of world to help the subject advance from consciousness to self-consciousness. The fleeting supersensible world is now an unreliable and even absurd "inverted world" (*verkehrten Welt*).[18] This world of absolute inversions or total differences turns and changes (verkehren) *in itself*. It enacts a "pure change" without needing to refer to "a different sustaining element."[19] This radical self-turning or pure auto-alteration reiterates that the supersensible world of "Force and Understanding" only functions to facilitate consciousness turning *to itself*. In this rather oblique fashion, world generates the first step in taking consciousness from appearance to actuality.[20]

## Actuality and the World

Having contributed to the rise of self-consciousness, the concept of world plays a relatively minor role in consciousness gaining freedom through taking itself as its own object. As Terry Pinkard has suggested, this is due in part to Hegel's definition of self-consciousness. For Hegel, self-consciousness is not formed by a subject in relation to external objects. In Pinkard's own terms, this means that we should not be seen as passively "*representing* the world" but as active "social creatures forming *concepts* of ourselves as already world-related."[21] For Pinkard, moving beyond the traditional subject-object relation also means that we can see "ourselves as *participants* in various historically determinate social practices."[22] Because Hegelian self-consciousness is able to gain a view of its world *as a whole*, it is more able to be *in* the world in an authentic, active and historical manner.

The world only becomes a focus of the *Phenomenology* again when consciousness turns to reason. This is no doubt a response to the traditional metaphysical account of world and its Kantian critique, but it is also due to self-consciousness now turning toward the external and encountering resistance as it attempts to impose its inner truth or rational thought on the external. This process will lead to the insights and limitations of rational self-consciousness. It will also initiate the critical link between the world and actuality that will ultimately produce the world *as* spirit. At the same time, as Pinkard suggests, after the development of self-consciousness we are dealing with the world as a concept.

Having been preoccupied "only with its independence and freedom," Hegel notes at the start of his account of reason, self-consciousness has sought "to maintain itself for itself at the expense of the *world*."[23] It is not exactly clear what kind of world is at stake here. This may be the supersensible world that has separated itself from the world of appearances or it could simply be shorthand for the manifold external world. It is more likely to be the former because Hegel goes on to link this neglect of the world to the relation of self-consciousness to "its own actuality" (*Wirklichkeit*). Reason's great presumption is that "everything actual is none other than itself." Again, Hegel is most likely criticising Kant's regulative world when he observes that for reason, "apprehending itself in this way, it is as if [*als ob*] the world had for it only now come into being."[24] In such circumstances, Hegel goes on to say, reason "discovers the world as *its* new actual world" (*als* seine *neue wirkliche Welt*).[25] The world here is no more than the world *of* reason.

This is one of two very specific instances before the advent of spirit that Hegel directly refers to the actual world. It is only through the movement from reason to spirit that the world will become *actual*. At this stage, at the start of the experience of consciousness with reason, this "actual world" is a limited and problematic world. If anything, this world is a projection of rational self-consciousness. As Hegel remarks, "The *existence* of the world becomes for self-consciousness its own *truth* and *presence*."[26] To put this in Kantian terms, it is a regulative world confined to the subjective ideas of reason: the unity of reason with itself is not enough to ensure that the true objectivity—the actuality—of the world has been grasped. In the *Phenomenology*, only spirit can do this. All that self-consciousness can hope for at this stage is a kind of limping Kantianism that only asserts an "empty idealism" in which the priority of the "pure category" is still, ultimately, reliant on an "absolute empiricism."[27]

It is in these conditions that the first stage of reason, observing reason (*Beobachtende Vernunft*), looks to things that are ostensibly "in the world" and finds, again and again, "the consciousness only of itself."[28] In a pejorative sense, there is no world here, no objective world, only the endless subjectivities of reason. The apparently rational aspects of world at this stage register a simple difference or immediate being that lacks the dynamism of a mediating and absolute difference.[29] Observing reason is preoccupied with the seemingly impossible task of finding *itself* as an object that is actually and sensuously present in the world. It is precisely this search for the actual *in* the world—as opposed to establishing a vantage point that can think of the world *as a whole*—that frustrates the attempt to link world and actuality as a project of reason. Reason will need to turn from observing the flora and fauna of nature to taking the activity of individual rational self-consciousness as its own object.[30] This will bring self-consciousness closer to its own actuality and to the actuality of the world.

Hegel's critique of observing reason raises one of the critical problems for what I have called the Kantian categorical world. As we have seen, the construction of *a* world that has been imbued with the authority of *the* world must grapple with the association of world with the *already given* (*der vorgefundenen*). Even if it claims a privileged association with the already given, the categorical world is not entirely given: it is also made. Seeking the actual in the external as a perfect reflection of itself, reason—as an aspect of pure psychology at this stage—claims the capacity to construct "an other world."[31] For Hegel, once again, the world becomes an issue when it is a matter of *turning away* from the external and moving toward a new form of the internal.

The construction of a world here facilitates the move from the mediated to the absolute difference of observing reason: we are on the horizon of reason taking itself as rational self-activity. At the same time, we are also still in the midst of the limitations of observing reason and, more specifically, of a self-consciousness individuality that believes that it needs to form the actual in its own image. At stake here is also the promise of a new social or political domain. In these conditions, Hegel observes, "Individuality is what *its* world is, the world that is its *own*." Having the apparent freedom to represent *itself* "as actuality," this individuality believes—erroneously—that it has achieved "the unity of the world as *given* and the world it has *made*" (*des* vorhandenen *und des* gemachten Seins).[32] For Hegel, this marks the clear limits and obvious failings of pure psychology.

One can take from this instance of a mistaken assumption of the unity of self-consciousness, actuality and world that Hegel is already concerned about an overly precipitous unification of actuality and world. We have still not reached the actual or objective world, and the world *itself* will not be found in the developing stages of reason. From this insight one could broadly say that the concept of world is evoked in the *Phenomenology* to illustrate either the true movement of consciousness from the external to the internal or the false assumption by consciousness of a unity of the external and the internal. Hegel repeatedly insists, "Consciousness is only *actual* to itself through the negation and abolition" of "what merely *is*."[33] The actual world must be more than "what merely *is*."

**The Shapes of Spirit**
In moving away from observational reason to an active reason (*tätigen Vernunft*), self-consciousness finally undergoes a process of actualization (*Verwirklichung*).[34] The world now appears not as something made but as "something *given*." Rational self-consciousness is prompted to a new activity by stepping "into its world which it finds already *given*" (*in seine vorgefundene Welt*).[35] In contrast to assuming that the merely made world can be opposed to and unified with the given world, the task of this second stage of reason is to reach a point where the given can also be taken as the actual *for* self-consciousness. This trajectory will lead to another series of erroneous claims by consciousness to the actuality of the world, notably when it declares that it has established the so-called "way of the world" (*Weltlauf*).[36] This evocation of the actuality of the course of the world (*der Wirklichkeit des Weltlaufs*) is no more true than the claims made at the start of observing reason.[37] Like Kant, Hegel warns against the infinite capacity of reason to create its own delusions when it takes up the concept of world.

However, unlike Kant, Hegel follows this narrative of errors and limitations with the world *itself* finally being grasped fully by self-consciousness as it moves from reason to spirit. According to Hegel, neither consciousness, nor self-consciousness or reason alone can register the actual world. The world itself is only found in the equation of *Welt* and *Geist*.[38] "Reason is spirit," Hegel argues, when "it is conscious of itself as its own world, and of the world as itself."[39] This leads to a critical moment in the *Phenomenology*, which famously unfolds its argument both progressively and retrospectively. We the readers *now* understand the possibility of the discrete shapes or moments that informed each developing stage of the whole work up to this point. From its inception, the world *as* spirit has provided the *Phenomenology* with *all* these shapes. In this sense, the concept of world has made the *Phenomenology of Spirit* possible. For spirit, each of its "shapes" or moments will now be recognized as "shapes of a world" (*Gestalten einer Welt*).[40]

Hegel goes on to describe what amounts to a Hegelian categorical world. The world as a shape of spirit constitutes in its first stage "the ethical world."[41] Culture, the second shape of spirit, will be delineated into spiritual "masses or spheres" (*geistige Massen*) of "self-conscious actuality" that display themselves, once and for all, "as a world" (*als eine Welt*).[42] The shapes of culture (as the mediating difference) will begin to split between the actual world and the world beyond and, at last, the world itself will start to gain objectivity.[43] This will lead to the third and final unifying shape of spirit as a moral world.[44] These three forms of world set up the conditions for the closing stages of the *Phenomenology*: religion and absolute knowledge. The world *as* spirit ensures both the primacy of consciousness and the actuality of the world *for* consciousness.

### The Objective World as Idea

Seven years later in the *Science of Logic*, Hegel is far more explicit about the need to convey an *objectivity* onto the world itself as a necessary step in securing the objectivity of the subject. Having delineated the actuality of the phenomenological world, he now turns to the logical world. Hegel notes at the outset of his work that Anaxagoras was the first to argue that "the essence of the world is to be defined as thought."[45] By taking an "intellectual view of the universe," he argues, it ultimately became possible to formulate the principles of logic as an exclusive attention to "the necessary forms of thinking."[46] Logic entails taking the essence of the world as thought and shifting one's perspective from mere being (both empirical immediacy and rational abstraction) to essential becoming and the concrete idea. In this sense, the science of logic as a whole constitutes a world. As Hegel observes in his introduction, the system of logic is "the world of simple essentialities, freed from all sensuous concretion."[47] Once again, this is a new form of the categorical world, of a world that is constituted by the thought of man.

For Hegel, objective logic (which will be followed by subjective logic) replaces traditional ontology and redefines the metaphysical treatment of the self, the world and God.[48] Hegel again argues that Kant's reworking of the concept of world was limited by his reliance on the "already *concrete* form of cosmological determinations."[49] In contrast, the world in a science of logic can only be taken as purely *in itself*. Kant's assertion of the Transcendental Aesthetic at the outset of the *Critique of Pure Reason* placed the apparent contradictions of the concept of world not in the world itself but in the intuitions of the subject gained through the *a priori* forms of space and time.[50] In Hegel's terms, the Kantian concept of world is not sufficiently dynamic, and the inevitable contradictions in this concept should not be left to consciousness alone but should take account of the world as both a concept and an *idea*.[51]

In the *Science of Logic*, the world *itself* must become an idea or objective world and be treated objectively by the subject. Hegel traces this development through the elaboration of an objective logic of being and essence and a subjective logic of concept and idea. The objective world contributes to the development of the subject as it attains the objectivity of the concept. For Hegel, the "absolute idea" is achieved when the objective world with its "inner ground and actual subsistence" is taken as the concept (*Begriff*).[52] In other words, the concept of world affirms the objectivity both of the world and of the subject. The Hegelian evocation of the world itself once again enhances and expands the powers of the subject.

This final goal is made possible by a critical but brief stage of development in the *Science of Logic* that echoes the similar stage in the movement from consciousness to self-consciousness in the *Phenomenology*. In the *Science of Logic*, this progression takes place in book 2, the *Doctrine of Essence* (1813), and in the second section of this book, which charts the movement from appearance to actuality. Essence must appear, and its appearance (*Erscheinung*) creates a conflict between essence and appearance in the form of "the world of appearance" and "the *world* that *exists in itself*." This conflict is resolved when "that which is in itself is in the appearance."[53] This conflict will ultimately lead to essence gaining actuality (*Wirklichkeit*).

We start with the contested relation between appearance and concrete existence generating a limited and inadequate representation of the content and form of the world *as* "multifarious diversity and manifoldness."[54] As Hegel observes, from this perspective "'world' signifies in general the formless totality of a manifoldness."[55] The task for the subject is then to give this world an essential—and true—form. The disjunction between the laws of appearance and the content of the world both ruptures this initial configuration and facilitates the emergence of "a *world* that *discloses* itself above the *world of appearances* as *one which is in and for itself*."[56] For this development to take place, the "diversified content of the concretely existing world" must be registered as "a content holding itself together essentially."[57] While the language here suggests something more tangible than the Kantian regulative world as an idea of reason, Hegel is still only concerned with the "suprasensible world" itself.[58] This world will eventually *reflect* the essence of the concretely existing world, and this is what Hegel calls the actuality of the world in the *Science of Logic*. To put this in Kantian terms, the world is actual when we objectively determine the unconditioned itself at work *in* the world.

The emergence of the suprasensible world begins this process by allowing the world to be taken *as a whole*.[59] This in turn facilitates the resolution of the disjunction between the ideal form and the real content of the world. The world can now be described as "a world distinguished within itself, in the total compass of a manifold content."[60] This real content must then be raised to the level of an ideality. For Hegel, the *idea* announces the final unity of the concept and reality of the world. The actuality of the world is found when the objectivity of the concept of world expresses the unconditioned reality of *the world itself*.[61] This ambitious reinterpretation of the Kantian world would inspire a wide range of political readings of Hegel throughout the nineteenth and twentieth centuries. At the same time, the use of world as a means of establishing a new form of subject-oriented objectivity would be systematically refuted in later philosophy.

## 2. Anthropology and Phenomenology

The Hegelian world remains primarily a question of spirit and logic in the vast three-part *Encyclopaedia of Philosophical Sciences* (1817, 1827, 1830). Hegel devotes half as much space to the concept of world in the *Philosophy of Nature* (Part 2) as in the *Encyclopaedia Logic* (Part 1) and the *Philosophy of Mind* (Part 3). The attention given to the world in the *Encyclopaedia Logic* in the sections on the transition from appearance to actuality reflect the earlier work in the *Science of Logic*. It is the status of world in the *Philosophy of Nature* and the transition to the world of the *Philosophy of Mind* that presents the most influential treatment of world after the *Phenomenology*.

The Hegelian world may be described as a way of viewing nature—from a logical or spiritual vantage point beyond nature—but it is not found *in* nature. The scattered references to world in the *Philosophy of Nature* primarily function as a generic term of containment—the animal world, the vegetable world—or as a means of illustrating the different levels of external and internal interaction found in plants and animals. Nonetheless, the *Philosophy of Nature* is significant because it gives an implicit account of how the world as the "outer world" both *enhances* and *disperses* organic beings. It also announces the wider problem of the relation between a refined concept of world and the status of humans, animals and things. This will become an increasingly significant issue in the work of Husserl, Heidegger and Derrida.

**Plants, Animals and the Outer World**
Having examined mechanics and physics, Hegel turns in the final part of the *Philosophy of Nature* to organics. It is here that he develops a *hierarchy of access* and reaction to "the outer world" (*die Außenwelt*) from plants to a range of increasingly sophisticated animal organisms. Without a relation to its self as a differentiated self, the plant "lacks the inwardness which would be free from the relationship to the outer world."[62] Without being a "veritable subjectivity," the plant cannot interrupt the influence of the outer world and "its individuality [thus] always falls apart into its particularity." The plant is unable to resist the influence of the outer world because it "does not hold on to itself as an infinite being-for-self."[63]

In contrast to the plant, the animal is able to form a limited subjectivity. The animal "preserves inwardly the unity of the self."[64] In the face of the outer world, the animal maintains a discrete and distinctive internal domain or realm. One might be tempted to call this a kind of world. Hegel merely calls it a soul. It is a soul that is "not aware of itself in thought, but only in feeling and intuition."[65] As we shall see with Heidegger, the denial of world to animals is a critical aspect in asserting that the world is uniquely a human sphere. For Hegel, the animal also has mobility and vocalization, which gives it an external and interior freedom. It has a "self for itself" and can interrupt the influence of the outer world, though its notion of self is still entirely defined by its relation to the external world.[66] The greater the development of the animal organism, the more that its natural functions—such as digestion and sexual reproduction—reinforce a structure founded on complex "inward and outward aspects."[67] If an animal becomes ill, for example, it loses the ability to interact with or to consume properties of the outer world and can only "digest its own self."[68]

The human being will be differentiated from the animal by his or her ability to overcome a distinction between the outward and the inward that is only "directed towards the outer world." The limitation and "true externality" of the animal is that it "turns in anger against what is external."[69]

The animal is tied to the *outer world*. The animal "must therefore posit what is external as subjective, appropriate it, and identify it with itself."[70] Hegel traces this relation to the outer world through assimilation (ingestion and digestion), externalization (excretion), sexual reproduction and death.[71]

As Werner Hamacher has noted, Hegel moves from the philosophy of nature to the philosophy of mind or spirit when the outer world as a whole has been ingested, digested and transubstantiated.[72] Matter will be transformed into the non-external and the nonmaterial, and the outer world will become a concept (*Begriff*) and an idea (*Idee*). For Hegel, the "death of Nature" leads ultimately to "a more beautiful Nature, *spirit*."[73] One might even say that to leave the animal stage, the human being must "eat" the world. As Hegel had already remarked in the *Encyclopaedia Logic*, human consciousness must "crush" the world when it is taken merely *as* the outer world: "What human beings strive for in general is cognition of the world; we strive to appropriate it and to conquer it. To this end the reality of the world is to be crushed as it were; i.e., it must be made ideal."[74]

**From the Soul to Spirit**
The most concentrated discussion of world in the *Encyclopaedia* is found in the sections in the *Philosophy of Mind* that immediately follow the *Philosophy of Nature* on anthropology as a form of the soul. The rather abrupt shift from the zoological to the anthropological is facilitated, as Michael Inwood has noted, by Hegel drawing a clear distinction between the *soul* as an index of the merely living organism and *spirit* as the uniquely human capacity to differentiate itself "from the external world of which it is consciousness."[75] The elusive difference between the soul and spirit secures the clear difference between the world of animals and the human world. As we shall see, Husserl will make much the same gesture at the start of the twentieth century in *Ideas Pertaining to a Pure Phenomenology and to a Phenomenological Philosophy: Second Book*.

The opening part of the *Philosophy of Mind*, the subjective mind, is divided into three sections: anthropology, phenomenology and psychology. The anthropology is concerned with a "natural mind" that precedes the dynamics of consciousness. The presence of a concept of world in the anthropology is particularly interesting because it suggests the constitution of the world directly *before* turning to the experience of consciousness in the *Phenomenology of Spirit*. In reading the *Phenomenology* as a treatise on world, one should begin with the opening section of the *Philosophy of Mind*.

In all these stages, Hegel remarks, the mind "has not as yet made its concept an object for itself." At the same time, this mind should be seen "even at the beginning" as an idea or a "unity of the subjective and objective."[76] This distinction suggests, in contrast to the philosophy of nature, we should assume at the outset of exploring the subjective mind a wider perspective or vantage point of the world *as a whole* and not take it for granted that a phenomenology of spirit begins merely *in* the world. As a shape of the soul, anthropology describes an immediate and abstract universality, a universality that precedes particularity and individuality. This universality emerges from a reality that is still taken as already given, external and tied to nature.[77] The world of the anthropology is structured by a "soul tied to its natural determinations."[78]

At its most basic level, the mind as the natural soul "takes part in the universal planetary life [and] feels the difference of climates, the changes of the seasons, the periods of the day."[79] For Hegel, human beings must liberate themselves from passivity in the face of nature. He reinforces this by anticipating the sophisticated worlds of the objective mind—"the world of ethical freedom" and "a world created by self-conscious human freedom"— immediately before starting his account of the most primitive form of the subjective mind.[80] As he warns, it would be "a complete mistake" to treat this "universal life of nature" as "the highest object of the science of mind." This passive interaction between the mind and "planetary life" leaves the mind entangled in "merely natural life," when the true task of the Hegelian mind is to subject "the world to its thinking and creating it from the concept."[81] The Hegelian world should always be seen as a categorical world, a realm that can and ought to be made by the subject *in relation to* the objectivity of the idea.

Hegel treats the stage of "the universal life of nature" as the province of the solar system and the earth.[82] As the mind develops through the stages of the anthropology of the soul toward the phenomenology of spirit, its focus leaves the earth and hones in on the world. Hegel is still preoccupied with refuting the unavoidable influence of the outer world that he introduced in the *Philosophy of Nature*. The mind is not influenced by the solar system or by the earth.[83] It can interrupt the power of these vast external forces, Hegel argues, by determining its own world and "creating it from the concept."

Having delineated the natural determinations of the individual—predispositions, temperament and character—Hegel goes on to give the world a distinctive role in its natural alterations in time (youth, maturity and old age). The external world is taken to reflect "distinct states" or "*ages of life*" in this natural passage of time.[84] As Hegel observes, in the transition from childhood to youth, "the child in gaining a feeling of actuality of the external world, begins to become an actual human being itself and to feel itself as such."[85] The child appears to have a strictly harmonious relation to the world, while the youth experiences it as limitation and disappointment when "the existing world . . . fails to meet the ideals." It is only in adulthood that the world can be taken as complete for the individual who has shaped it through his or her work and own activity. This relatively brief period is then followed by old age and a unification with the world that is at once the fall into "the inertia of deadening habit" and a liberation that comes from a loss of interest in the "entanglements of the external present."[86]

One could of course challenge every aspect of this characterisation of an entire human life in relation to the world. For example, Hegel's exact contemporary William Wordsworth was developing a very different theory of the dynamic interaction between childhood and the natural world in *The Prelude* (1799, 1805).[87] At the same time, the concept of world is given a critical role by Hegel in the development of the individual soul. The child moves from "a feeling of the actuality of the world" to the introduction at school of "the supersensory world."[88] The individual's development is then marked by a preoccupation with "an ideal of a universal state of the world," the necessary recognition of "the world as an independent, essentially *complete* world" and a final "insight into the rationality of the world."[89] This development ends when the individual forgets the world and returns once again to its "oppositionless childhood."[90] What is striking about Hegel's description of the different ages of life is that the world is registered chiefly as limitation (*the* world) that is then transformed into a discrete domain or realm through the actions of the individual (*a* world).

One can see the antecedents here of Karl Marx's early reading of Hegel and of Alexandre Kojève's influential interpretation of the *Phenomenology* in the first half of the twentieth century.[91] For the Marxist, the Hegelian world is always an actual world—actuality and world are taken as a unified concept—and this actual world is akin if not to the empirical or natural world then to the real, objective or concrete world as an imperative for practical political action. In broad terms, this reading of Hegel tends to give the world as spirit a self-evident tangibility and anthropological grounding that is not apparent in the *Phenomenology*, though it is clearly a focus of Hegel's later *Elements of the Philosophy of Right* (1821).[92] As Hegel himself emphasizes in the *Encyclopaedia*, phenomenology follows anthropology and gives rise to the philosophy of right (of property, law, ethics and the state). Phenomenology is not concerned with the mere outer world (nature). Nor is it preoccupied with the natural influence of the world on the individual (soul). Phenomenology is the experience of consciousness constructing itself through the determining of the world *as spirit*. We will come back to Kojève's reading of Hegel in chapter 6.

As Hegel makes clear in the *Philosophy of Mind* in his account of the transition from the natural soul to the feeling soul (before the actual soul leads to phenomenology), the individual can now be understood as "a *world* of concrete content with an infinite periphery."[93] In other words, even in this basic form before the advent of phenomenology, the human soul itself *constitutes* a world. As the summation of the nature that preceded it, the anthropological soul has internalized this world. "In relating to this world," Hegel notes, "it relates only to itself." In this sense, the soul "may be described as the soul of a world."[94] The feeling soul generates an unmediated relation to the external world that the actual soul will break. As it leaves this interconnection with the immediate and turns back to itself, the actual soul creates the conditions for the soul to reach consciousness. Hegelian phenomenology emerges as "the I excludes from itself the natural totality of its determinations as an object, as a world *external to it.*"[95] For Hegel, nature as a whole constitutes the world as soul, and the soul as a whole produces the world *as* spirit.

From an early age, Hegel argues in the *Phenomenology of Mind*, the individual soul is driven, primarily by gaining mobility and speech, "to reflect itself into itself out of its immersion in the external world."[96] This recognition of the outer or external world as a kind of immersion is notable because it is entirely absent from the start of the *Phenomenology*. Indeed, the opening of Hegel's *Philosophy of Mind* could be said to provide an explanation for the relative absence of the world from the beginning of both the *Critique of Pure Reason* and the *Phenomenology of Spirit*. Neither work can start with "planetary life" because they *already* see the world as a world *for* consciousness and reasoning. In both works, the world is implied at the outset but is not formulated in any detail until a full account can be given of the subject objectively constructing its own world. The proper place and status of this *implied world* is in turn only established retrospectively in other, later works. Kant and Hegel both reject an immersive world, and it will only be with Heidegger that the so-called outer world will be rethought in philosophy.

In this context, to understand the concept of world in Kant and Hegel one must read the *Opus Postumum* before the *Critique of Pure Reason* and the *Philosophy of Mind* before the *Phenomenology of Spirit*. However, to place an elaborated world at the beginning of these works is to misunderstand the radical challenge of the regulated and categorical world and of the world as spirit and idea. Kant and Hegel construct a philosophy that *cannot start with the world* because it must first construct a subject that can create a world. At the same time, this inability to give an explicit account of the world at the start of a philosophical project would prompt Schopenhauer and Nietzsche and later Husserl and Heidegger to insist that philosophy cannot begin if it does not start with the world.

## 3. World-History

In the last stages of the *Phenomenology of Spirit*, spirit gains knowledge of it-self as "the actual World-Spirit" (*der wirkliche Weltgeist*).[97] In his later works, Hegel uses the realization of the actual world-spirit as the basis for recon-structing world-history as a *history of spirit*. Hegel's notion of world-history is significant because it reflects his attempts to give a historical development and shape to his principal philosophical concepts and demonstrates that the concept of world accounts for the most complete synthesis in his philo-sophical project. His own specific determinations of what constitutes world-history are also of course the most antiquated aspects of his philosophy. In the *Philosophy of Mind*, for example, he makes it clear that only Caucasians have produced world-history because they alone have asserted their absolute independence from nature.[98]

As Rodolphe Gasché has recently emphasized, there is a long tradition of equating the concept of world with the idea of Europe.[99] Hegel certainly reinforces this tradition when he argues that out of the Caucasian races, "the European [alone] is interested in the world." Uniquely striving to es-tablish a unity "between itself and the external world," the European mind has achieved "the mastery of the world." This recognition of the colonial-ism of the early nineteenth century is mirrored in the *Aufhebung* of the world by the European mind. The European mind produces world-history by initially opposing the world, asserting its independence and then re-internalizing this dynamic relation as a whole into itself, making the world *its* concept and idea.[100]

In the recently translated 1822 lectures on world-history, Hegel argues that there are three forms of historical writing: original, reflective and philo-sophical.[101] The first type of historical writing is limited to the accounts of those who were present at the historical events that they record. This form of history is akin to an immersive world in which the historian "stands and lives in the material itself, [and] does not elevate himself above it."[102] The second type of historical writing, which is written by those looking back at events that they did not witness, offers a first vantage point above and be-yond the immersive world. The impartial scope of this reflective history can provide "a *survey* of the whole of a people or of world history," but its very lack of particular, present-at-hand knowledge also leaves it prey to abstract generalization. This second form of history produces the world as a whole, but it is still "a distant and reflected world."[103]

World-history requires a historical writing that is wholly reliant on neither an immersive world nor a distant world. World history needs a *double perspective* in which the historian is at once truly *in* the world at hand and has a commanding perspective of the world *as a whole*. This balanced and effective double perspective is the province of the third and final type of historical writing, which Hegel calls "philosophical world history."[104] Philosophical history embraces both the immersive and the distant world as forms of spirit. In this sense, philosophical history is concerned with "a *concrete* universal" and also recognizes that "the *idea* is the guide of peoples and of the world." World-history, Hegel concludes, provides "the totality of all particular perspectives" and "the totality of the one world spirit."[105]

World-history is the culmination of the Hegelian world. It relies on the structure of a categorical world to contain the totality of actual human experience. At the same time, in the name of the world it constructs a wonderful and rather dubious filter to organize all of this historical material. History can be described in discrete periods and aggregates to serve the apparent "world-historical significance of peoples." World-history allows Hegel to privilege "the most spiritual form to which the natural mind dwelling in the nations ascends."[106] The *Weltgeist* oversees the *teleological* analysis of the rise and fall of the political, cultural, intellectual and religious development of historical groupings in terms of the Oriental *world*, the Greek *world*, the Roman *world* and the German *world*, the latter naturally accounting for the history of the modern period since the Reformation. As one might expect, all of this is based on excluding those peoples who do not enjoy the status of world-history.[107] At the same time, as Terry Pinkard reminds us, for Hegel these epochs also denote progressive stages of the idea of freedom.[108]

If nothing else, Hegel's concept of world-history provides a salutary justification for the all-too-common reliance on a concept of world to describe an apparently self-evident linguistic, cultural or national grouping. However, the use of "world" as an umbrella term for the unification of the most disparate and complex historical relations is perhaps the least convincing—and the most dangerous—use of the concept of world. The concept of world-history can easily appear as a blunt instrument for simplistic ethnic generalizations, virulent nationalisms and aggressive imperialisms. It can also be the conceptual framework for the always equivocal call for political transformation and revolution, as seen by Marx's early insistence that "the liberation of each single individual will be accomplished in the measure in which history becomes transformed into world history." According to Marx, world-history is accomplished only when every individual is brought into "practical connection with the material and intellectual production of the whole world."[109]

For Hegel the world-history of the *Encyclopaedia of Philosophical Sciences* signals the completion of the objective mind, after anthropology, phenomenology and psychology have passed through the social and political stages of rights, morals and ethics. The mind has not yet reached absolute mind, but at this stage the concept of world can be said to be complete. Hegel describes this completion of world as the process of consciousness gaining its own actuality and seeing itself "become the externally *universal* spirit, the *world-spirit*." The perspective of world-history allows us to see this movement not only as a history or as a development "in time and in reality" but also *as a whole*. According to Hegel, from the vantage point of the world-spirit we can truly say that "the absolute final aim of the world is realized in the world."[110] The world-history of the world-spirit gives us the one thing that Hegel believed had always eluded Kant: the world itself.

We will return to Hegel and the reading of the *Phenomenology of Spirit* in the twentieth century in chapter 6.

## CHAPTER THREE

# Husserl and the Phenomenological World

## 1. The Suspension of the World

As Husserl explains in the introduction to *Ideas Pertaining to a Pure Phenomenology and to a Phenomenological Philosophy: First Book—General Introduction to a Pure Phenomenology* (1913; hereafter *Ideas* 1), phenomenology is a "new science" and should be seen as "remote from natural thinking."[1] Much of the treatment of the concept of world in *Ideas* 1 is preoccupied with this distinction between a natural and a phenomenological attitude. Husserl will famously argue that pure phenomenology requires a suspension or reduction (*epokhē*) of the natural attitude toward the world. At the outset, it is important to note that the phenomenological *epokhē* is not a suspension of the world itself but of a *natural attitude* toward the world. In a gesture that has obvious Cartesian resonances, Husserl states that a phenomenological attitude should "elevate . . . the natural attitudes into the scientific consciousness."[2] For phenomenology, the concept of world registers a particular attitude (*Einstellung*) that must be overcome.[3] At the same time, in his later work Husserl will insist on the central importance of the life-world (*Lebenswelt*).

### The Flow of the Flux

As we have already seen in Kant and Hegel, the concept of world raises the problem of securing a discrete domain and of establishing a higher vantage point from which to see this domain as a whole. For Husserl, pure phenomenology should not be confused with the limited range of empirical psychology. The difference between phenomenology as a "science of ideas," and psychology should be seen as the difference between geometry and natural science.[4] When phenomenology has risen above the natural attitude it should provide us with "the free vista of 'transcendentally' purified phenomena." Like Kant before him, Husserl describes the domain of this unique vantage point as a "new world."[5] As much as the phenomenological reduction is concerned with reconfiguring the "natural standpoint" in relation to the world, phenomenology will always claim a discrete realm for itself as the *phenomenological world*.

This phenomenological world will be constructed not on individual empirical facts but on general essences. Importantly, these essences are not confined to our experience of reality "in the real 'world.'"[6] In this sense, the phenomenological world is also *"irreal"* as it can embrace both what is experienced and what is not actually experienced. In addition to a phenomenological analysis of lived experience (*Erlebnis*), there is therefore a phenomenology of fantasy, fiction and memory.[7] This distinctive phenomenological world cannot be described merely as "the sum-total of objects of possible experience."[8] It is also not limited to the subject-oriented level of existence. The domain of pure phenomenology is the universal essence of our spatio-temporal experiences in the world. With its focus on the universal essence of sensible phenomena, Husserlian phenomenology is also a remarkable attempt to move beyond the traditional categories of empirical particularity and rational universality.[9] At the same time, phenomenology is primarily focused on what arises from the operations of consciousness.

Phenomenological consciousness is concerned with an intuition of the general essence or unifying possibility of a particular experience.[10] The possibility of this particular, contingent experience must always be seen in the larger context of a coherent and consistent unifying structure. There will be variations and modulations, but there must always be an explanation for what remains the same through these constant changes. Husserl will base this general intuition or wider perspective on what he calls a phenomenological reduction of our natural attitude to the world as a whole. In other words, from a general intuition of an individual experience in the world we are given a vantage point of the world *as a whole*.[11] As Husserl explains, it is a matter of not seeing from one side or many sides but of seeing *all* sides.[12]

To see from all sides is to have a vantage point that recognizes a constant flux and "changeable multiplicity of manners of appearing" in any given perception that consciousness can grasp. However, it also affirms that there is an essential flow to this flux. There is, Husserl argues, a "synthetic unity" to every perception.[13] Each perception can be taken as "one and the same" even in the midst of the inevitable temporalities of consciousness that spread out the present perception into varying continuous degrees of retention and protention, of recollection and anticipation.[14] Phenomenology recognizes the essentially indeterminate nature of perception and also believes that it has an underlying *"determinate structure."*[15]

## The Limitations of Subject-Object

This general intuition of objects is never grounded simply on an investigation of physical and material properties. The perspective of general essences includes both the ideal unvarying forms of geometry and unreal but regulated ideas of imaginative fantasy.[16] The intuition of general essence or what Husserl calls the "consciousness of something" gives rise to an objectivity that cannot be reduced to the traditional epistemological relation between a subject apprehending an object. However, this objectivity is also more authentic than the factual data gleaned from the objects of modern science. This challenge to the limitations of the subject-object relation will have a profound influence on Heidegger and his ontological treatment of world. As Husserl puts it in one of his late works, one must grasp "the attitude *above* the subject-object correlation which belongs to the world."[17]

The natural attitude toward the world is based on the immediate response to what is *"simply there for me"*: space, time, the senses, things and beings.[18] This self-evident or immediately given world is in truth already divided between my immediate surroundings and the intimation of a far wider "obscure indeterminateness" in the world as a whole.[19] This is apparent through my constantly varying degrees of attention and focus at any given moment. This spatial difference between what is proximate and what is distant is also found in the varied temporal differences between the present moment and the past and future. Nonetheless, according to Husserl, I am always "in relation to the world which remains one and the same."[20]

The *"natural* world" itself is always already there and by and large its objects have already been given clear definitions and uses. For Husserl, the natural attitude toward the world is grounded on the basic experience that I always find myself in the world and always find myself as a *cogito,* as a living, thinking thing in the world.[21] Even if I give my attention elsewhere—to more abstract, less immediate concerns—the natural attitude toward the world remains constant. We all live, he insists, in an "objective spatiotemporal actuality."[22] In its most basic or bare form, the world can be understood as an index of time and space. The actual, material and natural world is first and foremost for Husserl a spatio-temporal world.[23] This definition of world will have an influence on both Heidegger and Derrida.

The limitation of this natural attitude is evident in treating world entirely in terms of factual actuality. As Husserl observes, "From matters of fact nothing ever follows but matters of fact."[24] At the same time, one could question Husserl's assertion of this seemingly homogenous and self-evident natural attitude. Phenomenology *needs* the natural attitude and the sciences that are built on it to justify its sweeping phenomenological reduction. Importantly, the suspension of the natural attitude is not a general negation of the world or an instance of a radical universal Cartesian doubt. It is rather the bracketing or placing in parentheses of the natural attitude toward the world.[25] As Husserl remarks, the phenomenological reduction *"shuts me off from any judgement about spatiotemporal factual being"* and *"the whole natural world."*[26] This suspension of judgement in relation to the immediately given enjoins us not only to reexamine the ontological properties of the *"natural* world" but also to think about a consciousness that can undertake this *epokhē* of the world *as a whole.*

## Two Perspectives of the World

Husserl argues that if the world as a factual actuality has been pushed away, we are left with other worlds, with "the *world as Eidos"* or the spheres of general essence.[27] However, at this stage in his argument he is primarily interested in delineating the transcendental pure consciousness that is apparent in this gesture of stepping back from the attitude of merely being in the world. For Husserl, we are now dealing with two perspectives: one that is truly *in* the world with all its shifting nuances and one that can take an unbroken purview of the world *as a whole.* Transcendental consciousness is then not simply determined by objects in the world. Rather, objects are registered by the intentionality of consciousness, which is also often shaped by its own relation to memories and fantasies.[28] This intentionality or *directing toward* something is always concerned with general essences and does not only describe a particular subjectivity defined by an immediately perceived object.[29]

In refining the mobile nuances of what takes place when we have "consciousness *of* something"—for example, in relation to a given object there can be both an "objectivating" and "valuing" of the thing, which also directs us to a general essence of objectivity and value—Husserl constructs a new relation to world.[30] As he observes, "An individual consciousness is involved with the *natural world* in a *dual* manner." Within the natural attitude, we now see that there are "not only mere things of nature but also values and practical objects." In other words, we now see that we both are *in* the world and have a wider perspective *of* the world as a whole. Practical objects with values and uses in the world such as "streets with street lights, dwellings, furniture, works of art, books [and] tools" all give us "consciousness *of* that world."[31]

This *"dual* manner" of being at once in the world and having a perspective of the world as a whole is unified through our sensuous perception. We have at once a sense of the world *and* a pure consciousness of general essences.[32] This structure maintains itself in relation to the inevitable flux of individual consciousness and is supported by the wider "horizon of determinable indeterminateness."[33] As Klaus Held has observed, the phenomenological *horizon* describes the wealth and range of shifting but "regulated referential interconnections" that form any perception.[34] The world is then not determined by the sum total of objects *in* the world. The stability and coherence of the world as a whole or "the horizon of all horizons" arises from our belief in the inexhaustibility of the given horizons of possible experience.[35] In his later work, Husserl will call this the "universal horizon."[36]

The stability of this dual perspective—of being at once in the world and having a perspective of the world as a whole—is apparent in the famous section 49 of *Ideas* 1, which is entitled "Absolute Consciousness as the Residuum after the Annihilation of the World."[37] Husserl leads up to this apparent "annihilation of the world" by contrasting the contingency of positing the natural attitude toward objects in the world to the necessary positing of the pure ego in relation to the world as a whole. While the nonbeing of the world cannot be entirely ruled out, he argues, my own living being can never be doubted.[38] This *ontological* difference reinforces "the essential detachableness of the whole natural world from the domains of consciousness."[39]

As I have suggested, this "essential detachableness" describes not so much the denial of the existing world as the assertion of two coexisting, world-like spheres: the "whole natural world" and "the domains of consciousness." It is through the world-like "domains of consciousness" that the suspension of the natural attitude toward the world, toward measuring consciousness only through its immersive relation to objects in the world, gives us a wider perspective of the essential world, of the "whole natural world." As Held remarks, "The transcendental phenomenologist is interested in consciousness only as the site of the appearance of the world."[40]

**An Ontological Point of View**
For Husserl, part of this recognition of the vistas beyond the natural attitude to the world is an appreciation that the domains of consciousness also open "*a multitude of possible worlds*."[41] In section 49 Husserl argues that though consciousness is tied to experience in the world, it is not exhausted by it. In this context, the existence of the actual world is not in itself necessary for the domains of consciousness. As he declares, "*While the being of consciousness, of any stream of mental processes whatever, would indeed be necessarily modified by an annihilation of the world of physical things its own existence would not be touched.*"[42] This gesture of course brings to mind Descartes's moment

of radical doubt as to the veracity of any truths founded on external sense perception when he asserts the autonomy of the cogito.[43] We will come back to Husserl's critical views on Descartes's suspension of the world in his later *Cartesian Meditations* (1929).

To use Kantian terms here, Husserl's point is that in acting *as if* there is no world, consciousness now has the ontological authority both to reach a vantage point from which it can apprehend the world as a whole and to construct its own varied and complex worlds.[44] For Husserl, far from falling into a Cartesian duality where the mental and the physical realms are entirely separate or relying on a Kantian transcendental idealism where things in themselves remain entirely inaccessible, the necessary independence of consciousness reinforces the essential unity between mental processes and real being. Without consciousness there can be no actual world *for us*. Phenomenological idealism, as Paul Ricoeur notes, is "methodological rather than doctrinal."[45] Consciousness always begins as "consciousness of something."[46] In his preface to the 1931 English edition of *Ideas* 1, Husserl insists, "Phenomenological idealism does not deny the factual existence of the real world. . . . Its only task and accomplishment is to clarify the sense of this world."[47] To put this in Husserl's terms, "The whole *spatiotemporal world*" is "a being *for* a consciousness."[48] Without anticipating Heidegger, one can also read this as the assertion of a more fundamental ontological relation to the world as a whole beyond the immersive limitations of the empirical, epistemological and scientific tradition.

From an ontological point of view, Husserl argues, reality as merely constructed from the perception of objects in the world is nothing in itself. It is only when they are taken as an object of consciousness that the different constituents of reality can be grasped as essential, as general essences. The phenomenological attitude is focused on the "*absolute* being" of what is experienced *in* the actual world.[49] The phenomenological reduction and the suspension of the world allow us to see that consciousness is not a derivative being but rather constitutes "the whole of absolute being" and ultimately grasps the world *as a whole*—or what Husserl will later call "the spiritual world" and "the life-world."[50] Importantly, for Husserl the suspension of the world also suspends the self-evident "I" or ego of the subject and leaves us with the pure ego of transcendental consciousness or "the pure act-process with its own essence."[51] As Merleau-Ponty observes, the suspension of the natural attitude toward the world "does not withdraw from the world toward the unity of consciousness as the world's basis." On the contrary, "it steps back to watch the forms of transcendence fly up like sparks from a fire."[52]

## 2. The Spiritual World

It is in *Ideas Pertaining to a Pure Phenomenology and to a Phenomenological Philosophy: Second Book—Studies in the Phenomenology of Constitution* (1912–1928; hereafter *Ideas* 2), that we get a more developed sense of what the phenomenological reduction means for the concept of world. This work was first published in 1952, fourteen years after Husserl's death. In contrast to *Ideas* 1, the second book is divided into three sections arranged in what appears to be a rather conventional sequence: material nature, animal nature and the spiritual world. The first two sections are concerned with an elaboration of the naturalistic attitude, and the final section, the spiritual world (*geistige Welt*), addresses the domains of pure phenomenology after the suspension of the natural attitude toward the world.[53] This is obviously not the spiritual world of Hegel, but we do need to ask what the *spiritual* world—which is neither material nor animal—means for Husserlian phenomenology, not least because the problem of the access of the animal to the world will play a significant role in both Heidegger's and Derrida's accounts of world.

### The Body and the World

As Ricoeur reminds us, despite its emphasis on the material, animal and spiritual world-like domains, *Ideas* 2 is still primarily concerned with how these domains are constituted "in consciousness." The project of transcendental phenomenology establishes the possible relations for us between these world-like domains.[54] At the same time, in *Ideas* 2 these discrete domains or regions are given a heightened ontological status.[55] They present consciousness with regions that have a world-like stability.[56] Husserl devotes relatively little space to world itself in the first part of *Ideas* 2 on material reality. The most striking aspect of this section, which will have a marked influence on Merleau-Ponty's phenomenology, is the emphasis on the *body* in constituting the phenomenological world "as world."[57] For Husserl, the general essence of material, extended and spatial things in the world is grasped through a flexible and unifying schema.[58] The body and its senses—above all the sense of touch and of sight—are "the zero point" and "center of orientation" for this unifying schemata.[59] As Husserl remarks, "By means of the sense of touch, I am always in the world perceptually, I am able to find my way around it, and I can grasp and get to know whatever I want."[60] At a basic level, the body constitutes the stability of the "*the true world*" for the solipsistic subject.[61] This can mean that if one sense is impaired or a sense is altered by a prosthesis—such as coloured spectacles—the body can produce "world-change."[62]

At the same time, the phenomenological body is always mediated by the general structures of consciousness, its directed intentions, essences and the suspensions of the natural attitude.[63]

Husserl's aim in this opening section is to establish the consistency and reliability of constituting material nature in the face of constant variation, accidental change and relativity. In the closing pages he finds a more secure level beyond the merely sensuous and solipsistic subject by insisting that the "*physicalistic thing*" reveals the unvarying properties of geometry and that the "intersubjective experience"—our relation with others—takes us beyond the limitations of a world constituted by the necessary methodological fiction of an isolated subject.[64] For Husserl, the body itself has an inherent capacity for intersubjectivity, being able to constitute "one objective world" in the midst of a multiplicity of changing, individual perceptions. The body is the possibility of "a multiplicity of subjects sharing a mutual understanding."[65]

For Husserl, a phenomenology of material nature reinforces that objects and the world maintain their identity and remain the same in the midst of a series of differences. While the physicalistic thing is always the same, regardless how one or many treat it, the material, extended thing has a different status in relation to the one and the many. This difference, Husserl argues, does not preclude that "the true thing . . . maintains its identity within the manifolds of appearances belonging to a multiplicity of subjects."[66] Since the world is "*spatiotemporal* from the first," this coherence and consistency is founded primarily on the operation of "one and the same space" which ensures "one and the same system of *location*."[67] The world is ultimately formed not by a sensuous space but by an *idealized* space. As Derrida would note in his 1962 introduction to Husserl's later essay "The Origin of Geometry" (1936), Husserlian idealization is apparent when, "on the basis of a sensible ideality," Husserl "makes a higher, absolutely objective, exact and nonsensible ideality occur."[68] The "one and the same" world has now been raised to the level of "geometrical purity."[69] Taken from a common intersubjective point of view, the sensible world can now be raised to a higher level beyond material nature. The world can be seen from the objective perspective of "the physicalist world-view or world-structure."[70] We are no longer merely in the world.

## The World at the Psychic Level

In the second section of *Ideas* 2, animal nature, Husserl turns to the psyche or soul, which can be best described as a level of "quasi-reality" that registers the ego.[71] The essential "*priority*" of the psychic realm over the bodily is exemplified by a higher level of intersubjective stability being found in the experience of empathy.[72] This priority also reinforces the unity of the psychic and the bodily within the domain of animal nature: the soul animates the body and facilitates its role in constituting the world of animal nature as its *own* world.[73] Giving us an intimation of what he will eventually mean by the spiritual world, Husserl describes the spiritual ego here as the non-corporeal ego, or ego that is grounded by the cogito and unified in all its varied lived experiences by the "pure ego" or nonpsychological ego.[74] As Ricoeur notes, for Husserl psychology cannot understand the psyche as that which constitutes the world after the suspension of the natural attitude.[75] Once again, in his account of the pure ego Husserl describes a structure where differences are subsumed in a consistent but mobile sameness that can always "discover itself as identical."[76] The world is constituted at this level by the "unities of lived experience" confirming the continuity of the ego.[77]

In contrast to the spatial unities or schemata oriented by the body that allow us to grasp things in *"one and the same form"* as they continuously change, the soul provides a "higher level" of phenomenological analysis by bringing to our attention the flux and unity of the form itself as an aspect of our lived experience.[78] In moving our attention from the body to the soul, we turn much like Descartes from the material form or the general essence of extension to the psychic form of consciousness. This move from extension to consciousness can also be described in broad terms as a change in emphasis from spatial locations to temporal fields.[79] The world constituted by the soul will display a new kind of unity. As Husserl notes, material extension always suggests a possible fragmentation, but the soul "has no places, no pieces."[80] Material realities have no history; psychic realities have a history, and the soul—in its inherent unity with the body—will give this history *a world.*[81] These discriminations will facilitate the final distinction between a being that lives in the world and finds itself "an environment of things" and "man as *spiritually real* and as a member of the spiritual world."[82]

Husserl leaves animal nature by defining empathy as a uniquely human activity. Beyond the "primal presence" of registering actual bodies there is an "appresence" in which the unity of the body and soul experiences "the interiority of the psychic."[83] Playing on the difference between touching and being touched, Husserl treats empathy as the end of a limited "solipsistic view" of the body-soul unity through the appearance of another person and the emergence of a formative "presentified co-presence."[84] With a distinctly Hegelian resonance, this co-presence allows man at last to define himself *as* man. As Husserl observes, "it is only with empathy . . . that the closed unity, man, is constituted."[85] The third and last section of *Ideas* 2, the constitution of the spiritual world, will focus on man as an object of the human sciences (as opposed to the natural sciences), which for Husserl means locating human beings in "the *world of the spirit*."[86]

## The World, Myself and Others

The spiritual world emerges from the phenomenological suspension of "the whole world of the naturalistic attitude."[87] We are now dealing exclusively with general themes and essences beyond the natural view of both subject and object. We are now also on the level of pure transcendental consciousness and an objective ideality that marks a shift in emphasis from space to time, from spatial location in the world to the temporalities of consciousness that give us a vantage point of the world as a whole.[88] For Husserl, the natural attitude to the world is restricted by a "determinate index," which includes an unavoidable "relative sense."[89] What is now required is a far larger perspective of "the whole world." As Husserl observes, the natural scientist "does not realize that the natural attitude is not the only possible one, that it allows for shifts of focus whereby there emerges the absolute, nature-constituting, consciousness, in relation to which, in virtue of the essential correlation between constituting and constituted, all nature must be relative."[90] This absolute perspective promises not only the clarity of "absolute consciousness" but also a deeper ontological understanding of "being and sense."[91]

Part of the way that one departs from the "nature-attitude" is to stop treating men and animals as "animated bodies" and "objects of nature." We must move away from not only zoology but also anthropology. We must start with what Husserl calls "the *personalistic attitude*," or the intersubjective attitude "we are always in when we live with one another, talk with one another, shake hands with one another in greeting, or are related to one another in love and aversion."[92] As a *first stage* of the spiritual world, this world must be taken exclusively as a personal world, a world in which the individual is "always the subject of his *surrounding world*."[93] This world is my world and a world that is always available or "on hand" for me.[94] Above all, the things of this personal world are taken as "intentional objects of personal consciousness."[95] Suspending *the* world, I constitute *a* world through what I mean, intend and direct toward something or someone.[96] The world thus becomes "my thematic horizon."[97]

In what again appears to be a quite Hegelian model of successive stages or distinct shapes, Husserl follows this initial stage with what he calls the "*communicative*" world, a world in which the personal is absorbed to varying degrees into a "mutually understood" social world.[98] This is a world of moral norms in which the physical world as a whole is given a "spiritual significance."[99] In contrast to Hegel, for Husserl this is not a matter of actuality *as* spirit but of "actuality *for* spirit."[100] The communicative world in turn enables the constitution of a new, higher level of personal world and opens a relation between "the world of *social subjectivities*" and "the *world of social objectivities*."[101] These interrelated but discrete levels of personal, social and personal-social worlds constitute "the idea of a world as *world of spirit*."[102]

At the same time, Husserl reiterates that the spiritual world is not an isolated or absolute realm, as one would find in Hegel. *"Even as spirit,"* he observes, *"I find myself and others in a spatial and temporal world."*[103] The *world* of spirit remains part of the spatio-temporal and natural world, not least because spirit has an unbroken relation to the body.[104] As Husserl explains, "The flux of the stream of lived experience" demonstrates the dependency of spirit on the soul and of soul on the body.[105] The spiritual world thus includes unified and idealized aspects of the physical world that can be both real and unreal.[106] For Husserl, the concept of world indicates a discrete domain, but these domains *coexist* in various strata with a series of other worlds, depending on our attitude, intent and comportment.[107]

## 3. The History of the Life-World

Having delineated in *Ideas* 1 and *Ideas* 2 the suspension of the natural attitude toward the world and the constitution of the spiritual world, Husserl amplifies and extends the range of the phenomenological world in his later works, the *Cartesian Meditations* (1929) and *The Crisis of European Sciences and Transcendental Phenomenology* (1934–1936). His *Cartesian Meditations* is extremely important for our understanding of the phenomenological world because it takes up the apparent similarities between the phenomenological suspension of the world and Descartes's radical doubt of all things given by the sensory world to establish the absolute autonomy of the cogito. As Descartes famously writes in the Second Meditation, "I have convinced myself that there is absolutely nothing in the world, no sky, no earth, no minds, no bodies."[108] Descartes sought to establish a new form of objectivity within the thinking subject that did not rely on the vagaries of the empirical world. It is also worth recalling that Descartes did not see his project as a denial of the actual world, but as a demonstration that the arguments supporting the existence of the material world and the physical body were "not as solid or as transparent as the arguments which lead us to knowledge of our own minds and of God."[109]

In Husserl's opening summary of Descartes's work, which he describes as a "radical turn" from "naïve objectivism to transcendental subjectivism," one can already see Husserl's criticism of the Cartesian reduction of the world.[110] Descartes has presumed an "ideal of science" to guide his radical doubt and assertion of the cogito. Husserl is interested here in the *prescientific conditions* that would allow for the emergence of the ideal sciences, such as geometry and mathematics.[111] Descartes has ignored the problem of the genesis and history of geometry as an ideal or unchanging science.[112] Husserl is already gesturing here to the life-world (*Lebenswelt*) as the authentic possibility of the phenomenological world. As Dagfinn Føllesdal has suggested, Husserl was preoccupied for more than thirty years with what finally became known as the "life-world."[113]

Far from presenting a contradiction, Husserl's interest in both the suspension of the natural attitude toward the world and the life-world illustrate a dominant theme in the treatment of world in twentieth-century philosophy. To put it in quite simple terms, one must be at once truly in the world itself from the outset and have a reliable framework above and beyond this world from which to view it properly as a whole. There must be an explanation for both natural genesis and transhistorical idealities. Husserl explores these distinct but intertwined challenges in terms of the contingency of the world and the unbroken, ideal perfection of the natural sciences.[114] Our haphazard experience of the world is evidently not of a level to support the timeless truths of geometry. It is within this specific context of the inadequacy of both subject and object that we must once again think about the world. As Husserl comments, "The being of the world, by reason of the evidence of natural experience, must no longer be for us an obvious matter of fact."[115]

The crucial point here is that in the necessary suspension of the natural attitude toward the world, the *life-world* appears as a "phenomenon of being." The phenomenologist may not accept the self-evident existence of the world, but he or she registers that the life-world has always been there. From this new vantage point, the phenomenologist can now see the world as the life-world. Husserl emphasizes here what was implicit in *Ideas* 1. The suspension of the world is primarily about changing the self-evident "position-taking" of a subject in relation to "the already-given objective world."[116] He also takes pains here to stress that the *epokhē* of the world always gives more than it takes. From the suspension of the natural attitude toward the world, I gain "my pure living," which entails an apprehension of the "pure ego" and a "consciousness *of* 'the' world" above and beyond a mere subjectivity or deterministic object. In short, in "the life-world *epokhē*" as he calls it in *The Crisis of European Sciences*, Husserl argues that we are given a wider or transcendental perspective of both the self and the world.[117] The life-world here is "an *index* or *guideline*" for the self in the world.[118] This wider perspective on the self and the world also shows me that the life-world is antecedent to the natural world and provides the true grounds for both the natural and the human sciences, for both genesis and idealization.[119]

## Being, Ego and World

Husserl's chief criticism of Descartes is that after refuting the reliability of all sensuous knowledge and affirming the authority of the cogito he is left with a "kind of solipsistic philosophizing."[120] For Husserl, the reduction of the natural world and the recognition of the primary life-world must be seen as a form of *transcendental* subjectivity.[121] We have gone beyond the limitations of the mere ego and its solipsistic constructions.[122] The life-world will become apparent only in the "realm of *transcendental-phenomenological self-experience*."[123] Husserl's project will now be focused on justifying the life-world as a distinct domain that both engenders the ideal and exact mathematical sciences and remains a product of the transcendental ego. The transcendental relation to the life-world requires a new thinking of the interaction between ego and world.[124] This stretching out of the old categories of subject and object is perhaps Husserl's most lasting legacy in relation to the concept of world.

To understand the life-world, we must now concern ourselves only with universal structures and with a pure science of subjectivity that will lead to an absolute objectivity.[125] The transcendental idealism of the phenomenological world is apparent when a transcendental subjectivity constitutes the objective world.[126] Once again, this will in part be facilitated by the recognition of "*intersubjective* world."[127] This is the case not least because others are experienced as both objects in the world and as "*subjects for this world*."[128] The experience of other egos and of a wider "*ego-community*" is an essential confirmation of the objective world in general and of a specific "*cultural world*."[129]

Husserl's insistence that a relation to "*the 'other' ego*," which has to be registered but not produced by my ego, plays a critical role in the "constitution of an objective world" and adds an implicit ethical dimension to the phenomenological world.[130] This will have a marked influence on the ethical philosophy of Emmanuel Lévinas.[131] Recalling the terms of *Ideas 2* and the different phenomenological relations to the body, the soul and the spirit, Husserl also argues in the *Cartesian Meditations* that I must treat the other ego as having a body and an ego like mine, but while I can be in a state of co-presence with another body I can only have an analogous appresence of an other ego.[132] The other for me is an "identical unity" that also always *remains other*. It is the same *and* not the same.[133] As we shall see, this description of the other *as* other will also play a critical role in Derrida's treatment of the concept of world.

For Husserl, in contrast to the narrow parameters of Descartes's meditations, transcendental subjectivity takes the cogito beyond "the identical ego" and concentrates on "the flowing conscious *life* in which the identical ego . . . lives."[134] In these terms, in relation to the life-world, my consciousness of something is always on the universal or essential level of a phenomenon and not simply on the level of a mere actuality.[135] Our attention—our intent— must be directed to the "perceiving itself" and not to the object perceived.[136] Husserl calls this an act of reflection that refrains from taking a position.

Phenomenological reflection will lead us from subjectivity to the possibilities of scientific objectivity because Husserl associates it with a certain disinterest.[137] Reflection gives the ego the status of a "*disinterested on-looker*" in contrast to a perception that is merely "'*interested*' *in the world*."[138] A disinterested perspective gives us a view of the world that checks our natural immersion in the world. In this sense, the transcendental phenomenologist should also be able to look "at himself" in the act of looking at the world *as a whole*.[139] This perspective becomes the basis for "a universal description" and the "foundation for a radical and universal criticism" that will unify the prescientific and scientific worlds.[140] The disinterested perspective gives us both "the life of pure consciousness" and the "meant world" as a whole, or what Husserl will henceforth call the life-world.[141]

## Ideality and the World

At the end of the *Cartesian Meditations* Husserl reminds his readers that "phenomenological explication does nothing but *explicate the sense this world has for us all, prior to any philosophizing*."[142] With the writings gathered in *The Crisis of European Sciences and Transcendental Phenomenology*, Husserl explicitly turns to this fundamental life-world and the necessary connection it illuminates between the ideal, exact sciences and transcendental subjectivity. In this late work, not fully published until 1954, Husserl is broadly focused on the *possibility* of "reason in history," of the historical consistency and future of ideal rational and scientific disciplines, concepts and objects.[143] At the same time, the description of the "world as existing through reason" requires an elaboration of the prescientific world as the coherent possibility of not simply a singular objective world common to all but also of an ideal *and* historical world.[144] A "world of idealities" is not simply founded on a contingent event that was at one time invalid or may be superseded in the future. The unity of an ideal world can only reveal "what in itself already exists in truth."[145]

This ideal world is demonstrated in Galileo's idealization of nature. Galileo's idealization of nature as mathematics and the assertion of pure idealities stand as an example of moving beyond what is found simply *in* nature to a vantage point where one can think of nature *as a whole*.[146] This process entails a shift of perspective from particular bodies experienced in the world to the measurement of general fluctuating shapes to the calculation of universal invariant forms. Geometry will give rise to "an infinite and yet self-enclosed world of ideal objects."[147] This ideal world attitude can then be extended to an analysis of the world as a whole.[148] We are dealing here with the concept of world in its most discrete, exact and specific designation of a coherent, untouchable sphere, domain or realm. As we shall see, one can contrast this with Heidegger's formulation of being-in-the-world. One might also compare the phenomenological world of ideal objects to the Kantian categorical world and the Hegelian world as spirit. These ideal objects are not describing the world, but they are describing the possibility of a discrete, absolute and whole world. We are presented with world as the epitome of exactitude.[149]

However, as Klaus Held has pointed out, it is also important to note that Husserl juxtaposes modern science, which treats the idealized world as no more than an "infinite idea," with the life-world that is both enriched and contained by its many possible horizons.[150] For Husserl, this exact, ideal and transhistorical world *arises from* the life-world. He describes the life-world in general terms as "the surrounding world of life" that can become an objective and ideal world.[151] This prescientific "everyday life-world" is not just a name for the natural physical world. It is a world that must be open to the general intuitions of consciousness that *constitute* the bodies, souls and spirits of the phenomenological world. It is also "the only real world," which must not be lost in the abstractions of natural science.[152] Husserl is drawing a very clear distinction here between the idealizations of nature and "prescientifically intuited nature."[153] The natural sciences have failed to keep in touch with the very object that they were intended to describe: the *life*-world. A phenomenology of the life-world should take us back to "the ultimate purpose" that inaugurated the great natural and mathematical sciences and now informs the human sciences.[154] At stake is the possibility of a new and, ultimately, more accurate science of the world.

Turning in this late work to "the actually experienced and experiencable world" or "the world constantly given to us as actual in our concrete world-life," one can compare Husserl to Kant: neither starts with the world but both end with the world.[155] These very different forms of transcendental idealism are both driven by the continuing problem of giving an account of the world itself without relying on the terms *within* the world to coordinate the analysis. Heidegger's audacious being-in-the-world will be an attempt to give a more nuanced phenomenological account of the world that still eludes Husserl. Despite the evocation of the actual life-world, Husserl is still primarily interested in how this world has been mediated and idealized into a methodological *idea*.[156]

For Husserl, the modern distortion of the relation to the prescientific world begins with Galileo and Hobbes—and with empiricism in general— taking the sense impressions that arise from external objects as being first and foremost subjective. This inaugural and seemingly unavoidable subjectivity is then counterbalanced by the apparently self-evident mathematical properties of nature itself. These determinations then give rise to the subjective empiricism and innate rationalism that dominates seventeenth- and eighteenth-century philosophy. This in turn leads to a secondary division between a pure science of spatio-temporal forms and the natural sciences.[157] As the possibility of an authentic and new science, the phenomenological life-world will provide a common unified source for these apparent divisions without returning to the old categories of the subject and object.[158]

One of the significant aspects of Husserl's account of the history of geometry is that he offers a *history* of the concept of world, and this recognition that world has a history will become a key aspect of Heidegger's hermeneutical phenomenology (Heidegger of course had already been working on the problem of world for more than a decade when Husserl was writing *The Crisis of European Sciences* in 1934–1936). As Husserl observes, the scientist must recognize the need "to *inquire back* into the *original meaning* of all his meaning-structures and methods, i.e., into the *historical meaning of their primal establishment*."[159] Phenomenology shows us that every concept of world has a history. In the aftermath of Husserlian phenomenology, Heidegger and Derrida will both treat world as a historical concept that is not given at the outset or resolved in the end but remains an ongoing problem.

### The History of the Concept of World

As we have seen, Husserl argues that the modern history of the concept of world begins with Galileo. It is Galileo who first treats nature "as a really self-enclosed world of bodies."[160] As much as this is a gesture toward modern cosmology and physics, it also reinforces the far older history of world as an index of containment. In the aftermath of Galileo, a fundamental division appears between the empirical and the rational which will reach its heights in Cartesian dualisms or the insistence on the complete separation of the sensible and the intelligible. For Husserl, this generates a "split" within the concept of world itself: there are now "two worlds," the world of nature and the psychic world.[161] This is the foundation of the metaphysical world of the seventeenth and eighteenth centuries that Kant will first embrace and then challenge in his critical philosophy.

Husserl's history of the "rational world" raises the question once again of using the concept of world to designate a discrete "domain" or "closed special regions."[162] Significantly, Husserl links this modern use of world to the appearance of a new *subject-oriented* psychology that combines the short-comings of both empiricism and rationalism to generate "a psychophysical anthropology in the rationalistic spirit."[163] The modern idea of the self and its worlds appears with the modern idea of world. For Husserl, this is the legacy of Cartesian thought. After Descartes, the life-world is subsumed into projects of objectivism and subjectivism.[164] Despite his critical gesture, Kant is unable to escape these determinations because he inherits the Cartesian definition of world as the possibility of "a rational systematic unity."[165]

Husserl also praises Descartes in *The Crisis of European Sciences* for being the first philosopher to call into question sciences that are founded on *the* world and the hitherto self-evident link between experience and "the world itself."[166] At the same time, the phenomenological suspension of the natural attitude toward the world should allow consciousness to penetrate "into the sphere of being which is prior in principle to everything which conceivably has being for me."[167] The *epokhē* reveals an ontological depth beyond the limits of experience. For Husserl, a truly radical suspension of the natural attitude toward the world should also never stop.[168] On this basis one can say that a *phenomenological history* of the concept of world can never assume that world is "taken for granted."[169]

In this context, Husserl argues that Descartes's greatest fault is that he constructs a completed rational ego that can never *live* in the world.[170] A phenomenological history of the concept of world will not only overcome the old opposition between empiricism and rationalism but also have the breadth to embrace at once the spiritual world, the ideal world and the life-world. From this perspective, Husserl can criticize Kant for his inadequate concept of world at the start of the *Critique of Pure Reason*. Kant misunderstood Hume's insight that the life-world is not the world of empirical sensibility. For Hume, world is a subject-oriented concept that must rely on the fictions of the imagination to create the necessary illusion of an unbroken and coherent impression of the world.[171] Hume's failing is that he treats mere "sense data" as perception.[172] At the same time, Husserl credits Hume with being the first philosopher to recognize "the *naïveté* of the scientist of nature or of the world in general" who speaks about an objectivity without admitting that this so-called objective world is only possible because of "his own *life-construct* developed within himself." For Husserl, this limited perspective is "no longer possible as soon as *life* becomes the point of focus."[173] The *life*-world demands a more authentic understanding of subjectivity and objectivity. However, as Derrida will later point out, this leads Husserl to give a new status to life as the ground and horizon of the world.[174] As Husserl remarks, "To live is always to live-in-certainty-of-the world."[175]

Husserl goes on to argue that Kant partially addresses the limitations of Hume's empiricism by asserting the *a priori* forms of space and time, but the transcendental aesthetic implies that "the whole world of natural sciences . . . is a subjective construct of our intellect."[176] The Kantian world leads to a cul-de-sac where "objective knowledge cannot be objectively knowable." In this sense, critical philosophy produces a new division between philosophy and science.[177] However, Kant also recognizes that a philosophy of world must take account of a "knowing subjectivity as the primal locus of all objective formations."[178] As the extensive appendices to the incomplete manuscript of *The Crisis of European Sciences* suggest, Husserl concludes that the Kantian world has failed to take account of the life-world because it has excluded the body from transcendental philosophy.[179] The essential coordinates of the phenomenological life-world are found in the relation between the body, the soul and spirit as elaborated in *Ideas 2*. The history of the concept of world teaches us that beyond the physical body (*Körper*), the living body (*Leib*) and its essential relation to the soul and spirit constitute the life-world as the true origin of the phenomenological world.[180]

## A Constant Horizon

Despite the avowed need for leaping and zigzagging between different historical periods, Husserl's history of the concept of world is driven by a teleological rigour toward the unification of the various forms of the phenomenological world: the life-world; the spiritual, animal and material worlds and the suspension of the natural attitude toward the world should be taken together as a whole.[181] This gives us the ultimate conceit of Husserlian phenomenology: there is a "constant horizon" or unbroken vantage point for *all* of these worlds. The history of the concept of world from Galileo to Kant gives us the essential, ideal and constituted worlds of a transcendental subjectivity in relation to an objective world that remains in touch with its authentic life-world.[182] As a concept for understanding the history of philosophy, the life-world reassures us that we do not have to choose between science and life.

The history of the life-world in *The Crisis of the European Sciences* establishes the possibility of a single unity or *horizon* for the many worlds of phenomenology.[183] It is this unified horizon, this constant background that operates as a wider context, which allows Husserl to think once again of a final vantage point "*above* the whole manifold but synthetically unified flow" and "*above* the universal conscious life" that constitutes the life-world.[184] It is only in such conditions, he insists, that "the gaze of the philosopher in truth first becomes fully free."[185] As each new form of world is constituted and in turn suspended, the history of the concept of world ultimately serves to affirm the freedom of the philosopher to stand above and beyond its own worlds. This is the essence of the phenomenological world: "I stand *above* the world, which has now become for me, in a quite peculiar sense, a *phenomenon*."[186]

Phenomenology is distinguished by its challenge to the natural attitude to the world while elaborating a new, shifting mobility of perspectives to reach the real world itself. As Husserl observes at the end of *Ideas 2*, "The world of things in which spirits live is an objective world constituted out of subjective surrounding worlds and is the objectively determinable surrounding world of the spirits."[187] This variegated path to the one true world is transformed by the affirmation of a new range of constituted and possible worlds. Husserl rejects the Kantian regulative world, since he believes that the world itself can be reached, but he also gives a new dynamism and perceptual mobility to the static absolutes of the Kantian categorical world. He always begins with the world that is already constituted and requires the phenomenological *epokhē*, but he always ends with a world that has been constituted by the general intuitions of consciousness and transcendental subjectivity.[188]

First formulated at the same time as the birth of cinema at the end of the nineteenth century and the start of the twentieth century, Husserlian phenomenology can be seen as the philosophical articulation of the possibility of *coexisting virtual worlds* that we readily embrace today, but it is a virtual world that always defines its parameters in relation to the consciousness *of* something in the real world. At the same time, despite the recognition of constantly changing perspectives and the challenge to the traditional designations of subject and object, phenomenology retains the singular perspective of the world. It treats the world as a self-evident concept, affirming that an authentic vision of the world as a whole allows us to be truly in the world. Husserl never questions the ability to establish the essential "difference between the manner of being an object in the world and that of the world itself."[189] Despite the influential history of the concept of world in *The Crisis of European Sciences*, phenomenology never questions the concept of world itself. For Heidegger, the world will always remain a problem.

CHAPTER FOUR

# Heidegger and the Problem of World

## 1. Being in the World

Heidegger does not start with the world in *Being and Time* (1927). He begins his most famous work with the question of being, and it is from this framework that he turns to the phenomenon of the world. To reach the world, one must accept that "the Being of entities 'is' not itself an entity" and that *Da-sein* (being-there) is a particular form of being "which includes inquiring as one of the possibilities of its being."[1] Dasein is distinctive because being is "an *issue* for it" and, specifically, as the question of "its existence."[2] It is only "through existing itself" that Dasein can address the question of being. It is at this point, after having introduced the question of being and Dasein, that Heidegger makes his first reference to the world.

Heidegger is quite precise at the outset in his treatment of the world: "being in a world . . . belongs essentially" to Dasein. This means not only that "Dasein's understanding of Being" involves "an understanding of something like a 'world'" but that it also gives Dasein an understanding of "the Being of those entities which become accessible within the world." In other words, world gives Dasein access to beings "whose character of Being is other than that of Dasein."[3] World functions to give Dasein a relation to beings other than itself. At the same time, it is important to note that *Being and Time* does not start with a self-evident access to the world but opens far more cautiously with "something like a 'world.'" Heidegger will later clarify that these beings with a different kind of being are predominantly things *in* the world

67

that can be taken merely as present-at-hand (with a self-evident theoretical immediacy) or ready-to-hand (with a habitual immediate access).[4]

Things in the world are commonly treated as objects that one can merely look at as self-evidently present-at-hand. Heidegger begins to question this traditional assumption of phenomenology by emphasizing that things in the world that are ready-at-hand already involve a sense of active and problematic utility.[5] In contrast to what we found with Husserl, beings that have some kind of relation to being also hold back or withdraw themselves to varying degrees, and the extent to which they are not merely present-at-hand registers their relation to being. "Existent Dasein," Heidegger argues, "does not encounter itself as something present-at-hand within-the-world."[6] World in general then describes the relation of Dasein to itself and to others as *its* question of being. In other words, the "way world is understood" *as an immersion* can only be registered through Dasein and its interpretation of itself.[7] World will be demarcated in the relation between Dasein and time "as the horizon for all understanding of being."[8]

Seeing the world *through* Dasein, world takes on the structure of the ontic-ontological difference. Because "we *are*" Dasein, in raising the question of being, what is ontically closest to us is also ontologically farthest away. In this sense, Dasein's being "remains concealed."[9] The crucial point here is that we are not dealing with the world itself but with Dasein's interpretation or hermeneutic of the world. At the same time, Heidegger emphasizes that Dasein tends to rely on the "reflected light" of the world "to interpret itself."[10] He associates this reliance on the world with a limited philosophical tradition that interrupts Dasein's attempts to claim the past as its own.[11] Heidegger links this conventional treatment of the world and nature as the locus of being with the privileging of the present and presence.[12] This limited concept of world can only be counteracted by delineating the world through Dasein's own investigation into the question of being. The world is not constructed by Dasein, but it is only Dasein's relation to the world that can transform our understanding of the concept of world. This exclusive reliance on Dasein and its questions will also lead to Heidegger's later attempts to clarify the human relation to world *as a transcendence* that is confronted with the ongoing problem of a world that is shared with animals. This tension between immersion and transcendence in relation to world is already apparent in *Being and Time*.

## The Hermeneutic of Dasein

As Heidegger noted in 1929, *Being and Time* was the second of three different approaches to the *problem* of world.[13] The first, in "On the Essence of Ground"

(1928–1929), is concerned with the historical development of the word and concept of world. The second, in *Being and Time* (1926–1927), addresses "the *phenomenon of world* by interpreting the *way in which we at first and for the most part move about in our everyday world*."[14] The third, discussed in *The Fundamental Concepts of Metaphysics—World, Finitude, Solitude* (1929–1930), focuses on "a comparative examination" of man, animals, plants and stones.[15] What makes *Being and Time* distinctive is its emphasis on the world as not a concept but as a *phenomenon* (*das Weltphänomen*). A phenomenon describes something that "shows itself," something that becomes "manifest" and "*shows itself in itself*."[16] The world as a phenomenon should give us the world *itself*. However, for Heidegger the manifestation of the world in "our everyday life" reveals "the phenomenon of world as a problem."

This problem arises in *Being and Time* because Heidegger approaches the world from the vantage point of Dasein, and we therefore find "that which is so close and intelligible to us in our everyday dealings is actually and fundamentally remote and unintelligible to us."[17] However, the world is also "a problem" because in section 7 of *Being and Time* Heidegger offers a remarkable reinterpretation of Husserlian phenomenology. For Heidegger, the relation between phenomena and logos does not describe a self-evident "beholding."[18] It is not enough to base a phenomenology on the transparent immediacy of "just sensing something, or staring at it."[19] Heidegger contrasts this to what he later calls a "circumspective concern," a phenomenology of the wider context rather than a Husserlian phenomenology of focused intent.[20] This circumspection (*Umsicht*) is in turn determined by a necessary interpretation—a hermeneutics—of the being of beings which "for the most part does *not* show itself at all," which "remains *hidden*" and "*covered up*."[21] As Heidegger observes, "And just because the phenomena are proximally and for the most part *not* given, there is need for phenomenology."[22] It is from this recalibrated phenomenology that he will analyse the phenomenon of world—or being-in-the-world—as part of the "hermeneutic of Dasein."[23]

Heidegger may not start with the world but he gives being-in-the-world an unavoidable and fundamental status.[24] Being-in-the-world (*In-der-Welt-sein*) is "a fundamental structure in Dasein" and it is therefore "not pieced together, but is primordially and constantly a whole."[25] Heidegger adds, "The whole of this structure always comes first." As he later suggests, being-in-the-world can only be understood as a deduction.[26] Heidegger makes this critical point in a short paragraph between the end of the introduction and before the beginning of the first part of *Being and Time*. Being-in-the-world is always "*unitary*" and whole.[27] From the perspective of Dasein's relation to its own existence and to the question of the meaning of being, one can say that *Being and Time* starts with *the world as a whole*.[28]

Heidegger insists that one should begin the hermeneutic of Dasein correctly, and this means recognizing that we can never treat the being of Dasein as something "merely present-at-hand within the world."[29] If we can only approach the world as a whole *through* Dasein, we should not treat the primary wholeness of being-in-the-world world as present-at-hand. There may be things that are present-at-hand or ready-to-hand in the world, but the world *as a whole* cannot be taken as *Vorhandenheit* or *Zuhandenheit*. Heidegger will go on to make a series of distinctions to differentiate between mere things that are spatially taken as present-at-hand and Dasein's fundamental relation to the world. Things are simply *in* the world while Dasein is, on the contrary, in a state of "'being alongside' the world."[30] This particular distinction will lead to one of Heidegger's most revolutionary steps as he attempts to extend Husserl's work and to take the relation to world beyond the traditional spatial designations of subject and object and internal and external.

Being alongside or being-amidst (*Sein bei*), as Hubert Dreyfus translates it, does not describe a spatial side-by-side relation: Dasein is not merely *in* the world but neither is it *beside* the world.[31] Being-amidst is a form of Being-in (*In-Sein*). Heidegger illustrates this through the example of touching. Things can never touch because touching requires an encounter between beings that have both Da-sein *and* a world. For a being to touch or be touched, Heidegger insists, "something like the world is already revealed to it, so that from out of that world another entity can manifest itself in touching."[32] Without "something like the world," there is no touching. We will return to this proposition on touching in the reading of Derrida.

Dasein produces or reveals the world, and the world in turn facilitates the showing or manifestation of another being. Heidegger contrasts this with beings that are "present-at-hand within the world" but also "*worldless* in themselves" and can therefore never touch.[33] He does not mention animals here, but this is most likely the beings that are in question. This important passage, which first raises the grave problem in Heidegger's thought of an inevitable *hierarchy of access* to the world, gives us a critical insight into the difference between being merely *in* the world (as a worldlessness) and being-in-the-world (as having a world). Being-in-the-world is not simply in the world.

Beyond touching, any kind of meeting between Dasein and another being is only possible because Dasein can "show itself within a *world*."[34] In these encounters, world provides a structure for self-display, for a being to show or manifest itself. One could describe this structure in a classical logic of containment: it is only "within a *world*" that Dasein can "show itself."

However, for Heidegger, the phenomenon of world itself is also structured by registering what is covered up and does not show itself. It remains to be seen whether being-in-the-world is another form of containment. At the very least, predicated on the hermeneutic of Dasein, the phenomenon of world produces distinct and seemingly clear-cut boundaries between beings having a world and being worldless.

Nonetheless, Heidegger's being-in-the-world is a revolutionary innovation in the history of the concept of world. It offers a concept of world beyond the conventional thought of the internal and external. Being-in-the-world, one is neither *in* the world (as a subject in the external or outer world) nor is one *out* of the world (as a subject inside itself and cut off from the world). Being-in-the-world can be described as a mode of "Being-already-alongside" (or being-already-amidst) and it is worth quoting Heidegger at some length as he explains the world that cannot be thought or known as only external or internal. He writes,

> When Dasein directs itself towards something and grasps it, it does not some-how first get out of an inner sphere in which it has been proximally encapsu-lated, but its primary kind of Being is such that it is always "outside" alongside entities which it encounters and which belong to a world already discovered. Nor is any inner sphere abandoned when Dasein dwells alongside the entity to be known, and determines its character; but even in this "Being-outside" alongside the object, Dasein is still "inside," if we understand this in the cor-rect sense; that is to say, it is itself "inside" as a Being-in-the-world which knows. And furthermore, the perceiving of what is known is not a process of returning with one's booty to the "cabinet" of consciousness after one has gone out and grasped it; even in perceiving, retaining, and preserving, the Dasein which knows *remains outside*, and it dies so *as Dasein*.[35]

Heidegger overturns the epistemological conventions of knowing the world through a discrete subject, or what Dreyfus calls a "self-referential conscious-ness," which registers its own internal activity in relation to an established external world.[36] As Heidegger had argued in 1925, "A *science of conscious-ness*" privileges "inner experience" and reduces "the whole man" to the ap-parent clearly defined difference between an inner and outer perception.[37] Dreyfus characterizes being-in-the-world as the revolutionary articulation of a "non-self-referential mode of awareness."[38] In this sense, the Heideggerian world is a displacement of the Cartesian model of the mind's autonomous activity in relation to an entirely separate external world.[39]

Dreyfus himself argues that being-in-the-world offers the alternative of a "socially defined 'subject' relating to a holistically defined 'object.'"[40]

However, Dreyfus's emphasis on socialization is somewhat problematic, not least because Heidegger draws careful distinctions between the nonsocial ubiquity of the aroundness of the environment, the intricacies of being-with others and the necessary limitations of the public world.[41] Nonetheless, he is right to emphasize that the "object" is recast in a holistic or wider context and that being-in-the-world curtails, if not subdues, the claims for an "isolated" self-forming subject.[42]

Being-already-amidst can also be read as a criticism of the use of world to designate the self-evidence of sensible and intelligible realms. In its relation to the world, Dasein does not begin from "an inner sphere" but neither does it leave this "inner sphere." Dasein is always alongside or amidst the world: both inside *and* outside the world at once. Being-in-the-world registers the rupture of the barrier between the internal and the external. As Heidegger later observes in the midst of a critique of Kant, the true "scandal of philosophy" is that it still relies on "an ontologically inadequate way of starting with *something* of such a character that independently *of it* and 'outside' *of it* a 'world' is to be proved as present-at-hand."[43] However, it is also important to recall that at the very moment that he gestures to a new, fluid model for rethinking the relation between the self and the world, Heidegger also introduces a new barrier between beings that have a world and those that are worldless.

As he goes on to remark, this relation to the world that is at once inside and outside the world relies on a mode of being-in-the-world that must precede the world. Taking the world itself as a *phenomenon* does not entail an account of what "shows itself" in the world, such as "houses, trees, people, mountains, stars."[44] Rather, the phenomenon of world must be understood "as that which shows itself as Being and as a structure of Being."[45] As Heidegger notes, one would then expect that the world will be concerned with "the Being of the Things of Nature" and with "Things 'invested with value.'"[46] These "things" are only given as present-at-hand, but since Dasein is asking about being, and the world is Dasein's world, we can also address the question of the being of these things. At the same time, these things are already *within* the world and therefore cannot tell us about the world *as a whole*.[47] Heidegger later argues that Descartes's chief error is identifying the things in the world (*res extensa*) "with the world in general."[48]

## Contextual Immersions and Widening Vistas
Beyond its possible meanings—the totality of beings that are present-at-hand, a collective designation for multiplicities and public and private domains—world only "shows itself as Being" and "as a state of Dasein"

through what Heidegger calls "*the worldhood of the world as such.*"[49] The worldhood (*Weltlichkeit*) of the world, he argues, will be apparent by focusing on "everyday Being-in-the-world" because it is "*closest* to Dasein."[50] At this point Heidegger still retains the phrase "something like the world," suggesting some latitude in this stage of his inquiry. Through focusing on "average everydayness," he writes, "something like the world will come into view."[51] The worldhood of the world is predominantly focused on Dasein's *orienting* itself in its world through various interactions with the things it uses and values. The relation to what Heidegger calls in general terms "equipment" (*Zeug*) arises from an immediate, practical use that opens a wider referential context. This can be distinguished from the traditional mediated observation of static things by a discrete subject.[52] Heidegger uses this "totality of equipment"—and the "work-world" it constitutes—to begin to map out Dasein's wider environment (*Umwelt*) and aroundness (*das Umhafte*).[53] At the same time, his main task in these opening sections of *Being and Time* is to demonstrate the elusiveness of the most proximate and the inherent unfamiliarity of the familiar.

This mapping out of the world through the daily encounters and practical actions of Dasein is only one aspect of the worldhood of the world. As Heidegger clearly states, "The world itself is not an entity within-the-world."[54] Dasein's understanding of the world arises from its being-in-the-world and its ability to take a "pre-ontological" vantage point or "glimpse" of the world *as a whole* in relation to beings that have "their character within-the-world."[55] By grasping this larger perspective, by thinking of the world *as a whole* in relation to what is merely *in* the world, Dasein can define itself and its understanding of the world. For example, in section 40 Heidegger draws a critical distinction between fear and anxiety. The former is concerned with beings "within the world," while the latter addresses Dasein itself, being-in-the-world and "the world in its worldhood."[56] This anxious glimpse of the world as a whole is what Heidegger means when he says, "Something like the world show[s] itself for concernful Being-in-the-world."[57] In this way, beyond the possibilities of equipment that is "ready-to-hand," Dasein has "a possibility of Being in which the worldhood of those entities within-the-world with which it is concerned is, in a certain way, lit up for it."[58]

The vantage point of worldhood of the world as a whole gives us a unique insight into "the worldly character of what is within-the-world."[59] As Heidegger suggests in section 16, the implicit task of the worldhood of world is to use the "totality of equipment" to "go beyond the Being of what is within the world."[60] Heidegger describes a number of possible strategies to achieve this vantage point. For example, when what is assumed to be ready-at-hand becomes unusable and is registered as obtrusive and obstinate it raises the general larger "context" of equipment. As Heidegger comments, "With this totality . . . world announces itself."[61] Heidegger later turns to the more so-phisticated level of signs that indicate the wider context and totality of what is ready-at-hand and facilitates an "orientation within our environment."[62] He follows this with another level for reaching the broader context beyond individual things that he calls "the totality of involvements."[63] This structure of totality in turn gestures toward an even larger context beyond all involve-ment in the world: the worldhood of the world and being-in-the-world.

Again, it is important to emphasize that for Heidegger the world can only be taken *as a whole*. The world cannot be "pieced together."[64] It is only when a totality is glimpsed in the world or when one can abstract a series of totali-ties that afford an ever-widening perspective that one has anything like an intimation of the world or, to put it in Heidegger's terms, of the common view of the being of Dasein, the worldhood of the world and being-in-the-world. At the same time, Heidegger is quite clear that taking the world *as a whole* (*im Ganzen*) is not about assuming a world-view (*Weltanschauung*) or world-picture (*Weltbildes*) as some self-evident "map of the world" that grants us "a universal and uniform orientation."[65] These uses of world are still lim-ited, to varying degrees, to an orientation *in* the world and cannot provide a perspective of the world *as a whole*. This is a vantage point which can only be approached by thinking from the more original ontological difference between being and beings.

Heidegger's emphasis on a series of steps to secure Dasein's *world-like* perspective of the world describes two interrelated but distinct structures of immersion and transcendence: Dasein's absorption in the world and the glimpse of the world as a whole.[66] The glimpse of the world as a whole is made possible by the interruption of habitual, everyday use. When some-thing that we use all the time and hardly notice is suddenly missing, there is "a *break*" in the customary "referential contexts" and we become aware of the surrounding environment (*Umwelt*).[67] The *Umwelt* is then found to be *already there* and extends beyond the limitations of the "referential contexts" that only address being within the world.[68] Heidegger is also concerned here with giving the announcement of world the unique ability to check the tra-ditional phenomenological authority of the ready-to-hand and the present-at-hand. The announcement of the world offers the possibility of a different framework from the conventional claims for beholding a readily given full presence in the present moment.

This is the first time in *Being and Time* that Heidegger turns to the criti-cal problem of the world as something that is *always already* there. As he later observes, "In anything ready-to-hand the world is always 'there.'"[69] In effect, to have an understanding of the world that is always already there, we must already have an understanding of the world *as a whole*.[70] For Heidegger, this entails a synthesis of the wider perspective of the world and the already there. The worldhood of the world is "an involvement of something in something beforehand" in which Dasein already "understand[s] itself beforehand."[71] Heidegger calls this final "relational totality" a form of "significance," and this completes the trinity of totalities for reaching the worldhood of the world.[72]

## Fleeing from the World as a Whole

In his account of the worldhood of the world Heidegger also begins to set out the related structure of Dasein's familiarity (surface) with the world and the constant announcement of the unfamiliarity (depth) of the world in relation to itself, to others, to time and to death. One might say that the world for Dasein is always *(un)familiar*. This becomes apparent in Heidegger's examination of the "the aroundness of the environment" and spatiality of being-in-the-world.[73] Once again, Heidegger's task is to link the positioning of the totality of what is ready-to-hand into a larger framework, in this case into "something like a region."[74] This region in turn indicates an aroundness (*Umhafte*) in which "things present-at-hand are never proximally given."[75] Spatiality does not provide a static mode for theoretical observation. Spatiality registers the un(familiarity) of the phenomenon of world for Dasein. For example, in being-in-the-world in relation to others (being-with), Dasein is at once here *and* over there. As Heidegger observes, "In the 'here,' the Dasein which is absorbed in its world speaks not towards itself but away from itself towards the 'yonder' of something circumspectively ready-to-hand; yet it still has itself in view in its existential spatiality."[76]

What is merely *in* the world can be described through its position and place. However, since the being of Dasein cannot be taken as simply present-at-hand, what is spatially closest can only be registered *as* close through its relation to what is spatially farthest away. Heidegger calls this form of spatiality "de-severance," or "de-distancing" (*Ent-fernung*).[77] De-serverance also means that "close" and "far" are relative terms that alter in relation to Dasein. Being-in-the-world tells us that Dasein is first and foremost spatial.[78]

For Heidegger, these constant spatial alterations in the aroundness of the environment are not indicative of some nascent subjectivity: they demonstrate *"the Being-in-itself of the 'true world.'"*[79] It is from this dynamic interrelation between the close and the far that Dasein finds its sense of direction and orientation.[80] Heidegger conjures a remarkable vision of the "true world" as a being-in-the-world that is coordinated neither through the subject nor the object but within the relation between what is in the world and the world-like perspective of Dasein that encounters the spatial remoteness of what is closest.[81]

Being-in-the-world is also an emphatic rejection of thinking of world as a world of nature. Nature is nothing less than the loss of worldhood.[82] At the same time, it is now apparent that one cannot describe being-in-the-world as a Kantian regulative world or as a traditional metaphysical world. "As Being-in-the-world," Heidegger observes, "Dasein has already discovered a 'world.'"[83] If these Kantian categories are still applicable, being-in-the-world is perhaps closest to the categorical world, to a constituted or instituted world that is not the world but takes on an authority that is akin to the world. In Heidegger's case, this categorical world suggests a series of deep structures, widening perspectives and dynamic relations that take it beyond the previous phenomenological attempts to grasp the authentic relation between consciousness and the world. We may find this the most compelling account of *absorption* in the world since Kant, but its careful calibrations and methodological hierarchies also reinforce the truism found in Kant that *one cannot use what is in the world to grasp the world itself.*

In his subsequent analysis of Dasein's absorption in the world through its interaction with others and its relation to time and death, Heidegger reinforces this implicit tension between contextual immersion and the need for a larger frame of reference. In section 28 he argues that Dasein's relation to the world is defined by distinguishing itself from both things and the levelling neutrality of the dominant public or social domain in which "everyone is other, and no one is himself."[84] This leads once again to the necessary error of interpreting Dasein as something only within the world. Heidegger writes, "Because the phenomenon of world gets passed over in this absorption in the world, its place gets taken by what is present-at-hand within-the-world, namely, things."[85] It is striking how easily the phenomenon of world gets overlooked here through Dasein's absorption in the world. From the point of view of what is merely in the world, everything—including others—is taken by Dasein as immediate, self-evident and entirely given "as presence-at-hand."[86] At the same time, this error is necessary because it defines "the closest everyday Being-in-the-world" and provides the conditions for a reaction that leads to the more profound question of the occulted being of beings.[87]

While Heidegger explicitly turns away in section 28 from the world and the focus on "a steady preliminary view of the structural whole," he nonetheless makes a point of linking each stage that follows *back* to "the unitary phenomenon" of the world.[88] The many fluctuations of Dasein's "being-in" refer to its being-there, to the there in which it finds itself or what Heidegger calls thrownness (*Geworfenheit*).[89] Dasein finds itself *there* amidst its shifting and enigmatic states of mind or moods (*Stimmung*). For Heidegger, despite these constant alterations and variations, "*The mood has already disclosed, in every case, Being-in-the-world as a whole.*"[90] The world, he argues, *always* provides a "steady . . . view" of a "structural whole." The moods of Dasein register moments of disjunction that reveal in turn the series of totalities that lead to glimpsing the worldhood of world. As he remarks, "It is precisely when we see the 'world' unsteadily and fitfully in accordance with our moods, that the ready-to-hand shows itself in its specific worldhood."[91]

This series of totalities that always refer back to the worldhood of the world culminates in being as care (*Sorge, besorgen*) or the *totality* of the "structural whole" of Dasein.[92] The unity of this structural whole facilitates Dasein's relation to itself, though Heidegger pointedly describes this new relation and its various possibilities as one of Dasein finding itself "*already ahead of itself*" and always in the midst of the world.[93] The "structural whole" of Dasein remains a totality *in relation to* the vantage point of the world as a whole. The full range of Dasein's ongoing possibilities or the "not yet" includes being-toward-death and the possibility *of* the impossible as its ultimate, authentic and individual "being-a-whole."[94] This wholeness of Dasein is reinforced by Heidegger's account of time. Every manifestation of the wholeness and unity of being-in-the-world *in relation to* the worldhood of world is supported by the "*temporality* [that] *temporalises itself as a whole*" or "a future which makes present in the process of having been."[95] Being-in-the-world is understood not in what is taken as present-at-hand but in the wider horizons of "making-present."[96] As Heidegger observes, "In so far as Dasein temporalises itself, a world *is* too."[97]

At the same time, being as care supports the critical relation of Dasein to the world as a whole through the form of anxiety (*Angst*). The world preoccupies and slightly overwhelms Dasein in the midst of its varied projecting possibilities of understanding.[98] Nonetheless, Heidegger insists, "*in every case*" there remains "an understanding of the world."[99] He describes this world-related understanding as an interpretation that goes beyond merely beholding and draws an important distinction between an *apophantical* discourse and a *hermeneutic* interpretation.[100] The former always shows itself *as* itself and exhibits "something in such a way that we just look at it."[101] The latter is mediated by circumspective concern and does not show itself but is still manifested *as* something occulted. In *Kant and the Problem of Metaphysics* (1929), he refers to this showing that holds itself back as "the constant although mostly concealed shimmering of all that exists."[102] When Heidegger

turns to Dasein and the phenomenon of truth, which will become the dominant focus of his later work, he describes truth as a relation between *apóphanis* and *alētheia*, or a showing-itself that relies on and manifests an uncovering
of what has been covered.[103]

Taken in this larger sense, the apophantic logos also displays a "synthesis-
structure" that does not simply merge something with something but rather
lets "something be seen in its *togetherness* with something—letting it be
seen *as* something."[104] This describes the unique ability of Dasein to take
something *as* something, to register "the explicitness of something that is
understood."[105] While this "as-structure" can be reduced to the "merely present-at-hand," Heidegger argues that Dasein also can take the table *as* a table
because it understands the series of wider contexts and temporalities that
manifest the relation between what is shown and not shown and gestures to
the fundamental difference between beings and being.[106] Dasein can take the
table *as* table because it understands the world *as* a whole.

As much as *Being and Time* provides an innovative account of the world
as an immersive context beyond the traditional designations of subject and
object, it always keeps in sight this vantage point or frame of reference
above and beyond the world. In distinguishing anxiety *of* the world as a
whole from fear *in* the world, Heidegger argues that anxiety is concerned
with "the *world as world*."[107] This anxiety takes Dasein away from the
daunting expanse of the world *as* a whole and facilitates its individualiza-
tion, its possibility and its finitude.[108] *Being and Time* is concerned not only
with the phenomenon of world but also with confronting the world *as* a
whole.[109] Dasein is never simply in the world: it remains in an anxious and
(un)familiar relation to the world.[110]

Heidegger's distinctive insight here is that Dasein is always trying *to get
away from* this uncanny perspective that places it beyond what is most familiar.[111] As he observes, Dasein "does not flee in *the face of* entities within
the world; these are precisely what it flees *towards* . . . we flee *in the face of*
the 'not-at-home.'"[112] This constant flight from the uncanny is also part of
Dasein's being toward death and the affirmation of its propriety, conscience,
freedom and wholeness.[113] As much as the anticipation of its indefinite finitude enables Dasein to make "certain of its ownmost Being in its totality,"
the relation between world and anxiety is rather different.[114] For Heidegger,
having a vantage point of the world *as* a whole is not an affirmation of a God-
like point of view, of Cartesian cogito or Husserlian transcendental pure consciousness. This glimpse of the world *as a whole* is rather to encounter what
one most wants to avoid: "the uncanniness which lies in Dasein—in Dasein
as thrown Being-in-the-world, which has been delivered over to itself in its

Being."[115] In terms of the history concept of world, this is Heidegger's most revolutionary stance in *Being and Time*.

In the traditional logic of containment that informs the treatment of the world in the history of philosophy, the task of unifying what is *in* the world is always driven by the need to establish the grounds for a larger perspective on the world. Securing a vantage point of the world as a whole empowers the reasoning subject in relation to the complexity and range of external objects. It also reinforces the view that the task of philosophy itself is to provide this larger perspective or logic of containment to resolve the problem of world. Despite his association of anxiety with the most authentic possibilities of Dasein, Heidegger's insistence that the sight of the world as a whole exposes Dasein to an unfamiliarity that it cannot escape would have a lasting influence on thinking about the concept of world in the second half of the twentieth century.

## 2. The Historical World

For Dasein the meaning of world as a whole is always a question of the meaning of being.[116] It is precisely this problem of the exact relation between being and world that will lead Heidegger to turn away in his later works from the phenomenon of world as elaborated in *Being and Time*. Two years after *Being and Time*, Heidegger offered quite a different account of world in "On the Essence of Ground," which was written in 1928 and published in 1929.[117] It is worth noting that in his subsequent 1929–1930 lectures, Heidegger makes a point of changing the order of his different approaches to the problem of world. As we have seen, Heidegger says in these lectures that he has first dealt with the historical world then turned to the world as a phenomenon and is now dealing with the comparative world.[118] In terms of his publications, he first deals with the world as a phenomenon in *Being and Time* and then turns to the historical and conceptual world in "On the Essence of Ground."

Heidegger's alteration of his sequence of publications to explain how best to address the problem of world can be taken as indicative of a wider difficulty in coordinating the phenomenal world and the conceptual or historical world. The comparative world of the 1929–1930 lectures can be seen as an attempt to resolve this apparent difficulty. At the same time, Heidegger had already made the proper sequence of analysis abundantly clear in his 1925 lectures on *History of the Concept of Time* when he states that an understanding of the phenomenon of time must always precede an understanding of the concepts of time.[119]

In his 1929–1930 lectures, Heidegger offers an overview of his three different approaches to the world that gives us some insight into his methodology.
The question "*What is world?*" must begin with "the *history of the word* 'world'
and the historical development of the concept it contains."[120] However, this
limited approach of "the history of the word" can only offer "the exterior."
It must be followed by an "inner history" through an analysis of the "history
of the concept of world which is not expressed in the history of the word at
all."[121] As the range of the concept of world exceeds that of the word "world,"
the world as phenomenon goes beyond the limitations of the concept of
world. It is by seeing the history of the concept of world within the larger
framework of the world as a phenomenon that the world can be taken as a
problem.[122] For Heidegger, this now means treating world exclusively as an
issue for human Dasein and its relation to "beings as a whole."[123]

This issue of exclusivity will also inform his treatment of the comparative
world as an analysis of the difference between man and animal "having"
world.[124] I have suggested in the previous section that Heidegger's treatment
of anxiety in *Being and Time* offers a radical change in the traditional philosophical accounts of the world as a structure of containment. However, one
could argue that Heidegger's later thought on the world attempts to establish
a new logic of containment through its focus on world as the unique domain
of human Dasein and its relation to the truth of being. The problem of the
truth of being requires that Dasein have an explicit and exclusive vantage
point of the world as a whole; a vantage point that it does not flee but must
recognize in its totality.

In the extraordinarily condensed argumentation of "On the Essence of
Ground," Heidegger bases his case for the world belonging "legitimately and
exclusively to Dasein" on a larger discussion of essence and ground.[125] He is
primarily concerned here, as he is in his later work on Leibniz, with challenging the metaphysical union of the essence of ground (*Wesen des Grundes*)
with the principle of reason (*Satz vom Grunde*).[126] Heidegger argues that
Leibniz's reworking of the Aristotelian categories of predication asserts—as
an apophantic logos—truth as a "unitary accord" and "self-'grounding.'"[127]
As in *Being and Time*, in contrast to the apophantic logos, he makes the case
for a "*more originary* truth," a hermeneutical "making-manifest" or treating
the essence of ground as the transcendence of beings.[128] This transcendence
of beings provides a more emphatic version of the distinction between entities that are merely in the world and Dasein's glimpse of the world as a whole
through its being-in-the-world.

The essence of ground as transcendence provides a framework for a concise account of the history of the words and concepts of world. It also allows

Heidegger to move away quite quickly from his previous immersive analysis of the intricate relation between Dasein and things in the world. Dasein's being-in-the-world and its relation to being is the essence of ground *as* transcendence. Dasein has a "*distinctive*" relation to world because being-in-the-world is "the *problem* of transcendence."[129] In this sense, Heidegger insists, world should not be mistaken as a concept for "everything that is" or as a concept that takes Dasein and other beings "together."[130] World now only registers the transcendent relation of Dasein to "*beings as a whole*" and to the essence of ground as an intimation of the occulted truth of being.[131]

### Heidegger and Kant

It is within this context that Heidegger turns to the historical world, covering a wide historical range from Heraclitus to Kant in a few short, remarkable pages. The Greeks were already on the way to recognizing the world as an index of Dasein's unique transcendence. *Kósmos* is not concerned with particular beings or designating an orderly collection of beings. It is rather about the being of beings "*as a whole*" in relation to human Dasein.[132] With the rise of Christianity, *kósmos* loses this broad sense of totality and becomes a theologically determined anthropological concept to describe the isolation and earthly limitations of man in relation to God.[133] Heidegger then addresses the pre-Kantian concepts of metaphysics and rational cosmology where world designates a reductive "totality of what is present at hand" as created by God. This metaphysical cosmos is an onto-theological articulation of the "highest unity," as it uses a traditional notion of substance or general essence to *ground* a theological imperative.[134]

It is at this point that Heidegger turns to Kant. Throughout the important years of 1925–1930 Heidegger devoted a number of works to an extended critique of Kant. At the same time, Heidegger's discussion in "On the Essence of Ground" demonstrates that Kant remains a central figure in thinking about the concept of world in the twentieth century. His criticisms of Kant may be summarised very broadly as the need for a new ontology to supersede an inadequate epistemology.[135] In his 1927–1928 lectures on the *Phenomenological Interpretation of Kant's* Critique of Pure Reason, Heidegger is emphatic about "Kant's failure to recognize the phenomenon of world and to clarify the concept of world."[136] He had already argued in *Being and Time* that Kant makes the mistake of measuring Dasein merely from the perspective of things that are present at hand.[137] However, he also reinterprets Kant and uses his *Anthropology* in particular to support his own reading of an inherent finitude in Kant's critical philosophy.[138] It is also in his reading of Kant that Heidegger moves away from the external history of the word "world" to an internal history of the concept of world. The key issue for Heidegger is then "the conceptual structure of the *concept* of world" in the *Critique of Pure Reason*.[139]

Heidegger takes the Kantian distinction between appearances (the finite) and things themselves (the absolute) as a new relation to finitude that both reinforces traditional metaphysics and opens a "more originary" interpretation of the concept of world.[140] He suggests that one can discern both an old epistemology and a new ontology in the *Critique of Pure Reason*. Kant relies on more conventional notions of ground and substance in formulating synthetic *a priori* knowledge.[141] However, Heidegger recognizes that the ideas of reason as pure concepts of systematic unity representing the unconditioned possibility of any conditioned series gesture to quite a different notion of ground. The regulative idea of the world describes "the unconditioned totality of a realm of beings."[142] In Heidegger's reinterpretation, the regulative world indicates an underlying ontological framework for understanding world.[143]

Heidegger concludes that the Kantian concept of world is situated between two forms of transcendence: one that exceeds appearances but remains within the limits of experience (the regulative idea) and one that seeks a higher unity beyond the finite world (the transcendental ideal).[144] Kant's concept of world is distinguished by its innovative recognition of "the totality of the finitude that is *human* in essence."[145] This conclusion allows Heidegger to return to the concept of *kósmos* and to describe world as the basis for Dasein's distinctive relation to the essence of ground.[146] It is significant that Heidegger leaves his history of the concept of world by citing the opening of Kant's *Anthropology from a Pragmatic Point of View*. As we saw in the first chapter, pragmatic anthropology is founded not on "*things* in the world" but on "knowledge of the human being as a *citizen of the world*."[147] In affirming the exclusive claim of Dasein to world and moving beyond the world as a complex interaction of things and beings by defining being-in-the-world as transcendence, Heidegger seems quite close here to the more conventional Kantian treatment of the world.[148] In this sense, one may move beyond theological cosmology but still rely on a persistent anthropocentrism. For both Kant and Heidegger, humans alone are "*of the world*."

### In and beyond the World

In this context, one could say that Heidegger's historical world is a narrowing of the more radical possibilities of the world as a phenomenon. However, he goes on to offer a striking challenge to the traditional logic of treating world as a substantive grounding for the subject.[149] In the same way that he sees the Kantian concept of world situated "*between*" two gestures of transcendence, we can read Heidegger's essay as both an *opening* of the concept of ground and the *closing* of the concept of world. It should be said that this clear distinction between opening and closing is not straightforward, not least because Heidegger intertwines the concepts of ground and world in "On the Essence of Ground." Nonetheless, we can broadly say that being-in-the-world may not support an isolated, autonomous subject but it does insist on the unique anthropological *capacities* of man to make and have a world.

It is here that we first encounter a key theme of the comparative world in the 1929–1930 lectures: human Dasein as world-forming (*weltbildend*). As Heidegger observes, "'Dasein transcends' means: in the essence of its being it is *world-forming*, 'forming' in the multiple sense that it lets world occur, and through the world gives itself an original view that is not explicitly grasped, yet functions precisely as a paradigmatic form for all manifest beings, among which each respective Dasein itself belongs."[150] While Dasein's exclusive claim to be world-forming will become problematic when we come to the comparative world, it is important to note that world-forming does not just mean that Dasein forms its world. As a product of Dasein's world-forming, world must be thought here as something that is both within *and* beyond Dasein.[151]

Heidegger himself uses Dasein's unique capacity as world-forming to bring together his new interpretation of the world and the essence of ground. As that which is both *within* and *beyond* the world, Dasein encompasses a transcendence that cannot be determined as merely either subjective or objective.[152] This leads to one of Heidegger's most famous pronouncements on the concept of world. *Finding itself* at once in and beyond world, human Dasein discovers its projective possibilities and its freedom. Arising within the structure of the *in* and *beyond*, this freedom for human beings is at once a liberation of self and the possibility of "something binding."[153] It is this *simultaneous* loosening and binding of Dasein that Heidegger goes on to describe by the well-known phrase "world never *is*, but *worlds*" (*Welt* ist *nie, sondern* Weltet).[154]

This striking reformulation of a concept of freedom in relation to the world leads Heidegger to the problem of the relation between Dasein and other things and beings. As the "projection of world," it is Dasein's being-in-the-world *as* transcendence that makes other things and beings "manifest in themselves."[155] These other beings and things have no capacity for transcendence. At the same time, Heidegger counterbalances this by reiterating that Dasein's transcendence is compatible with its unavoidable absorption in the world.[156] In this sense, Dasein's being-amidst and being-with *is* transcendence. In this fine balance between a surpassing that is always in the middle of things—and there is no sense here of the uncanny or the possibility of an unbalanced relation that we found in *Being and Time*—it is the "projection of world" and "absorption by beings" *as* grounding that coordinates these gestures. As Heidegger observes, "Dasein grounds (establishes) world only as grounding itself in the midst of beings."[157] For Dasein, the relation to world is at once immersive and transcendent.

The apparent new stability of these dynamic relations is demonstrated by the fact that Dasein never loses its capacities. As much as Dasein "exceeds itself" in "the projection of possibilities," this momentum is counteracted by the constant "*withdrawal*" of other possibilities.[158] As Heidegger has already argued in *Being and Time*, it is precisely what is missing or unavailable that gives the world to Dasein. As Dasein is both in *and* beyond the world and its freedom is at once a loosening *and* binding, "*transcendence at once exceeds and withdraws.*"[159] Each of these dynamic structures announces Dasein's finitude—its freedoms are finite, but they also confirm its unique powers in relation to the world.

Heidegger then turns to a third and last structure of grounding in relation to Dasein's being-in-the-world as transcendence. Challenging the Husserlian model of intentionality, Heidegger argues that Dasein's comportment "*toward* beings" can be better described as "*the grounding of something*" (reworking Husserl's dictum that consciousness is always "the consciousness of something").[160] For Heidegger, this third type of grounding addresses the key question of Dasein's new relation to other things and being. As the grounding of something, this grounding is concerned with "making possible the manifestation of beings in themselves."[161] For Heidegger, both previous structures of grounding included the comportment "toward those not having the character of Dasein, and toward oneself and those like oneself."[162] The third way of grounding thus opens the more fundamental question of Dasein's own relation not to beings but to being.[163]

We are now turning, Heidegger argues, to the "preconceptual" understanding of being in general or to the essence of ground as the unity of all three modes of grounding.[164] It is at this critical point that we formally take leave of the concept of world. Dasein's understanding of being as the possibility of making beings "manifest in themselves" is prior to any concept of world.[165] We have arrived not at the world as phenomenon but at being-in-the-world as a making manifest or the hermeneutical phenomenology of being and truth. As we have already noted, in contrast to Husserl's confident belief that "perfect clarity is the measure of all truth," for Heidegger the truth of being as the making manifest of beings is based on the transcendence of the concealed, of what shows or unveils itself by showing that it remains covered and hidden.[166]

Understanding the world both as a phenomenon and a concept brings us to a fundamental connection: "being (not beings) is given only in transcendence as a grounding that finds itself in a projection of world."[167] World is now the bridge between the possibilities of immersion and promises of transcendence. For Heidegger, Dasein's "factical existing" may expose it to "possibilities that gape open before its finite choice" and require that it "understand *itself* as an abyss of ground" (*Ab-grund*). However, this necessary journey only reiterates that its freedom is "*the ground of ground*" and that Dasein is "*a creature of distance*" that can always find its "true nearness."[168] At the same time, the implicit reliance here of being on the stability of the world-forming capabilities of Dasein is one of the reasons that Heidegger's later works turned from the larger problem of world and being to the more focused analysis of being and truth. As Jeff Malpas has observed, this shift from being-in-the-world to transcendence, ground and the truth can be seen as Heidegger's attempt to establish "the unity of being-in-the-world" that eluded him in *Being and Time*.[169]

## 3. The Comparative World

Heidegger's 1929–1930 lectures, *The Fundamental Concepts of Metaphysics—World, Finitude, Solitude*, is his most sustained work on the problem of world after *Being and Time*. As Derrida suggested in some remarks after a conference in 1997, what is striking about *The Fundamental Concepts of Metaphysics* is that after the great work on being-in-the-world in *Being and Time* and after the extraordinarily condensed exploration of world as Dasein's transcendence and the essence of ground in "On the Essence of Ground," Heidegger implies in this later work that he still "doesn't know what 'world' means."[170] This constant recasting and rethinking of the problem of world is Heidegger's most lasting contribution to the concept of world in the history of philosophy: *world remains a problem*. What is also striking about this last concentrated work on world is Heidegger's interest in the clear differences between *worldlessness*, *poverty in world* and *world-formation* as a "*fundamental problem of metaphysics*."[171]

As in "On the Essence of Ground," *The Fundamental Concepts of Metaphysics* is preoccupied by the world as a concept. A fundamental concept, Heidegger argues, is not concerned with universals that provide "determinative representations" of particulars as something placed simply "before us."[172]

Fundamental concepts should avoid the self-evidence of a discrete subject in relation to objects that are taken as present-at-hand. Instead of *Begriff* (concept), Heidegger uses *Inbegriff* (sum-total) here—a word often used by Kant—to designate concepts that *only* question "the whole."[173] At the same time, in his discussion of the history of philosophy as the essence of metaphysics, Heidegger returns to the differences between the history of a word and the history of a concept. The investigation of metaphysics, he argues, will require an examination of "the strange history of a strange word."[174] This complex distinction between word and concept is also placed increasingly within the larger context of the relation between being and truth.[175]

As his subtitle suggests, Heidegger is concerned in these lectures with a distinctive relation between world, finitude and solitude. In its attempt to grasp the essence of metaphysics, he argues, philosophy is only directed toward the world when world indicates "something as a whole."[176] As he states, "This 'as a whole' is the world."[177] This definition of world is significant. The concept of world should not be taken as a mere illustration or representation of the "as a whole": it *is* the "as a whole."[178] In other words, the "as a whole" itself—the world—is the fundamental structure for taking something *as* something. This emphatically places the concept of world within Heidegger's analysis of the logos and truth, *apóphanis* and *alētheia*.

This world-as-a-whole then accounts for "being as whole" as that which we are constantly driven toward and driven away from at the same time.[179] Heidegger defines this relentless oscillation in relation to world-as-a-whole as finitude. Finally, he defines the third and last of the themes of his lectures, solitude, as the proximity of man to this absent and elusive wholeness. Man is solitary. This announces an individuation that is not the affirmation of man's "frail little ego" but of "a nearness to world."[180] The trinity of world, finitude and solitude suggests a different relation to world from being-in-the-world and the historical world. As a fundamental concept of metaphysics, world determines human finitude and solitude.

World is no longer only concerned with an immersive always already existing relation to things that can be used to formulate an incremental wholeness or transcendence. World itself is now *an immediate wholeness that is entirely absent*. This immediacy and this absence are found within the framework of the essence of metaphysics as a "questioning" oriented toward the occulted truth of being.[181] In this sense, there is a clear shift of focus in Heidegger's work from *Being and Time* to *The Fundamental Concepts of Metaphysics*. World is no longer only the key referential structure of Dasein's immersive existence. It is now also one concept among others in the fundamental relation between being and truth. As Heidegger observes, "Everything that belongs to the existence of Dasein belongs just as essentially to the truth of philosophy."[182] It is on this basis that Heidegger will ultimately turn to the world through a *"comparative examination"* of humans and animals.[183]

## World and Truth

In the important third chapter of the preliminary appraisal Heidegger gives us another ambitious and detailed history of a range of classical Greek words and concepts. He takes us back to where we began with Kant: the problem of the metaphysical world. He argues that the word "metaphysics" has a complex history. In the scholastic and medieval period, which attempted to systematize Plato and Aristotle, metaphysics became explicitly associated with a *"knowledge of the suprasensuous."*[184] In this sense, all metaphysics assumes and requires a distinction between the sensible and the intelligible.[185] The scholastic interpretation of Aristotle in particular led to the equation of metaphysics with theology and to an inherent confusion in defining metaphysics as both the general universal *un*sensuous in relation to individual beings and the ultimate *supra*sensuous in relation to God.[186] It is precisely this supra- and unsensuous domain that will become the *mundus intelligibilis* of the pre-critical Kant.[187] In the modern period, Heidegger argues, this metaphysical tradition has become associated with an absolute knowledge of the subject and the mathematical natural sciences.[188]

Though he has not yet explicitly connected this history of metaphysics to the concept of world, one can already see the basis for a new interpretation of world. For Heidegger, the challenge is to think beyond the world as a discrete sphere, domain or realm to designate the intelligible, the theological, the subjective and the objective. He goes on to offer a compelling counter-history of classical Greek philosophy. The collection of notes and lectures that we call Aristotle's *Metaphysics*, he argues, was initially catalogued after Aristotle's death as a work that simply came after (*meta, post*) Aristotle's *Physics*. In time, metaphysics came to be described, erroneously, as a discipline that went beyond (*meta, trans*) physics, hence the commonly held view of metaphysics as the designation of a *discrete realm*—or world—beyond the physical.[189] From this history, one could argue that the use of the concept of world to designate a contained and self-sufficient realm or domain only arises from the need to describe the intelligible, the intellectual, the nonsensible, the supersensible and the transcendent.

In his attempt to reconstruct metaphysics, Heidegger calls Aristotle's work not *Metaphysics* but *First Philosophy*. First philosophy entails a thinking of the relation between *phúsis*, *lógos* and *alētheia*. Heidegger defines *phúsis* not as nature, but as the "prevailing of beings as a whole."[190] By the time of Aristotle's *First Philosophy*, the thinking of *phúsis* has been separated into two world-like domains: *onta* (beings in nature) and *ousia* (being as essence).[191] It is by recognizing the "prevailing of beings as a whole" in relation to the *logos* and *alḗtheia* that one can begin to understand *meta ta phusika* as *the province of being and truth*.

This province will determine Heidegger's final sustained attempt to resolve the problem of world. He now describes the structure of the herme- neutic phenomenology of *Being and Time* in slightly different terms. *Lógos* is the making manifest or revealing *of what prevails* (*walten*). *Alḗtheia* describes the wrenching of what prevails from its concealment.[192] Metaphysics is then the dynamic confrontation that occurs when being or "the prevailing of what prevails" is manifested *as truth*.[193] The truth of world is no longer found in a cosmology of containment but in *registering* an immediate wholeness that is entirely absent for human Dasein.

As is often the case, as Heidegger seems to be opening a provocative new way of thinking about the problem of world, he closes these very possibili- ties by relying on far more traditional concepts. At the very moment that he suggests we might be able to think of world beyond the traditional log- ics of containment, he evokes a traditional hierarchical order of distinctive capabilities for the stone, the plant, the animal and man which sounds as if it would be more at home in Hegel's *Encyclopaedia of Philosophical Sciences* and has obvious resonances with Husserl's delineation of material, animal and spiritual *worlds* in *Ideas 2*.[194] This sequence of developmental stages or different "kinds of beings" is introduced by Heidegger to address once again "the question concerning the structure of being," and it will *determine* the subsequent status of the world as a comparative world.[195]

As much as Heidegger's discussion of the various forms of Dasein's fun- damental attunement (*stimmung*) display his dynamic and revolutionary structures—which here attempt to exceed traditional distinctions such as internal and external, conscious and unconscious, subject and object—these structures remain *contained* by the apparently clear progressive differences between the stone, the plant, the animal and man.[196] One of Heidegger's most striking innovations in *The Fundamental Concepts of Metaphysics* is the definition of the fundamental attunement of human Dasein as that which has the capability to be at once there *and* not there.[197] At the same time, this extraordinary capacity for being-there (*Da-sein*) and being-away (*Weg-sein*) is founded on the rather ordinary distinction between man and stone. While *"being away is itself a way of man's being,"* the stone "in its being-away, is precisely *not* there."[198] It is such heavy-handed and clear differences—stable and absolute differences that appear to lack the dynamic quality of human

Dasein's *own* attributes—that will shape the relation of the stone, the plant, the animal and man to the world.

As much as Heidegger challenges the logic of world as an intelligible reality, there is now a seemingly unavoidable hierarchy of access to the world. These *"ways of access"* stand as an absolute, unshakable difference.[199] The stone, the plant and the animal can never have the same relation to the world as man. In truth, they have very little or no access to world. It seems as if a new kind of very traditional metaphysics is being installed here in which man's world, strictly speaking, has no stones, no plants and at best only a dim, fleeting intimation of animals.

This world is very rich for man and quite barren for anything that is not human. This is not to suggest that Heidegger has simply restored the very humanism he constantly criticizes but more to argue that his insistence on the "essential connection between being and truth" as the *gatehouse* to the comparative world restricts the possibilities of truly exceeding the concepts of world that we have seen from Kant to Husserl.

### The Stone, the Animal and Man

Heidegger devotes the first part of the main text of *The Fundamental Concepts of Metaphysics* to an extended discussion of boredom (*Langeweile*) and "passing the time" (*Zeitvertreib*) that will introduce a key step in constructing the comparative world between the human and the animal: Dasein's indifference to *beings as a whole*. There is a profound boredom that transposes a particular "passing the time" to a general indifference and delivers the individual subject to the "realm" of Dasein and the relation between being and truth. This analysis of boredom can be seen as the first step in constituting the distinct and discrete realms—worlds—of man and animal. In contrast to animals, man is not simply captivated (*benommen*) or *immersed* in what is present-at-hand. Man has the unique capacity and burden of registering the passing of time and Dasein's finitude through being left empty or bored by what is present-at-hand. Animals cannot be bored. Boredom arises when the "environing world" *as a whole* is taken as mere immersion (*Aufgehen*).[200]

For Heidegger, profound boredom leads us to pass the time and the unfamiliarity of this drawn-out temporal stasis pushes humans "back into the specific gravity of Dasein."[201] Ultimately, this return to Dasein will allow Heidegger to define man as "world-forming" in contrast to the animal that is merely "poor in the world" and the stone that is "worldless." Heidegger also describes boredom as a move into a general indifference in which we find ourselves *"elevated beyond* the particular situation."[202] In other words, this being drawn back down to Dasein and to a distinct "realm of power" can also be described as a rising above, even if this elevation has its origins in finding ourselves "in the midst of being as a whole, i.e., in the whole of this indifference."²⁰³ This movement recalls the logic of containment. In such moments of profound boredom, I am no longer simply *in* the world. The world, as an indifferent whole, provides me with a new vantage point of *the world as a whole*.

Heidegger founds the comparative world not just on general indifference but also on an emphatic "refusal" of *beings as a whole*.²⁰⁴ This distinction between beings as a whole (*das Seiende im Ganzen*) and Dasein is founded on what *manifests* uniquely *for* Dasein, or what Heidegger calls "Dasein as such."²⁰⁵ This manifestation of what shows itself as a whole for Dasein alone prefigures the new tripartite division of the world for man, animals and things. The world (of beings as a whole) *shows itself to* Dasein. This perspective of the world-as-a-whole manifests Dasein's *as such* (*als solches*) or its unique "potentiality for being."²⁰⁶ The "as such" registers Dasein's exceptional claim to "whatever is utmost and primary in making possible."²⁰⁷ One could argue that despite Heidegger's reworking of Husserlian phenomenology, there is a distinct link here between a capacity for showing or making appear and the access to being.

This withdrawal of beings *as a whole* and *as such* for Dasein leads to the recognition of human Dasein as world-forming. Heidegger is at pains to qualify this withdrawal (*Entzug*) of beings-as-a-whole. As he observes, "Beings as a whole withdraw, yet not at all in such a way that Dasein is left alone."²⁰⁸ He then reinforces his point: "Beings as a whole withdraw, this means: Dasein is indeed there in the midst of beings as a whole, has them around, above, and within itself, yet cannot give way to this withdrawal."²⁰⁹ Heidegger's resolution of the simultaneous need for a comprehensive immersion and for establishing a clear vantage point beyond this immersion is "the *temporal horizon*."²¹⁰ The temporal horizon keeps Dasein amidst beings as a whole and it ensures that Dasein itself is also "entranced by time."²¹¹ Time accounts for both Dasein and for all beings as a whole, and this common temporal horizon enables Dasein alone to be at once everywhere *and* nowhere, at once in the world and to have a wider perspective of the world as a whole.

Heidegger begins the second part of *The Fundamental Concepts of Metaphysics* by offering an initial definition of the world. Taking the withdrawal of beings-as-a-whole as the prompt for Dasein to turn toward "its Da-sein," Heidegger defines world as the manifestation of the "as a whole."²¹² His task will then be to *contain* this sphere of beings-as-a-whole and to explain how Dasein—in relation to its own Da-sein—has access to an entirely different world. This need to account for the clear division between Dasein's world and the world of beings-as-a-whole is in part why Heidegger will devote three chapters to the animal in this section of his lectures.

"The path of *comparative examination*," as he describes it, is based on a fundamental assertion and a series of questions. The assertion is that "man is not merely *a part of the world*" but also "*has* world."[213] The questions and the issue of comparison arise from asking if animals, plants and stones have the same relation to world. It is important to emphasize that Heidegger presents these comparisons as questions:

> But then what about the other beings which, like man, are also part of the world: the animals and plants, the material things like the stone, for example? Are they merely parts of the world, as distinct from man who in addition has world? Or does the animal too have world, and if so, in what way? In the same way as man, or in some other way? And how would we grasp this otherness? And what about the stone?[214]

Heidegger having elaborated in his account of being-in-the-world and the historical world that man has a dual relation to world, being at once a part of it and having world as a whole, it is this series of questions as the *culmination* of the problem of world that makes Heidegger's work most compelling.

One could say that though Heidegger begins with man he *ends* with the "otherness" of the animal and the lingering question of the stone. It is not the emphasis on man as world-forming that makes these lectures distinctive as much as Heidegger's engagement with the profound difficulty of thinking *worldlessness* (*weltlos*) for the stone and *poverty in world* (*Weltarmut*) for the animal. At the same time, we should not forget that Heidegger closes his 1929–1930 lectures with a discussion of the logos as a *realm* that is unambiguously the province of man. We should also keep in mind the problematic use of "three realms"—a world-like designation—to describe three very different relations to world itself.[215] For example, the stone is worldless but it is still denoted by Heidegger as a discrete world-like realm.

It is precisely the difficulties that Heidegger gets into when attempting to distinguish stone, animal and man that suggest the need for a very different way of thinking world. As we shall see, it is not fortuitous that Derrida would devote an extended seminar to Heidegger's 1929–1930 lectures and the question of the animal. Though I will concentrate here on the treatment of world, it is also worth noting that Heidegger gets embroiled in larger problems about life and death. For example, he argues that the stone "cannot be dead because it is never alive."[216] An animal of course is a living being according to Heidegger but it still has no relation to death. Only man is a living being that knows it will die and this gives it the fullest entitlement to *having* a world.[217] Heidegger's presentation of his "three theses"—"the stone is worldless, the animal is poor in the world, man is world-forming" is based on a range of rather frail presuppositions.[218] One could quite easily argue that the stone or the animal is world-forming and that man is both poor in the world and even worldless. In a different context, Heidegger's former student Hannah Arendt argued that some humans are indeed worldless due to their lack of political involvement and arduous economic circumstances.[219]

What makes Heidegger's "three theses" more interesting is that he places them all in relation to each other: world here is truly a *comparative* world. To have a world and to form a world, to be poor in world and *to have no world* are all interrelated.[220] Heidegger also evokes a circular rather than linear method of interpretation to address his three theses.[221] This circularity provides a relation between the periphery and the centre, the centre being the essence of the stone, the animal and man. But this also opens a relation to ambiguity, dizziness and the uncanny, as one goes around and around in circles.[222] To his credit, Heidegger keeps both this central orientation and this circular disorientation in view. In relation to "the *essence of the animal*" in particular, Heidegger does not minimise "the disquieting circularity of our thesis."[223] Without falling into zoology and biology, he suggests, philosophy can only go so far when it comes to a determination of the animal.

Nonetheless, Heidegger makes this determination and pursues his theses to their asserted ends. In comparison to man the animal has "less" world.[224] The animal has less of world because its "domain" is often specific and its range limited. More profoundly, its relative poverty in world is indicative of its inability to penetrate "to the extendability of everything."[225] In a terminology that we have already encountered in *Being and Time*, the bee has less world than man because it cannot know the stamens it visits *as* stamens that can be found in the world *as a whole*. This comparative analysis of less and more leads Heidegger to a *provisional* definition of world as "the sum total of beings accessible to man or animals alike, variable as it is in range and depth."[226] He then quickly rejects this definition both for its failure to account for the fact that "less" world may be better than "more" world and for its reliance on the obscure sense that man is "higher" and the animal "lower."[227] *Weltbildend* and *Weltarmut*, he insists, should not be differentiated on the basis of "a hierarchical evaluation."[228] It does seem, however, quite hard to avoid this.

Heidegger moves beyond this initial configuration by arguing that the animal's poverty in world should not be measured into a less-more relation. Being poor in world is rather a sign of "*being deprived*" that can be attributed to both man and the animal.[229] This deprivation is not a lack or absence but a "preeminent kind of having in which we seem not to have."[230] This redefi-nition of deprivation as a relation of having *and* not having also allows Hei-degger to separate world from its more traditional associations with quantity, sum total or degree of access.[231] The point here is that the comparative world is not defined by quantity of access but by the more fundamental capacity to "have a world."[232] This sense of *having* coordinates the three theses: the stone can never have a world, the animal can have world but is "*deprived*" of world and man always "has a world."[233]

Heidegger may reject hierarchy and quantity in differentiating man and animals, but he retains the framework of access. The stone has no world because "it has no possible access to anything else around it."[234] Without access to other beings *as* beings, it has no world as a whole and cannot register its lack of world. This rather odd formulation suggests that the hav-ing of world is not simply about an interaction with other beings but also requires a capacity to be deprived of what one can have. The animal can be deprived of life, the stone cannot. In this sense, the animal "has world," but it is world as "a specific set of relationships" and "a circumscribed domain."[235] The animal has access to other beings, but it does not have access to these "*as a being.*"[236] If anything, one might say at this stage that Heidegger gives the animal—as it is placed *between* the stone and man— the most dynamic relation. The animal is both stone-like and man-like and consequently "*both has world and does not have world.*"[237]

As Heidegger remarks, the concept of the comparative world has yet to be defined with any clarity because the animal, as the middle term, suggests a link between worldlessness and world-formation.[238] He ultimately resolves this problem of animal's ambivalent claim to world by drawing an unassail-able distinction between having capacity *for* something (*Fähigkeit*) and being captivated *by* something (*benommen*).[239] As an instinctual way of being, the animal's capability takes the form of an "intrinsic absorption" or captiva-tion.[240] The animal is poor in world because it is captivated by what it is related to at any given moment. Its capabilities culminate in subservience.[241] In this sense, the animal "*behaves within an environment but never within a world.*"[242] The animal is only *in* the surrounding world (*Umwelt*) because its behaviour and its drives cannot exceed its own captivation.[243] In contrast to the comportment of man, the animal's behaviour has no apparent "recogni-tion" of the dynamics of being, of the *play* of presence and absence beyond what is merely present at hand.[244] The animal is "*taken by things.*"[245] The animal is immersed without a possible relation to transcendence.

Heidegger suggests that having a world requires an ontological level of un-derstanding. The bee is "*never within a world*" because there is "*no apprehending* of honey *as* something present."[246] Having world is based on the capacity to take x *as* x, and human comportment alone can take a world *as* something present. The animal is poor in world because "the possibility of apprehending something as something is *withheld*."[247] Heidegger suggests that the ability to take something *as such* provides a barrier against being merely *taken* by things. The animal has world because it can access beings other than itself but it does not have world because it cannot take these other beings *as* beings.[248]

Heidegger now resolves the animal's ambivalent status of having and not having world—and the possible link between man and the stone—by insisting that because "the accessibility of beings as such belongs to the essence of world," the animal "essentially cannot have world at all."[249] The deprivation and poverty of the animal in relation to world arises chiefly from its *comparison to man*, even if it does perpetually confront the animal with something "other than itself."[250] Nonetheless, this failure of the animal to "comport itself toward beings as such" is the absolute barrier between man and animal.[251] The resistance against being entirely captivated or absorbed by things is the uniquely human possibility of having a world. Man can never be absolutely immersed.

At the same time, as Heidegger insists that the animal cannot be within a world because it cannot register beings manifesting *as* beings, he still relies on a world-like language to designate the animal's proper place. The animal is encircled or ringed-in by its own limitations. It encircles itself or ties itself up in an "*intrinsic self-encirclement*," and this "*opens* up a sphere" where it operates without inhibitions.[252] The animal has no world but it has a "sphere," or what Heidegger calls "the unity of captivation as a structural totality."[253] At the very least, this suggests that it is difficult to define an exclusive concept of world without also giving that which is excluded from world a world-like concept of containment. For Heidegger, "the animal is separated from man by an abyss."[254]

On the threshold of turning to man as world-forming, Heidegger leaves us with what seems to be a very traditional conclusion: the animal "has *no* world."[255] Without falling into a reductive trap of simply defining the human as the animal—as driven, instinctual, reliant on its reaction to other beings, disinhibited in its given sphere of activity—Heidegger's emphatic refusal of world to animals does raise the question of whether man can also not have world, of whether man both has and does not have world. Heidegger himself acknowledges this second possibility, noting that "at first and for the most part" man "does not properly know of the world as such."[256] He does not address the first possibility—that man also has "*no* world"—and we will come back to this beguiling but difficult proposition in chapters 5 and 6. This generation of a determined moment where there is "*no* world" for the animal in Heidegger's thought might be compared in a broad sense with the Kantian regulative world in which only the systematic unity of the ideas of reason allow one to act *as if* there is a world. On the margins of the construction of the concept of world in the history of philosophy there is always the *possibility* that there is "*no* world."

The relation between being, logos and truth provides the framework for man's relation to world. As Heidegger remarks, "The manifestation of beings as such, of beings *as* being, belongs to world."[257] As we have seen, the key to the human concept of world is the *manifestation* of "*beings as such as a whole*" (*als solchen im Ganzen*).[258] The double use of "as" here takes us back to the questions of language, truth and the logos that were raised at the start of the 1929–1930 lectures.[259] Heidegger once again draws a distinction between the logos as self-evident exhibition or "pointing out" (the apophantic) and the variegated process of unconcealment (*alētheia*) and argues for a more dynamic notion of "pointing out."[260] If world-as-a-whole is manifested for man by taking something *as* something, this process describes a showing or pointing out that is the possibility and unity of revealing and concealing (as a pointing toward *and* a pointing away).[261] Taking something *as* something is already indicative of a world-forming unity, of man taking the world *as* a whole. Following Aristotle's *De Interpretatione*, Heidegger insists that this world-forming unity has a distinctive dynamic. It is *at once* a combination and a division (*súnthesis* and *diaíresis*), "*a taking together that takes apart*" as a *whole*.[262] Heidegger is not that far from Heraclitus here—and it is no mistake that this seminar was subsequently dedicated to Eugen Fink, who attended the 1929–1930 lectures and later wrote extensively on Heraclitus.[263] The truth—and the being—of world as a whole *for man* is a unique "taking together" that also "takes apart."

This extended discussion of logic and language in the final chapter of *The Fundamental Concepts of Metaphysics* reinforces the Aristotelian separation of man and animal as the absolute difference between beings that can speak meaningfully (*lógos*) and those that can only make noises (*alogon*).[264] Language remains an essential difference between what is world-forming and what is poor in world. Heidegger concludes, "In the *lógos*, in language, and thereby within man's formation of world, being can be said."[265] This *saying* of being reinforces that world is a fundamental concept of metaphysics because it is connected to "a *pre-logical being open for beings*."[266] In this context we can now appreciate Heidegger's earlier definition of the logos as the *manifestation* of what prevails (*walten*).[267] The recognition of "the *prevailing of world*" is an intimation of the *being* of beings.[268] As Heidegger later observed in the

"Letter on 'Humanism'" (1946), "For us 'world' does not at all signify beings or any realm of beings but the openness of being."[269] Heidegger summarises man's world-formation in his 1929–1930 lectures as finding oneself at once bound to and oriented by being while keeping "beings as a whole" always in view. As being-in-the-world and keeping a wider perspective of the world as a whole, man's world-formation finds its unity and possibility in the fundamental difference between being and beings.[270]

## Opening and Closing the World

The "*problem of world*" for Heidegger after *Being and Time* may finally be located in the rather familiar realms of the stone, the animal and man, but it also presents the challenge of thinking the concept of world *in relation to* that which is at once a loosening *and* a binding, a unification *and* a separation.[271] Nonetheless, one could say that Heidegger partially closes most of his own radical openings. The possibility of world as a persistent unification *and* separation should also take us beyond the traditional opposition between what is merely *in* the world and the need to think of a vantage point that provides a view of the world *as a whole*. However, we must keep in mind Heidegger's rather prosaic insistence that "*ordinary understanding cannot see the world for beings*" when he writes, quite wonderfully in the last paragraph of his lectures, of projecting man as "thrown" into his possibilities and in a constant state of "*transition*" that leaves him as "essentially absencing and never at hand, yet *existent* in his essential absence."[272]

This is the world for man when the concept of world chiefly accounts for an immediate wholeness that is entirely absent. But this is also a world that only some men can truly grasp. Ordinary understanding, Heidegger concludes, cannot see world because of a "failure to distinguish in its comportment toward beings."[273] As he remarks, for such limited views, "beings are the beginning and end of its accomplishments."[274] In contrast, more-than-ordinary human understanding is precisely that which can distinguish that man is uniquely at once existing and absencing *in* the world *as such* and *as a whole*.

This distinction between ordinary understanding and non-ordinary understanding requires the same *presumption* of world-like discrete spheres, domains or realms that allows Heidegger to separate the stone, the plant and the animal from man. In this sense, Heidegger still relies on the categorical world as it first appeared in Kant and uses the same logic of world-like discriminations as Hegel and Husserl. At the same time, one can challenge this comparison when Heidegger speaks of the difficulty in locating "the very *dimension*" in which the distinction between being and

beings is apparent.[275] As his later work attests, Heidegger remained preoccupied with the problem of world as a problem of logos, truth and being
that both invites and refuses traditional designations and discriminations.
The difficulty of reading Heidegger is to keep both his radical innovations
*and* conservative reactions in mind without taking an emphatic gesture on
one side as the final word in the matter.

This difficulty in reading Heidegger is more apparent than ever when
it comes to what we might call his fourth and fifth concepts of world: the
darkened and spiritual world and the world seen in the relation between
world and earth. These concepts of world were formulated in 1933–1935
and remain entangled in Heidegger's active involvement with the Nazi re-
gime as the rector of Freiburg University (1933–1934). In his *Introduction to
Metaphysics* (1935), Heidegger is still concerned with the problem of "beings
as such and as a whole" in relation to the elusive but fundamental question
of being.[276] However, he is also more explicitly concerned with cultural and
political judgements, and he links the general "spiritual decline of the earth"
to "the darkening of the world."[277] He now argues that new "*spiritual* forces"
in Europe can only be manifested by restoring "the power of Being" to "historical Dasein."[278] World is now "always *spiritual* world," and its darkening a
sign of "a *disempowering of the spirit*."[279] This spiritual world is evidently not
the Hegelian world as spirit or the Husserlian spiritual world but a resource
and *exclusive* domain for "that depth from which the essential always comes
and returns to human beings."[280] This spiritual world signals the emphatic
end of the comparative world. One could say that the concept of world is
displaced in Heidegger's turn to the relation between spirit and being in this
period. As he observes, "Spirit is the empowering of the powers of beings as
such and as a whole."[281]

This displacement of world in the name of more direct or more fundamental structures in relation to being and truth is also apparent in Heidegger's other principal work from this period, "The Origin of the Work of
Art" (1935–1936).[282] Within the context of trying to think of art beyond
the history of aesthetics and an established subject standing in front of and
representing an established object, in this famous lecture Heidegger uses the
concepts of earth and world to describe the relation between being and truth.
The truth of the work of art is produced "in the opposition between world
and earth."[283] World here is the opening of the withdrawing-concealing
earth.[284] An artwork creates a true world, Heidegger argues, when "world is
grounded on earth, and earth rises up through world."[285]

This concept of earth may finally allow Heidegger to secure a nontheo-
logical or subject-oriented vantage point beyond the world.[286] However,

the full-scale incorporation of world into the structure of the truth of being is also a dramatic reduction of the rich complexity and philosophical
innovation of being-in-the-world, the historical and comparative worlds.
Despite Heidegger's critique of Husserlian phenomenology as a metaphysics
of self-evident showing, of an appearance that displays in the full light of
day the mechanisms of its appearing, Husserl's recognition of the contingent
phenomenological play of intermingled potentialities and actualities is perhaps a more rewarding analysis of the world than Heidegger's later sustained
emphasis on a withdrawn potentiality and a suspended actuality.[287] We will
return in more detail to "The Origin of the Work of Art" in chapter 6.

Heidegger's reformulation of world as being-in-the-world in *Being and
Time* opened a new range of possibilities for thinking the phenomenon of
world, not least the quite radical idea of being-amidst (rather than of a
subject in relation to an external object) and the recognition that the long-
sought-after vantage point above and beyond the world was not a source of
God-like power or autonomy but an unnerving and uncanny encounter that
man in his Da-sein is always attempting to avoid. At the same time, Heidegger's subsequent interest in the historical and the comparative concepts
of world demonstrates that being-in-the-world raised as many new problems
as solutions in regard to the traditional tension between an immersive and a
transcendent world. As an index of the truth of the being of beings, the concept of world ultimately becomes subsumed in Heidegger's constant attempts
to differentiate the closure of mere absorption in the world from the open
possibilities of a world-like perspective that is at once found in the world and
can grasp the depths and heights of the being of beings.

CHAPTER FIVE

# Derrida and the End of the World

## 1. The World, the Other and Death

The world (*haolam*, *tevel*) and the world to come (*haolam haba*) are often cited in texts from the Tanakh, but in the Torah there are only three references to something like a concept of world. Two of these occur in Genesis in the descriptions of the great Flood at the time of Noah. In Everett Fox's remarkable translation, inspired by the work of Martin Buber, God announces to Noah, "I will blot out all existing things" (*et col hayehkum*).[1] This concept of world is not created at the moment of creation—at the start of Genesis there are only "the heavens and the earth"—but at the moment of destruction.[2] I will blot out all existing things. This is only the first gesture in a long tradition. Imagine there is no world, no *kósmos*, no *mundus*, no *orbis* and no *universitas*. Imagine there is no world, if you can. From Descartes to Husserl and perhaps to Derrida, the disappearance of the world has become a persistent trope in Western philosophy.

Derrida insists on a certain "end of the world" in his later work, but one should not confuse this with either more traditional apocalyptic narratives or with the Cartesian or Husserlian erasure and annihilation of the world in the name of the *cogito* or the phenomenological reduction as the possibility of transcendental consciousness. According to Derrida, the end of *the* world is the only possible response to the death of the other. It is part of the task of marking death *as* other, of challenging the tradition of harnessing "the tremendous power of the negative" from Hegel to Heidegger.[3] Derrida is also very attentive to the fictions that arise from announcing the closure or the opening of a world, and in his reading of Kant in particular he attempts to counteract a programmatic fictionality linked to the concept of world. Nonetheless, he insists that the death of the other be treated as the end of the world, without any apparent leeway to act "as if" the death of the other is the end of *the* world. This link between the world, the other and death has its origins in Derrida's fifty-year engagement with the thought of Husserl, and he retains a phenomenological difference throughout his work to mark the world. At the same time, as his twenty-year reading of Heidegger's comparative world suggests, there is also a distinctive concept—or rather a difference—of world in Derrida's work.

## At the Origin of the World

In his work from the early 1960s, Derrida's reaction to the Husserlian phenomenological reduction or suspension of the natural attitude toward the world can be described as both a profound resistance to an attempt to put aside the world as an index of space and time and the evocation of the world as the chance of a total destruction. Derrida resists the disappearance of the world and imagines its end. For Derrida, it is Eugen Fink, Husserl's assistant and successor to Heidegger's chair of philosophy at Freiberg in 1946, who provides a critical step in rethinking the concept of world. In his influential essay on Husserl's late work in 1933, "The Phenomenological Philosophy of Edmund Husserl and Contemporary Criticism," Fink had insisted that phenomenology does not take the measure of the world through beings or things *in* the world but thinks of the world as a whole *from* "the *origin of the world*."[4]

For Derrida, Fink's evocation of "the *origin of the world*" will shape both his description of an ethics toward the other in the early 1960s and his emphasis on the death of the other as the end of the world in his late work. The death of the other is a question that must be addressed not from a self-evident position *in* the world but from the vantage point of the origin of the world and its end. As Derrida remarked at the funeral of Louis Althusser in 1990, "What is coming to an end, what Louis is taking away with him, is not only something or other that we would have shared at some point or another, in one place or another, but the world itself, a certain origin of the world—his origin, no doubt, but also that of the world in which I lived, in which we lived a unique story."[5]

In *The Problem of Genesis in Husserl's Philosophy*, his 1953–1954 dissertation, Derrida implies—perhaps under the influence of Jean Hyppolite—that Husserl's phenomenological reduction should be understood as a kind of Hegelian *Aufhebung*. As he writes of Husserl, "More and more, he insists on the difference that separates neutralization from pure and simple negation.

Reduction is not sceptical doubt or ascetic retreat into immanence as lived experience. It conserves what it suspends. It maintains the 'sense' of the object whose existence it 'neutralises.'"[6] Derrida goes on to highlight that Husserl's reduction of "the 'thesis' of the natural attitude" begins with the "spatio-temporal world" as "a total world." As Derrida notes, for Husserl the world of "my natural environment" is defined by a time and space that are "indistinctly mixed."[7] It is this natural spatio-temporal world that Husserl submits to the uplifting, the negation and conservation of the phenomenological reduction.

As we have seen, in his attempt to distinguish the perception of physical things from mental processes in *Ideas* 1, Husserl insists that while the positing of the pure ego is always necessary, the positing of the world is always contingent.[8] Eight years after his dissertation, in his 1962 introduction to his translation of Husserl's *The Origin of Geometry* (1936), Derrida attempts to register the contingency of the "world" without subscribing to what Husserl called "the essential detachableness of the whole natural world from the domains of consciousness."[9] In section 49—which from his first to last works Derrida referred to as the "famous" or "celebrated" section of *Ideas* 1—Husserl insists, "*While the being of consciousness*, of any stream of mental processes whatever, *would indeed be necessarily modified by an annihilation of the world of physical things its own existence would not be touched.*"[10] This end of the world, or this *fiction* of the end of the world as Derrida later emphasizes, registers for Husserl a pure consciousness "to which nothing is spatiotemporally external and which cannot be within any spatiotemporal complex."[11]

One can imagine *différance*, Derrida's innovative term for "the becoming-time of space" and "the becoming-space of time," as Derrida's sustained reaction to this profound exclusion of the spatiotemporal in the name of the disappearance of the world.[12] For Derrida, we are always confronted by the entangled and impure difference of spacing *and* temporalization. Derrida makes this point explicitly in his reading of Husserl five years later in *Voice and Phenomenon* (1967).[13] He treats the *Aufhebung* of the spatio-temporal world here as part of Husserl's *idealization* of language. He argues that it is the ideality of a voice that hears itself speaking and understands itself "in the absence of the world" that epitomizes Husserl's traditional delineation of the relation between the body, the soul and the spiritual world.[14]

## Language and the World
One can also see this link between language and world in Derrida's reading of Hegel in this period. As in all his works of the late 1960s and early 1970s, Derrida is primarily concerned with the inherent and unacknowledged

idealization of language—which he calls phonocentrism and logocentrism—that he sees still at work in contemporary linguistics and philosophy. Derrida's 1968 paper "The Pit and the Pyramid: Introduction to Hegel's Semiology" opens with a quote from the *Science of Logic* in which Hegel contrasts the "realm of bodies" and the realm of spirit, concluding that the spiritual realm is distinguished by its relation to language and to "the *sign* in general."[15] Derrida suggests that one of the ways in which Hegel designates spirit as a discrete and unique world is through his theory of signs. As Husserl had noted in *Ideas* 2, the possibility of the spiritual world rests on "the difficult distinction between *soul* and *spirit*."[16] For Derrida, it is their inherent assumptions about language that allow both Hegel and Husserl to establish idealized and hierarchical spiritual worlds.

In the *Phenomenology*, Hegel devotes a number of passages in the stage of reason to language, speech and the sign. He initially criticizes speech (*Rede*) as an "outer expression" or an externalization that leads consciousness to lose control of the inner or the meaning of the inner. It is only when he can find a mechanism to move beyond the corporeal structures of the mouth and the organs of speech that Hegel provides a more laudatory account of speech. When expression is placed in relation to reflection, consciousness maintains a form of internal speech. The sign supports what will ultimately be a spiritual level of language in which outer expression maintains the meaning of the inner. Hegel describes the indicative but protective nature of the sign as "a *visible* invisible."[17] It is only after consciousness reaches spirit that Hegel argues that language is the pure expression of the "I."[18] As an expression that retains, protects and carries its dynamic inner meaning, speech is "the *existence* of Spirit."[19] In his reading of Hegel, Derrida argues that the spiritual world and its ideal world-like demarcations are made possible by language. He also cites a minor work by Hegel stating explicitly that "language is the disappearance of the sensuous world in its immediate presence."[20] Derrida challenges the viability of language as a "*visible* invisible" and describes this erasure of the world as an instance of "the invisible ideality of a logos which hears-itself-speak."[21]

In *Voice and Phenomenon*, Derrida acknowledges that Husserlian phenomenology is distinctive in recognizing the difference between what is "in the world" and what is "outside of the world without being in another world."[22] As we will see, this structure influences Derrida's own characterisation of what he calls "the play of the world." However, Derrida also questions the discrete world-like domains that Husserl constructs in drawing this fundamental distinction. He is particularly interested in Husserl's equation of what is "outside of the world" with "the invisible ideality of a logos which hears-itself-speak."[23]

For both Hegel and Husserl, Derrida argues, what is not merely in the world is carried out of the world by the expression of an ideality that "passes outside of itself into another outside, which is still 'in' consciousness."[24] In tracing Husserl's distinction between an indication that remains in the world and an expression that is outside the world, Derrida offers a critique of the prevalent tradition in the history of philosophy to use the concept of world to establish a unique vantage point *for the subject*.[25] The voice takes what is in the world (sound) and produces the ideality of a phenomenological world that stands "outside of the world."[26] As he observes, "The unity of the sound and the voice . . . allows the voice to produce itself in the world as pure auto-affection."[27] This voice is then untouched by the world and becomes the possibility or unity of any idealized world.[28] Derrida's work suggests that this entire tradition of drawing a distinction between what is in the world and the need for a perspective or vantage point of the world as a whole—including Heidegger's emphasis on its uncanniness—ultimately enhances the authority and autonomous powers of the subject.[29] Language is one more form of the idealization of the world in a long history of idealization.

Derrida's readings of Husserl suggest that the inseparability of the *differantial* relation between time and space cannot be excluded from the possibility of consciousness or reduced to a matrix of external reality. Most significantly, it cannot give rise to a perfect phenomenological world of "hearing-oneself-speak." Husserl entitled section 49 of *Ideas* 1 "Absolute Consciousness as the Residuum after the Annihilation of the World," and Derrida implies that one can begin to think of the "world" as the *residuum*, the remainder that resists, the remainder that accounts for the chance of a disruption of the phenomenological relation between consciousness and world. In the wake of his account of the phenomenological voice as a self-sustaining auto-affection that is untouched by the world and yet can establish a commanding perspective on the world as a whole, Derrida attempts to work out the possibility of the "end" of the world. In the first case, this is a question of the threat of its destruction.[30] This must also be a possibility in which contingency does not merely confirm the necessary.

One can see the first outline of this work in Derrida's 1962 introduction to *The Origin of Geometry*. He opens the introduction with the problem of the "life-world" that is taken as the site of both the "sensible" and "the unity of ground and horizon."[31] However, he is primarily interested here in the phenomenological world as the "infinite horizon of every possible experience," of a world in which all objects can be taken as theorems.[32] Anticipating *Voice and Phenomenon*, Derrida argues that the phenomenological world must be thought in relation to both the ideality of speech and the problem of writing. In contrast to the voice, writing is "in the world."[33] In other words, writing *catches* on the junction between the world as an ideal possibility and the world as an empirical and historical reality. While the voice carries a self-contained domain or realm across the world, writing inhabits a more equivocal and porous space that at once is in the world and supports a disconcerting vantage point of the world as a whole.

The key for Derrida is that unlike the phenomenological voice that is exclusively found in the living present (*die lebendige Gegenwart*), writing unavoidably stands in relation to a concept of world that both promises immortality—the written work that lasts the test of time—and is profoundly mortal. As Derrida remarks, "Factual destruction does not interest Husserl at all," and he brings to his reading of the origin of geometry the recognition that writing is part of "the factual worldliness of inscription."[34] Writing is an aspect of the constant danger of "worldly accident," of a contingent chance, destruction and death that differs from the ideality of the truth, of Husserl's celebration of the historicity of ideal objects that remains "absolutely independent of the whole world."[35] Husserl cannot think of the destruction of all existing things.

In contrast, within the context of the vulnerability and contingency of all inscriptions, of something less than the uninterrupted transmission of the history of the truth, Derrida can *imagine* "a world-wide burning of libraries" and a "catastrophe of monuments."[36] As the Torah first suggested, the concept of world registers at once the reality, the possibility and the fiction of the end of the world. Derrida's response to Husserl implies the need for a concept of world that can account for these three different registers: reality, possibility and fiction. In other words, there is the need for a concept of world that does not itself—as a concept—require a singular and self-contained realm, domain or sphere.

### Imagine There Is No World

Imagine there is no world, if you can. It seems that this is what the world does for Derrida, from his earliest writings on Husserl in 1953 to his final readings of Heidegger and the poet Paul Celan in 2003. In a number of different works from 2002–2003, Derrida explicitly focuses on the end of the world (*la fin du monde*). The end of the world marks the reality, the possibility and the fiction of a destruction that is at once unthinkably total and entirely individual. In "Rams: Uninterrupted Dialogue—Between Two Infinities, the

Poem" (2003), meditating on a line from Celan, *"Die Welt ist fort, ich muss dich tragen"* (The world is gone, I must carry you), Derrida links the end of the world as a whole to the death of the other.[37] It is worth quoting this dense and rich passage at some length. He writes,

> For each time, and each time singularly, each time irreplaceably, each time infinitely, death is nothing less than an end of *the* world. Not *only one* end among others, the end of someone or of something *in the world*, the end of a life or of a living being. Death puts an end neither to someone in the world nor to *one* world among others. Death marks each time, each time in defiance of arithmetic, the absolute end of the one and only world, of that which opens as a one and only world, the end of the unique world, the end of the totality of what is or can be presented as the origin of the world for any unique living being, be it human or not.
>
> The survivor, then, remains alone. Beyond the world of the other, he is also in some fashion beyond or before the world itself. In the world outside the world and deprived of the world. At the very least, he feels solely responsible, assigned to carry both the other and *his* world, the other and *the* world that have disappeared, responsible without world (*weltlos*), without the ground of any world, thenceforth, in a world without world, as if without earth beyond the end of the world.[38]

Derrida argues here that the individual and singular death of the other should be taken not as a death *"in the world"* but as "the end of *the* world." In other words, the death of the other must be registered from the vantage point of the world *as a whole*. When it comes to the death of the other, we are not dealing with one event among others in the world but with the wider perspective at the "origin" and the "end" of the world. That we are confronting once again the traditional space in the history of philosophy that provides a unique vantage point of the world as a whole is apparent in Derrida's emphasis on the fact that the death of the other as the "end" of the world also entails an ongoing relation to the world. As a survivor who has endured the death of the other, I find myself variously "beyond" the world, "before" the world and "without" the world. In marking the death of the other we can never simply dispense with the world.

After "Rams," his paper delivered in memory of Hans-Georg Gadamer in February 2003, Derrida returned to the end of the world in the foreword to *Chaque fois unique, la fin du monde*, a collection of memorial tributes and funeral orations and one of his last publications before his own death in October 2004.[39] He clarifies here the relation of the survivor to the world in the wake of the death of the other. The death of the other, Derrida remarks, must be distinguished from the possibility of a world that can be encompassed, from a world that can be known in its entirety by a living survivor. The death of the other is rather "la fin du monde en totalité."[40] Once again, it is a question of accepting the possibility of the total destruction of the world. However, this insistence on the end of the world *en totalité* is precisely to counteract the traditional assumption of the vantage point of the world as a whole as a position that enhances the capabilities and powers of the subject. One can see this gesture as a significant extension of Heidegger's recognition of the uncanniness for Dasein of this world-like perspective in *Being and Time*.

Importantly, Derrida also adds here that it is a matter of a total destruction of the entire world each time that there is a death of the other. *Each time* there is a total destruction of the world. The death of the other registers an infinite, helpless, repetition of the singular. Each time, there is "another end of the world . . . and each time it is nothing less than an origin of the world."[41] Derrida ends the opening paragraph of his foreword with an audaciously short sentence of summation that I would read as a knowing joke, as a recollection of the many other worlds in the history of philosophy that have been held in parentheses: "*Voilà ce que voudrait dire 'le monde.'*" That's it, that's what "the world" means, or means to say. That's the whole story.

It is unsurprising that Derrida's insistence on the end of the world coincides with his call for the "the annihilation" of the "as such" in the work of Husserl and Heidegger. We have already seen Heidegger's evocation of the "as such and as a whole" to demarcate the unique privileges of human Dasein. In his 1992 work *Aporias: Dying—Awaiting (One Another at) the "Limits of Truth,"* Derrida argues that for *Dasein*, "the disappearance, the end, the annihilation of the *as such*, of the possibility of the relation to the phenomenon *as such* or to the phenomenon of the '*as such*'" is "nothing less than the end of the world."[42] Eleven years later in "Rams," Derrida repeats this phrase but with added emphasis: "Death is nothing less than an end of *the* world."[43]

It is striking that in these works on the death of the other Derrida refuses to treat this end of *the* world as a quasi-fiction. It would appear that the death of the other as the end of the world marks the annihilation of the "as such" but also the silence of "as if." In the face of each death being an absolute end of the world, we cannot it seems act *as if* the death of the other is the end of the world. As we will see, this absence of the fictions of the "as if" is also notable since it plays such a critical role in Derrida's reading of Kant. One is also tempted to ask what it means for Derrida's work to exclude "some virtualization" in thinking the death of the other as the end of *the* world, not least because he argues elsewhere that a certain virtuality is always at work when it comes to the *trace*.[44] For Derrida, the trace cannot be included in the logic of the part-whole relation, and as both a mark and an erasure it exceeds the traditional opposition of the sensible and the intelligible. Traces of *différance* indicate an entanglement of spacing and temporalization that no longer resides in the traditional categories of matter and spirit, body and soul, graphic and phonic.[45]

These brief remarks in this foreword in 2003 also bring to mind Derrida's analysis forty years earlier in 1963 of "the hyperbolic audacity of the Cartesian Cogito" in his paper "Cogito and the History of Madness." In this well-known paper, which includes a pointed critique of Michel Foucault, Derrida treats the cogito as the common source of both reason and madness, a common source that is announced by Descartes's excessive declaration of the end of the world. As Derrida observes, for Descartes, "even if the totality of the world does not exist, even if nonmeaning has invaded the totality of the world, up to and including the very contents of my thought, I still think, I am *while* I think."[46] In other words, as I declare the perfect end of the world in the name of reason, I am also mad. For Derrida himself, the madness of the *cogito* has an echo in the phenomenological suspension of the natural attitude toward the world, which he describes in "Rams" as "the most necessary, the most logical, but also the most insane experience of a transcendental phenomenology."[47] After Descartes and Husserl, in the name of an emphatic response to death and to a death of the other, Derrida aligns himself with this hyperbolic and "insane" tradition.

Keeping in mind the equivocal relation to world as a reality, possibility and fiction, it is also important to note that Derrida himself describes the world as a possibility in the foreword to *Chaque fois unique*. Having in the past criticized Husserl's use of the world as the origin of the possible and his reliance on the teleological horizon and unity of the phenomenological world, Derrida retains the notion of the end of the world as a possibility. The end of the world, he writes, is "the always open possibility, indeed the necessity of the possible non-return." To insist on the end of *the* world each time there is the death of the other, Derrida must also insist on the *possibility* of an original finitude or total destruction of the world.[48]

Nonetheless, it must be said that having announced the unequivocal end of the world in "Rams," Derrida makes it clear that he is interested not only in the end of the world but also in the "distancing" of the world in Celan's work.[49] It is Celan who imagines that there is no world as the possibility and the necessity of my carrying you and the world after you have died.[50] Atlas-like, I will carry the world over and over again, after each and after all the deaths. As Derrida comments in his reading of Celan, "No world can any longer support us, serve as mediation, as ground, as earth, as foundation or as alibi."[51] As Derrida observed many years earlier, the world only becomes "an alibi or evasive transcendence" when I invoke the resource of "an *other world*."[52] This is not primarily a question of a traditional theological gesture as much as an ethical imperative. The irremediable loss of calling on this "*other world*" interrupts the blindness of a morality founded on my delusive good conscience as an ethical agent in relation to the other. As soon as I am satisfied that I have been ethical in relation to the other, I have already betrayed the very ethics that I evoked in the first place.

For Derrida, this evocation of a concept of world that does not act as an alibi for good conscience begins with the recognition of the death of the other as the end of *the* world. After the death of the other and the end of the world, one cannot avoid the solitude of the survivor: "the survivor, then, remains alone." This insistence on solitude and on drawing a link between one death and the destruction of the world as a whole was also articulated long ago by Talmudic scholars. As the *Ha-Aggadah* records, "The reason Adam was created alone in the world is to teach you that whoever destroys a single soul, Scripture imputes it to him as though he had destroyed the entire world; and whoever keeps alive a single soul, Scripture imputes it to him as though he had preserved the entire world."[53]

### Derrida and Husserl

In the last pages of his reading of Celan in "Rams," Derrida returns once again to the worlds of Husserl and Heidegger. Like Celan, Husserl and Heidegger have also imagined that there can be no world, that the world can disappear to announce the pure ego of transcendental phenomenology or that one can discern a hierarchy of access to the world among things and living beings and there can be no world for the animal, the plant or the stone.[54] Derrida had already traced in *Glas* (1974) Hegel's association of the Jew with a stone that has no feeling, no spirit—and no world.[55] In the name of the death of the other Derrida may insist on a certain end of the world, but this should not be confused with a tradition of imagining that there is no world based on philosophies of containment and exclusion.

As we have seen, Derrida's emphasis on the origin and the end of the world relies on a phenomenological framework that he took from both Husserl and Fink. It is in the name of a philosophical approach that does the most to recognize the difference of the other that Derrida retains the traditional distinction between what is merely in the world and a vantage point that can see the "origin" and "end" of the world as a whole. In the important early essay "Violence and Metaphysics" (1964), Derrida counters Emmanuel

Lévinas's reading of the Fifth Meditation in Husserl's *Cartesian Meditations* by explaining that "the other as transcendental other" must be seen as the "other absolute origin and other zero point in the orientation of the world." Husserl, he adds, "seeks to recognize the other as Other only in its form as ego, in its form of alterity, which cannot be that of things in the world. If the other were not recognized as a transcendental alter *ego*, it would be entirely in the world and not, as ego, the origin of the world."[56] Forty years later in "Rams," he again explains the importance of this section of the *Cartesian Meditations* for his own work, noting, "When the world has retreated [after the phenomenological reduction] . . . the *alter ego* that is constituted in the ego is no longer accessible in an originary and purely phenomenological intuition."[57] As Paul Ricoeur notes, in the *Cartesian Meditations* Husserl leaves us with the paradox of "constituting the other as 'outsider' and yet 'in' me."[58] For Derrida, this relation to the other *as* other—that is, beyond my projections, idealizations and self-orienting categories—is found not in the world but at the "origin" and the "end" of the world.

Derrida recognizes that this ethical relation to the other and to death at the "origin" and the "end" of the world also evokes a larger phenomenological framework.[59] This wider problem is addressed in *On Touching—Jean-Luc Nancy* (2000). At the start of the book, there are two voices in a dialogue and one of them observes that there is a phenomenological difference between the "*visible* (things or objects in the world)" and "*seeing* (at the origin of the world)."[60] Derrida is most likely offering an oblique criticism here of Merleau-Ponty, who argued that there is both "a circle of the touched and the touching" and "a circle of the visible and the seeing."[61] For Derrida, Merleau-Ponty "reinstates a symmetry that Husserl challenges between the touching-touchable and the seeing-visible."[62]

In the last pages of *On Touching*, Derrida returns to this difference between the visible and seeing, between what is "in the world" and what is "at the origin of the world."[63] In the midst of a long sentence, which starts with "I believe and accept," he draws out the differing relations of this difference. There are two interpretative paths to follow in this sentence. On the one hand, he writes, "one cannot see anything in the world . . . without the possibility, at least, of a reflecting surface that makes visible." In this sense, seeing *from* the "origin" of the world is blind "in the world." If the claim for a vantage point of the world as a whole is to see the world, it must admit "the possibility" of the visible, of what is merely "in the world." Derrida is challenging one of the critical distinctions in phenomenology here and offering an entangled or impure difference in the face of a seemingly absolute or pure difference.

Forty years earlier in his introduction to *The Origin of Geometry*, Derrida noted that phenomenology is founded on a clear difference between what appears and "the regulative possibility of appearing."[64] Husserl links this possibility of appearing to an infinite and teleological "idea in the Kantian sense," which does not itself appear. Not *x* but the possibility of *x*, the Kantian idea secures the unseen origin or pure possibility of phenomenology—which cannot itself undergo a phenomenological analysis. This pure possibility, this untouchable origin coordinates the phenomenological difference between the visible (finite evidence) and seeing (possibility in general). This difference, Derrida notes, also accounts for the possibility "of the world in general." Returning to this phenomenological framework in *On Touching*, Derrida argues that possibility in general "at the origin of the world" (which cannot be seen or touched in phenomenology) must be seen or touched if it is to be registered "in the world." The "origin of the world" cannot itself be an *untouchable* phenomenological origin for a history of touching. From his earliest work, Derrida challenged the traditional notion of the origin as something that is entirely separate from what it subsequently generates or produces.[65]

On the other hand, to follow the second interpretative path, Derrida adds a parenthetical comment in the midst of this long sentence in *On Touching*, an observation that is placed in parentheses or suspended as it talks about world. He writes, "One cannot see anything in the world (this is the origin and the possibility of the world that only a world can also give)."[66] Seeing (possibility in general) is blind without the visible (finite evidence) in the world, but the visible "in the world" is itself also already a structure "of the world," of "the origin and the possibility of the world," of an unseen possibility in general. Just as we cannot claim a pure vantage point beyond the world, we cannot grasp what is truly and only in the world: this is the *equivocal inheritance* of the phenomenological world. One could say that Derrida never stops touching this clear difference, of disturbing the not *x* but the possibility of *x* as the pure possibility of Husserlian phenomenology. At the same time, he maintains this difference. To assert the end of *the* world, Derrida must also mark the difference between what is *in* the world and a vantage point *of* the world as a whole. As the other of Husserl—as a differing and never absolute other—Derrida holds on to both the world and its end.

In a discussion at Villanova University in 1997 with Jean-Luc Marion, Derrida cites once again the passage from the Fifth Meditation of the *Cartesian Meditations* on the relation to the other at the origin of the world and describes it as "a limit of phenomenology that appears within phenomenology."[67] As he would later say in "Rams," the critical point here is that the other ego as defined by Husserl "is no longer accessible in an originary and purely phenomenological intuition."[68] In his 1997 discussion, Derrida goes on to define his own work as an attempt "to check the limits and possibility of phenomenology." Challenging what he sees as Marion's attempt at a pure escape from phenomenology that also claims to be a pure phenomenology, Derrida concludes, "I would like to remain phenomenological in what I say against phenomenology."[69] Always the other of Husserl, the other as other for Derrida becomes the possibility, the memory, the fiction and even the necessity of repeating this difference at the origin and at the end of the world. And one can still ask, after this heritage of the world, this world heritage from Husserl to Derrida, *why world*? Do we still need a concept of world?

## 2. Fictions of the Regulative World

In August 2002, Derrida delivered the paper "The 'World' of the Enlightenment to Come," placing "world" in the title in quotation marks. As far as I am aware, this is the only work by Derrida before *Chaque fois unique, la fin du monde* (2003) that had "world" in the title. Placing the "world" in quotation marks or bracketing the "world" of course evokes the Husserlian suspension of the natural attitude toward the world. But Derrida is also thinking of Kant here and of the regulative world in the *Critique of Pure Reason*. Derrida first made the regulative world an explicit focus of interest in the 1999 paper "The University without Condition," though there are references to this reading of Kant as early as 1982.[70] As Derrida notes in 2001, part of his intention in this paper was to challenge Kant's use of the "as if" (*als ob*) as a regulated instance of fiction in establishing the ability of the ideas of reason to form a systematic unity that can give us a regulative idea of the self, the world and God.[71] To recall Kant's argument, we can only grasp the idea of the world *as if* it is the world as a whole if we take "nature in general" as a pure systematic unity that has no relation to an object of experience.[72] The Kantian logic is wonderful here. We take an idea and treat it *as if* it gives us the object of experience which gives us the true gift: a pure transcendental idea. For Kant, this not only gives us the freedom to make use of nature in general as an idea of world, it also reinforces that the world is an idea that "opens up new paths into the infinite."[73]

### Mondialization: As If There Is a World
Derrida is interested in "the 'if' of a fiction that is heterogeneous . . . to so many 'as ifs' of tradition."[74] He also places this discussion of the fiction in Kantian regulative ideas in the wider context of an important distinction between *mondialization* and globalization. It is likely that the heightened

critical attention given to globalization in the 1990s prompted Derrida's marked emphasis in this period on Kant's regulative world. He argues that the term "globalization" has been taken up without sufficient attention to "the semantic history" of the concept of world and, particularly, to its "Christian history." Derrida makes it clear that *mondialization* reflects a concept of world that describes "neither the universe, nor the earth, nor the terrestrial globe, nor the *cosmos*."[75] In drawing the same distinction between globalization and *mondialization*, Jean-Luc Nancy has defined the former as claiming "a totality as a whole" and the latter as "an expanding *process*."[76] In addition to the common association of globalization with the power of international mass markets and the speed and reach of modern telecommunications, Derrida also emphasizes that *mondialization* is concerned with the international conventions, laws and judiciaries of human rights.[77]

This juxtaposition of a new kind of fictionality with the larger questions of international law and ethics may seem provocative, but of course this is precisely what Kant did in his own work. In my reading of Kant I've drawn a distinction between the regulative world and the categorical world, and it is in this latter sphere of the moral world that I argue Kant reinstates the more traditional quasi-metaphysical frameworks for the concept of world. Interestingly, Derrida insists on the term "mondialization" here because he believes that "the world . . . is neither the globe nor the cosmos."[78] In this specific context, he argues that the traditional concept of world facilitates "the concept of man, of what is proper to man" and a "humanization."[79] Derrida associates deconstruction here with "rethinking the concept of man, [and] the figure of humanity in general."[80] Whatever the concept of world is for Derrida, it has an ability to carry other concepts in a way that is quite distinct from the globe and its closer association with the earth as a tangible object.

Another level of complexity raised by Derrida in this 1999 paper is the question of the university and in particular of the possibility of the university "without condition." In other words, he is not only challenging Kantian regulative ideas and the marking of the differences between world and globe but also revisiting Kant's emphasis on the unconditional. As we have seen, in the *Critique of Pure Reason* Kant argues that the systematic unity of the ideas of reason can grasp the unconditioned possibility of any conditioned series. The unconditioned offers a unique vantage point to see the conditioned series *as a whole*. Derrida will suggest that the university "without conditions" is not an object of possible experience—it "does not, *in fact*, exist"—but it can have a productive relation with a certain "as if" that is no longer contained by Kantian limitations.[81] Importantly, Derrida also implies that the university does not constitute a world in itself but operates as an institution that demands constant negotiation between the public and the private.[82]

After his introductory remarks, Derrida begins the first part of his paper with a phrase that, as we have seen, links Kant to Fink's influential reading of Husserl. The phrase reads, "As if the end of work were at the origin of the world."[83] Derrida then goes on to note the difference between the "as such"—which we have already encountered in his reading of Heidegger—and the "as if." To anticipate his argument, Derrida distinguishes between a programmatic "as if" or a domestication through "legitimate fictions" that can "already be read, decoded, or articulated *as such*" and an irrepressible and nonprogrammatic "if."[84] For Derrida, such an "if" would not be confined to the categories of the conditional and the possible as a domain of assured self-orienting capabilities, powers and decisions. He contrasts this "if" without condition to the traditional metaphysical gesture of the "as such" in Hegel, Husserl and Heidegger. In a paper from 2002 he also contrasts the economy of the "as such" to another nonprogrammatic "if": the impossible event or invention that cannot be predicted, anticipated or foreseen. As he observes, "An event or an invention is possible only as im-possible. That is, nowhere *as such*, the phenomenological or ontological 'as such' annulling this experience of an im-possible that never appears or announces itself *as such*."[85]

Derrida's first comments on Kant are brief and concise. The "as if" facilitates the relation between the conditioned series (the order of nature) and the unconditioned (the order of freedom), and, subsequently, "this 'as if' would itself be something like an agent of deconstructive ferment, since it in some way exceeds and comes close to disqualifying the two orders that are so often distinguished and opposed, the order of nature and the order of freedom."[86] Having linked *mondialization* to a concept of world that supports the traditional concept of man and a general humanization, Derrida suggests here that the "as if" does not fit into the customary oppositions between nature and humanity that define "the proper of man."[87] In this sense, Derrida argues that the Kantian "as if"—which is the possibility of the regulative world—challenges the traditional designation of the discrete sphere or domain (the proper) of man. One can extend this hypothesis to ask whether the "as if" supports the Kantian concept of the regulative world as a marshalling of the conditioned and the unconditioned. Derrida himself goes on to cite an example of the "as if" from *Third Critique* which very much supports the clear difference—or world-like discrete domains—between nature and art. One must act, Kant argues, "as if" the work of art has the "purposiveness" of nature.[88] For Derrida, this is an instance of a programmatic *as if*, in which the *if* has very little force.[89]

While Derrida affirms the need for a conventional "as if" in the attempts to secure international laws and rights beyond the absolute authority of nation states, he also makes the case for a nonprogrammatic or predetermined "as if."[90] This "other mode of the 'if'" is a question of a conditional that is not *necessarily* conditioned and that can then be placed in relation to the unconditioned.[91] This opens the possibility of the fictions of the regulative world. At the same time, to act only as if the world as a whole is given, to open the chance of the *absence* of the world in critical philosophy—of the world as a whole being a fiction precisely of the ideas of reason—is to stray from the Kantian framework of the regulative world as a critique of the metaphysical world which ensures the ultimate authority of the categorical world.

Derrida addresses the link between world and the "as if" in the third and fourth sections of his paper. Returning to the phrase "*as if* the end of work were at the origin of the world," he contrasts the end or "disappearance" of a certain kind of work (*le travail*) and its relation to created works (*oeuvres*) with the emergence of "the *mondialisation du monde*."[92] However, he keeps this within the register of the "as if" in part to challenge the customary distinction between so-called real or actual work and the more performative, fictional and virtual works associated with the humanities. What is also interesting here is that, somewhat like Heidegger's analysis of the historical world in "On the Essence of Ground," Derrida emphasizes the theological implications of acting "as if" the "beginnings of the world originarily excluded work."[93]

Derrida is not describing a fully formed prelapsarian world that flourished before the advent and necessity of labour and work, but the "beginnings of the world." We are not dealing here with world as a given sphere but as a *concept* that could, mistakenly, be seen to preclude the concept of work. As Derrida remarks, "the concept of world" has a long and complex philosophical, religious and cultural history and he reiterates that this concept should not be confused with the cosmos as "the heavenly world above" nor should it "wrongly [be] identified with the earth."[94] Derrida also warns against treating world as a word "without concept."[95] Given the evident echoes here with Heidegger's 1929 essay, it is not surprising that Derrida goes on to speak of Heidegger's attempts "to remove the concept of world and of being-in-the-world from these Greek or Christian presuppositions."[96] As in an earlier paper, "Faith and Knowledge" (1996), Derrida suggests that these "Christian presuppositions" are still informing the talk in the 1990s "about a 'globalization,' a worldwide-ization of the world, [and] a becoming-world of the world."[97]

## The Limits of the Concept of World

Derrida's reading of Kant in "The University without Condition" suggests that Kant's need to rely solely on "legitimate fictions" in his account of the regulative world limits the possibilities of thinking world beyond the metaphysical world that he himself criticized in the *Critique of Pure Reason*. To challenge the security of the regulative world is also to question the assertion of the categorical world. This reading of the Kantian world is of course not new. Schelling remarked that following Kant one could act both as if there is a world and as if there is no world.[98] Derrida himself associates this programmable "as if" with the Husserlian notion of "a horizon of anticipation or precomprehension."[99] In this sense, the regulative world has a predetermined horizon and a secure but entirely static concept of world. Nonetheless, as Derrida's emphasis on the "as if" in the 1990s attests, what makes Kant's treatment of world so significant is that it announces a concept of world that can be taken beyond its own limits and puts into question the basic assumptions of any concept of world—namely, the easy assertion of a discrete and contained world-like domain, sphere or realm and the claim for a secure perspective or vantage point of the world *as a whole*.

Three years later in "The 'World' of the Enlightenment to Come" (2002), Derrida returns to "the fiction of the *als ob* honored in philosophy, and in the name of reason itself, by Kant and others."[100] Derrida once again criticizes the Kantian world as a regulative idea of reason, noting that the "as if" functions primarily as a unifying and totalizing agent. To act as if one can have an idea of the world as a whole is to affirm the overriding and centralizing logos of analogy and proportion.[101] As a fictional unity, the regulative world can even do "violence" to the heterogeneous pluralities within reason itself.[102] The limitations of the Kantian regulated world are in turn determined by the often unrealized but always sought "architectonic desire" of reason.[103] Derrida contrasts a series of "heterogeneous rationalities" to "the unity of the regulative idea of the world." He also refers here once again to the connection between Kant and a contemporary *mondialization*.

Rodolphe Gasché has offered a persuasive reading of Derrida's use of "*the* world" in relation to *mondialization*. In the last pages of his paper, Derrida speaks of the inequality and violence of globalization that is "actually less global or worldwide than ever, where *the* world, therefore, is not even there, and where we, who are wordless, *weltlos*, *form* a world only against the backdrop of a nonworld."[104] Derrida uses Heidegger's designation for the exclusion of animals from the world of human Dasein to describe the current economic, political and social exclusions of so many people from "*the* world" as it is constituted by "so-called globalization."[105] Derrida's em-phasis on "*the* world" highlights that we should also take care to distinguish this from the concept of world.

In *Europe, or the Infinite Task* (2009), Gasché argues that for Derrida there is "no such thing yet as the world" because *the* world today is not a "shared world," a world for all.[106] Gasché suggests that this political determination of the absence of the world and the "worldlessness" that it generates prompts Derrida's emphasis on the ethical chances of "the world to come." As an index of the birth, death and responsibility to the other as other, Gasché argues, the world "is only ever promised" in "an openness to the other in his or her absolute singularity."[107] In Gasché's reading, we are always waiting for the world: for its birth, its end and its promise. If anything, Gasché confirms the concept of world is indispensable for Derrida, as it was for Kant, Hegel, Husserl and Heidegger.

However, Gasché does not perhaps give enough attention to Derrida's marked emphasis on "*the* world" here and his evident attempts to distinguish *mondialization* from the terrestrial globe or the earth and a seemingly self-evident "vision of the world determined by the spherical roundness of the globe."[108] Derrida is clearly concerned with "*the* world," but he is also inter-ested in a concept of world that cannot be mapped onto the planet earth. As Derrida's reading of Kant suggests, there is an inherent fiction in all concepts of world—the Kantian *as if* is only one of the more prominent—and the history of philosophy has never stopped producing new fictions in its tireless efforts to open and close so many different worlds.[109]

One can see this important emphasis on the fictions of world in Der-rida's work by briefly turning to his magisterial reading of Hegel in *Glas*, a two-column reading of philosophy and literature together with Hegel on one side of each page and Jean Genet on the other side.[110] The concept of world does not appear until Derrida retraces Hegel's account of the Flood. It is not entirely surprising that Derrida describes the philosophical tradition of analysing the biblical Flood as the construction of a fiction. When it comes to the end of the world, we are always dealing with a certain relation to the fictional and the virtual. Derrida writes, "Like Condillac, like Rousseau, Kant and some others, Hegel resorts to a kind of theoretical fiction: the re-cital of a catastrophic event reconstitutes the ideal-historic origin of human society."[111] Glossing Hegel's account of Deucalion and Pyrrha and the Greek myth of a global flood, Derrida observes, "After the flood they invited men to renew their friendship with the world, with nature."[112]

What is striking about this first use of world in his reading of Hegel is that Derrida is clearly paraphrasing Hegel: this is a Hegelian *Welt*. The question of whether there is a concept of world in Derrida's thought in this period is even more acute when the next instance of world in *Glas* is explicitly put in the voice of others. In a dialogue between Hegel and "the doctors of cas-tration" (which may stand for Freud and Lacan), "Hegel" responds to their call to recognize "the truly feigned" castration by remarking, "If we are not concerned with a real event, all of you must talk at great length, even spin tales, in order to describe or fulfil the conceptual structure of what you call castration; you must recount a legend, make a whole network of significa-tions intervene; frankly speaking, you must make the whole world of signifi-cation intervene, beginning with the relief [*Aufhebung*], truth, being, law and so on."[113] On the following page, Derrida will formally quote Hegel using the always slightly tautological phrase "the whole world" (*monde tout entier*).[114]

According to Derrida's "Hegel," the legitimation of the "truly feigned" (*le vraiment feint*) requires the evocation or the construction of "the whole world." Speaking *as* Hegel, Derrida suggests at the very least that one can read the "whole world" as a phrase in quotation marks, as a phrase placed in parentheses, as a suspension of the "world." In his reading of Hegel, Der-rida takes care not to speak of the "world" or of the "whole world" in his own name. This caution around one of the oldest of metaphysical props is compounded by his emphasis on the traps and ruses of the fictionality of cre-ating—or ending—a world. Derrida attempts to displace the "truly feigned" fiction of the concept of world within the philosophical tradition.

As he later suggests in "The 'World' of the Enlightenment to Come," the relation between a plurality of reasons and a unifying concept of world is not straightforward. In the case of the regulative world, the concept of world is itself reliant on the ideas of reason ordering the systematic unity of the "as if." If we lose reason, reason risks "*losing itself as world.*" Derrida suggests that the architectonics or systemization of the concept of world in both Kant and Hegel—its discrete spheres and its vantage points—are reliant on the un-stable grounds of a rationality that has the capacity "to *autoimmunise* itself," to destroy itself in the name of protecting itself from its many *others*.[115]

Derrida goes on to turn to *The Crisis of the European Sciences*—where Husserl asserts the primacy of the life-world—to address the concepts of world and of the "end" of the world.[116] Again, it is important to stress here that Derrida treats the end of the world as a *concept*. This was already ap-parent in his earlier paper on Kant, "Of an Apocalyptic Tone Recently Adopted in Philosophy" (1983). In reading Kant's own essay on the dangers of apocalyptic rhetoric and religious enthusiasm as a means of reflecting on contemporary trends in twentieth-century philosophy, Derrida noted the influence of "numerology, mystic illumination, theophanic vision" and "all that indeed belongs to the apocalyptic world."[117] He refers to these various strands of apocalyptic discourse as "the vast and overabundant corpus of the apocalyptic 'genre.'"[118] This "genre," or what we might call *the concept of the world of world*, cannot be gathered into a retrospective unity, and this is particularly the case when it comes to announcing the futurity of "the end of the world."[119] As Kant himself suggested, to assume a vantage point that can take a view of the world and its end in its entirety presupposes a theological fiction. In such circumstances, Kant comments, one would need to act *"as if* this experience constituted an absolute unity," *"as if* the sum total of all appearances (the world of sense itself) had a single supreme and all-sufficient ground outside its range."[120]

In "The 'World' of the Enlightenment to Come" Derrida explores "a transcendental pathology" in Husserl's account of reason, concluding that "it is reason that throws reason into crisis."[121] As he notes, Husserl argues—in the shadow of Kant—that a specific historical world, "the European 'world,'" was "born out of the ideas of reason."[122] For Derrida, both Kant and Husserl therefore rely on a fundamentally *conditioned* relation to the *"unconditional rationalism of the unconditional."*[123] This conditioning of the unconditional also shapes their constructions of the concept of world. One of the ways that Derrida questions this tradition is to turn back to Plato and the recognizably metaphysical world with its clear and separate designations of "the sensible visible world," "the intelligible visible world, and the invisible."[124] He argues that these Platonic discriminations are also founded on the assumption of the apparent rationalism of the unconditional, and he implies that the Kantian regulative world is still tied to the metaphysical world.

Derrida also gestures here to a different concept of world or what he calls "the thought of the world to come." He indicates this other kind of world by arguing for the need to distinguish the theological imperatives of an indivisible sovereignty from the unconditional. Whatever this different concept of world might be, it will be divisible, unforeseeable and without condition.[125] In short, "to think, rationally, something like a future," Derrida argues, one must act *as if* there will be a concept of world without an overriding conceptual horizon.[126] In this way Derrida retains the fictive element of the regulative world without falling back into either the metaphysical or the categorical world.

## The Unconditionality of the Uncontained

Derrida concludes his 2002 paper by affirming "*the unconditionality of the incalculable*," and it is within these terms—which he associates with certain forms of the gift, hospitality, forgiveness and justice—that one will presumably find "the world to come."[127] What is striking about this is that Derrida's concept of world is clearly a concept and cannot be confused with the world as the globe or the earth. However, one could also add that within the history of philosophy the concept of world has always been associated with concepts of containment. If one wanted to challenge this dominant motif it would require the attempt to think *the unconditionally of the uncontained* rather than that of the incalculable. Of course, the danger here, which Derrida avoids, is the implicit association of world with a globe-like uncontained space, domain or sphere. This temptation to evoke the uncontained in relation to world can also lend itself to a problematic earth-centred theory in which the earth is uncontained and the world contained. We will come back to this in chapter 6.

Nonetheless, it is worth briefly exploring the difference between the *unconditioned* and the *uncontained*. Both concepts are defined negatively and suggest an unavoidable relation to the conditioned and the contained. Kant argued that the unconditioned cannot be part of a series in which each term is conditioned by the term that precedes and follows it. The Kantian unconditioned—when one acts as if the ideas of reason give us the world as a whole—requires a vantage point from which to see the whole series of conditioned terms. This is a vantage point outside the series that also operates as the possibility of everything that takes place within the series. To avoid as far as possible replicating the traditional metaphysical relation of the world as a whole created by a God that is found above and beyond the world, Kant situates this structure in the relation between nature and freedom.

It is important to point out that Derrida's evocation of the unconditioned is quite different from the Kantian unconditioned. From his earliest work on Kant, Derrida describes a countermovement to critical philosophy that challenges the logic of a philosophy that announces limits and boundaries and that claims, mistakenly, to determine what is both inside and outside its own self-instituted boundaries. In fact, Derrida argues, critical philosophy must constantly exceed its own limits to maintain the cohesiveness of its inside/outside distinction. In this sense, if one may so say, it de-constructs itself. As Derrida puts it in the introduction to *Margins of Philosophy* (1972), this is a philosophy that "has recognized, conceived, posited, declined the limit according to all possible modes; and therefore by the same token, in order better to dispose of the limit, has transgressed it. Its own limit has not remained foreign to it. Therefore it has appropriated the concept for itself; it has believed that it controls the margin of its volume and that it thinks its other."[128]

Derrida traced this unavoidable self-preserving and self-denying transgression in Kant's work in a number of remarkable essays in the 1970s and

1980s.[129] For our purposes, perhaps the most interesting is a short work entitled "Cartouches" (1978), which disrupts the whole Kantian logic of the conditioned as a contained series and the unconditioned as absolutely outside the series. The unconditioned for Derrida is not simply outside the series, it is "outside the series in the series" and—much like Heidegger's being-in-the-world—attempts to overcome the traditional boundaries and limits of the outside and inside, the external and internal.[130] The unconditioned in this sense would also disrupt the traditional concept of world as a structure of containment, allowing for neither discrete self-defined and self-contained spheres, domains or realms nor the possibility of a secure conceptual space, ground or place from which to view the world as a whole, as if the subject were standing in a god-like vantage-point beyond the globe or the earth. In this context, Derrida's readings of Kant offer the possibility of thinking of world in terms of *the unconditionally of the uncontained*.

Such an undertaking would no doubt have to begin again with Aristotle, who associates the uncontained with that which uniquely cannot be contained but which always enacts a containment. The traditional logic, which organizes its concepts in terms of a seemingly unalterable natural cosmology, suggests that one cannot reverse the sequence: the uncontained (the universe) always *gives rise to* the contained that contains (the world), which in turn always *gives rise to* the contained (beings, things). The order and teleology of this sequence cannot be changed: the contained (beings, things) could never give rise to the uncontained (the universe). However, part of what Derrida suggests with his rereading of the Kantian "as if" and his insistence on the term *mondialization* is that we need to avoid treating concepts of world as exclusively natural descriptors (without, of course, then seeing them as only cultural, fictional or virtual).

Aristotle's classical model of containment relies on a series of distinctive temporal and spatial determinations. There is a linear and teleological development from the uncontained to the contained (the universe, the world, things and beings). This nonreversible temporal sequence also describes a spatial order in which an infinite or indefinite magnitude progressively reduces itself to the finite and infinitesimal (the universe, the world, beings and things). This is the temporal and spatial limit of the traditional logic of containment. Following Derrida, if we act *as if* the concept of world is structured by the unconditionally of the uncontained, these limits have always been transgressed in the history of philosophy in the attempt to maintain the very logic of containment.

It is after listing the *aporia* of place in his *Physics* that Aristotle first refers directly to world. He remarks, "'Place' may refer either to the shared place which contains all bodies or to the particular place which immediately contains a body." He then uses the world as an example to account for this distinction in the concept of place. The world illustrates or represents—or *re*-presents as Derrida might say—the concept of place. Aristotle writes,

> For instance, you are now in the world, because you are in the air and the air is in the world; and you are in the air because you are on the earth; and by the same token you are on the earth because you are in this particular place, which contains nothing more than you.[131]

Aristotle suggests that there is a clear difference between finding oneself "in the world" and finding oneself "on the earth." He also implies that the earth provides an example for "the particular place" while the world illustrates the concept of "the shared place." At the same time, it seems difficult to maintain this clear difference between finding oneself "on the earth" and finding oneself "in this particular place, which contains nothing more than you." One is tempted to ask how one could not be *in* the world and *on* the earth at the same time and in the same place.[132]

As an example of the world as "the shared place," Aristotle also links the world, the air, the subject *and the now*: all these concepts can share the same place at the same time. Nonetheless, the subject does not have an immediate relation to the world. I am "in the air," and it is because "the air is in the world" that I am "now in the world." The world contains air, which contains me and contains me now. This suggests the possibility of a sequence of preconditions: to find myself in the world *now* I must *already* have found myself in the air, which was itself *already* in the world. First there was the world, then there was air, then there was me and now there is me now. As an example of place, the world suggests the possibility of a sequence of multiple containments that can also coexist *simultaneously* in a present moment. A series of spatial relations, which can also be described as a succession of temporal stages, culminate in "the shared place" that gathers itself into the now. As Derrida recognizes, the concept of world as a structure of containment illustrates the possibility of a subject-oriented presence, of a present moment, my moment, here and now, in the world, that has surmounted—for a moment—all its spatial and temporal differences.

It is worth pointing out that Derrida's interest in space as a dynamic spacing suggests that any notion of the world as ground or place is already shaped by the unconditionally of the uncontained. The *differantial* modes of "the becoming-time of space" *and* "the becoming-space of time" ensure that any assertion of place as *the* place is displaced and replaced.[133] Derrida explores this displacement in a number of different readings, including a notion of writing (inspired in part by Mallarmé) as a "taking the place of the place" and of the event without a predetermined horizon in which what *takes place* always takes away *the* place.[134] Following Heidegger, he also uses Plato's *Timaeus* to describe *khōra* as neither place nor space but the spacing that makes any placing and displacing possible.[135] As he observes in "Plato's Pharmacy" (1968), as a "receptacle that is never and nowhere offered up in the form of presence," *khōra* requires "that we define the origin of the world as a *trace*."[136]

For Aristotle, the key quality of place is its ability to separate itself from all the moving and changing bodies that pass through it. If one takes place as the possibility of a concept of world, the world contains and remains separate: it *auto-contains*. As Aristotle remarks in the *Physics*, "The place *is* separable. For, as we have already said, the place where air was before now contains water instead, as they replace each other, and the same goes for other bodies too; consequently, the place of any given thing is not a part or a state of that thing, but is separable from it."[137] World appears to be that in which we always find ourselves but which also remains separable from everything that we find. It is in this context that Aristotle first describes place as a "container."[138] The logic of containment requires that we continually think what contains the container—like a series of Russian dolls each placed inside the other—*until we reach a limit.* "Place is the limit of the containing body," Aristotle declares.[139] The container takes us to the limit, and as Derrida suggests in his reading of Aristotle in *On Touching*, this limit cannot avoid marking itself as a limit of what can be touched and which, impossibly, must itself also always be untouchable. In other words, at the necessary limit of all logics of containment one can never entirely separate the touchable and the untouchable—and the limit always exceeds itself.[140]

It would be very tempting here to act as if the world no longer operates as an Aristotelian term and can be relieved of mediating between the unconditioned (the universe) and the contained (beings and things). In this sense, the world would be a concept that is neither contained nor contains. It would no longer hold the place in place. World could then be thought in the unconditionality of the uncontained. However, one has to be vigilant about not treating the unconditionality of the uncontained as an untouchable or pure originating difference, as something simply outside the series.[141] As Derrida suggests at the end of "The 'World' of the Enlightenment to Come," the claim for a world that is exclusively unconditional still occupies the traditional position of the metaphysical world and reinhabits Plato's inaugural division of entirely distinct sensible and intelligible realms.

In his account of reason in "The 'World' of the Enlightenment to Come," Derrida concludes "*both* calculation and the incalculable *are necessary*."[142] A dynamic or differentiated concept of reason is found in the constant "transaction" between "the reasoned exigency and conditionality" and "the intransigent, nonnegotiable exigency of unconditional incalculability."[143] Derrida suggests that the concept of world can be thought of as both conditioned and unconditioned *at the same time*. In this sense, it would be apparent that the spatial and temporal limits of the traditional concept of world have always operated "outside the series in the series." The uncontained (the universe) has always been *in the midst of* the contained that contains (the world) and the contained (beings and things). Both the world and beings and things have always been exposed to the uncontained, and their own containments have always been breached or perforated.

Derrida's reading of Kant allows us to think of quite a different concept of world than that readily found in the history of philosophy. We clearly need structures of containment, of the designation of discrete realms, domains or spheres, but these structures can now be seen in relation to a concept of world that is *uncontained without being absolutely uncontained*. It is of course extremely difficult to think of the contained and uncontained together. At the very least, it suggests a "transaction without any rule given in advance, without any absolute assurance."[144] We can also call this a concept of *world without horizon*. While world without horizon enables us to think the uncontained *with* the contained, it does preclude the other dominant aspect of the traditional concept of world: the ceaseless attempt to use world to establish a secure vantage point beyond the world. There is simply not enough time or space for the subject to establish a transcendental perspective or god-like platform from which to view the world as a whole. Derrida's work opens the possibility of a concept of world that is always enacting an operation of (un) containment. As he suggests, this possibility is announced in the philosophical revolution of Kant's *Critique of Pure Reason*.

## 3. The Cohabitation of the World

While Derrida's evocation of the end of the world emerges from his reading of the relation to what is truly other in Husserlian phenomenology and he uses Kant's critical philosophy to think beyond the limits of the regulative world, his most sustained and direct treatment of world arises from his work on Heidegger. It is in his readings of Heidegger that Derrida comes closest to forming his own concept of world. To understand Derrida's critical account of Heidegger's comparative world, we must begin with Derrida's earliest work on Husserl and his interest in the notion of the *play of the world*, which had been highlighted in readings of Heraclitus by Nietzsche, Heidegger and Fink.

## The Play of the World

Derrida started his academic career by working on Husserl, and his first book-length publication in 1962 was a translation of and introduction to a short, late work by Husserl on the origin of geometry.[145] In *The Problem of Genesis in Husserl's Philosophy* (1954), Derrida's dissertation that he completed at the age of twenty-four, he is preoccupied with a critique of Husserl's notion of the life-world. For Derrida, there is "a serious ambiguity in the concept of 'world'" in Husserl's later thought because the concept of world accounts for both an "antepredicative" reality and the "predicative" possibility of judgements.[146] Husserl's concept of life-world is contradictory because it attempts to describe the preexisting reality of *the* world that is "always already there" while also being the basis for *a* world as the idea of "an infinite horizon" of as yet unrealized possibilities.[147] As the young Derrida observes, "A formal *a priori* possibility" cannot produce "an antepredicative moment of the existent or of an actual, that is to say, 'finite,' totality of existents."[148]

On the one hand, if one begins with world as possibility, consciousness has no origin in concrete existence, and it will invent and fabricate its pure world and terminate in a psychological and subjective cul-de-sac.[149] This is not only a question of hermetic fictional worlds worthy of Cervantes's *Don Quixote* but also of reality being described through the "idealization" of logical concepts. In such a case, the real world would disappear. On the other hand, Husserl still "presents the antepredicative world [ . . . ] as the always present actuality of the given," insisting that the life-world is also "the world of experience, in the most concrete and most everyday sense of the word." The life-world leaves us with two incompatible assertions: there is no world, there are only my fictional worlds; *and* there are no fictional worlds, there is only the one and everyday world.[150]

Thirteen years later in *Of Grammatology* (1967), encountering the inheritance of the suspension of the world in transcendental phenomenology and its intricate connection to *Dasein* in Heidegger's thought, Derrida can adhere neither to a clear denial nor to a persistent affirmation of world. As we have seen, Derrida formulates his own critique of the concept of world by addressing the relation between language and world. He writes,

> The system of "hearing (understanding)-oneself-speak" through the phonic substance—which *presents itself* as the nonexterior, nonmundane, therefore

nonempirical or noncontingent signifier—has necessarily dominated the history of the world during an entire epoch, and has even produced the idea of the world, the idea of world-origin, that arises from the difference between the worldly and the non-worldly, the outside and the inside, ideality and non-ideality, universal and nonuniversal, transcendental and empirical, etc.[151]

A phonocentric tradition casts language not *in* the world (the exterior, mundane, empirical and contingent) but as the "origin" of the world. Language is the transcendental possibility of the world.[152] It is itself entirely free of the world: intelligible, necessary and universal. In this sense, without the ideality of the *phonē* and the logos, there would be no "idea of the world."

Derrida offers a sustained critique in *Of Grammatology* of this use of language to construct an ideality of world. In his most well-known work, Derrida challenges the prevailing view in the 1960s that structural linguistics could give a comprehensive account of language and the other disciplines in the so-called human sciences. Far from advocating the supremacy of language, Derrida is interested in language *and* its many others. He also suggests in his analysis of linguistics that both Husserl and Heidegger have a problematic relation to the world. Despite the careful construction of a transcendental internal time consciousness, Husserl cannot avoid "the time of the world."[153] And despite his evocation of being-in-the-world, Heidegger still succumbs to a notion of language "which does not borrow from outside itself, in the world."[154] We are left with what Derrida calls "the *game of the world*" (le *jeu du monde*).[155] The challenge of le *jeu du monde* is to think of a writing "which is neither *in* the world nor in 'another world,'" of a writing that marks "the absence of another here-and-now, of another transcendent present, of *another* origin of the world."[156]

In his earlier influential paper "Structure, Sign and Play in the Discourse of the Human Sciences" (1966), Derrida associated le *jeu du monde* with Nietzsche's "joyous affirmation of the play of the world and the innocence of becoming."[157] He refers here to Nietzsche's description of the world as a "*game*" or "play of forces" in which world accounts for a continual becoming, passing away and destruction. To understand the context of Derrida's evocation of the play of the world in 1966–1967, it is worth briefly turning to the readings of Heraclitus by Nietzsche, Fink and Heidegger.

### Nietzsche and Heraclitus

Nietzsche insisted throughout his work on refusing the easy allure and theologically overdetermined value of "another world."[158] As Deleuze observes, for Nietzsche "the idea of another world, of a supersensible world in all its forms (God, essence, the good, truth), the idea of values superior to life, is not one example among many but the constitutive element of all fiction."[159] Nietzsche himself took his concept of world—a dynamic relation of forces that are in the process at once of becoming *and* being destroyed—from Heraclitus.[160] According to Nietzsche in his lectures on the pre-Platonic philosophers at the University of Basel, for Heraclitus there is "no thing of which we may say, 'it is'" in the world and he therefore "rejects *Being.*" Heraclitus "knows only Becoming."[161] However, this endless becoming of world is also an unavoidable "passing away."[162] Placed well beyond its theological narratives, the concept of world can be seen within the larger perspective of a "world-creating" game of perpetual building and destroying.[163]

Nietzsche argues that it is important to recognize that Heraclitus's account of the world still maintains the vantage point of an "intelligence prevailing over oppositions."[164] Heraclitus's depiction of the world as a becoming that also passes away still retains the traditional logic of the contained (the one, justice) and the container (opposing and mixing differences, injustice, periodic destruction, play). Nietzsche is interested in the finitude of a playing that builds and destroys without purpose or a larger divine order. He suggests the need for a concept of world that is no longer tied to the gods or to *kósmos* as the ordering of the world.[165] In one of his best-known fragments, Heraclitus compares the play of the world to the innocent play (*paidiá*) of a child. "Eternity [*aión*]," Heraclitus is reported as having said, "is a child at play, playing draughts: the kingdom is a child's."[166] For Nietzsche, the world here is like the play of a child because it describes "a becoming and passing away without any moralistic calculations."[167] In the later *Twilight of the Idols* (1888), Nietzsche contrasts this play of the world to the erroneous history of the so-called "true world" as world that is both truly available and truly unavailable.[168]

Derrida's understanding of the play of the world in the mid-1960s was also inspired by the work of Fink and his own readings of Nietzsche and Heraclitus.[169] In *Nietzsche's Philosophy* (1960), Fink observes, "The cosmos plays. . . . It plays joining and separating, weaving death and life into one beyond good and evil and beyond all value because any value only appears within the play."[170] As Fink implies, Nietzsche takes the concept of world beyond its delimitation within classical natural philosophy, the Aristotelian logic of containment and Christian theology. However, it is worth noting that in his own reading of Heraclitus in *Spiel als Weltsymbol* (1960), Fink is also very close to a Heideggerian account of the comparative world when he contrasts the relation of humans and animals to the world.

According to Fink, the play of the world is found in the unique ability of gods and men to be at once *in* the world and to have a perspective *of* the world as a whole. Humans are defined by their ability to secure a vantage point that is not only, thoughtlessly and animal-like, *in* the world.[171] Man's recognition of the play of the world—of what is at once in the world and has a view of the world as a whole without recourse to another world—allows him to form rather than be formed and to give above and beyond the merely given.[172] One can see the clear difference here between Derrida and Fink in Derrida's later pointed critique of Heidegger's emphasis on the uniquely human "power to configure the world" and of world as a confirmation of the holding sway or violent sovereign domination (*Walten*) of human Dasein.[173]

Fink's reading of Heraclitus and the play of the world can also be counterbalanced by Heidegger's own account in the last pages of *The Principle of Reason* (1956–1957). Heidegger does not return here to the problems of the comparative world from his 1929–1930 lectures but turns to the associations of world with ground or support. In his account of Leibniz, Heidegger explores the links between *Grund* (which means both ground and reason in German) and *Abgrund* (abyss or without ground). For Heidegger, the play of the world is primarily about how being—within the familiar dynamic of concealing and revealing—grounds or underwrites without taking on a traditional form of grounding or support that is akin to Leibniz's equation of reason and ground. Heraclitus's fragment on the play of the world emphasizes a pervasive connection between world, time and being. The "abyss" of being is intimated, Heidegger argues, by eternity (*aión*) giving us a finite time for "world-play" that just plays "because it plays." He concludes by associating the play of the world with human finitude and death as the "yet unthought standard of measure of the unfathomable."[174]

For Derrida, significantly, the play of the world suggests that one can avoid thinking of world within the traditional Aristotelian structure of container and contained. As he remarks in a discussion from 1979, "On the basis of thinking such as Nietzsche's (as interpreted by Fink), the concept of play, understood as the play of the world, is no longer play *in* the world. That is, it is no longer determined and contained by something, by the space that would comprehend it."[175] At the same time, Fink was closely associated with Husserl, and his argument for thinking "at the origin of the world" could be taken, as Ricoeur suggests, as the possibility of "the transcendental subject" discovering itself "as the foundation of the world."[176] In his 1979 discussion of Fink, Derrida pointedly emphasizes a different interpretation. "Once play is no longer simply play in the world," he remarks, "it is also no longer the play of someone who plays."[177] The play of the world is not subject-oriented and cannot be seen as yet another discourse on the world as the unfolding of human finitude.

For Derrida, the play of the world is registered by *différance* and the trace or the inextricable intertwining of space and time and the mark that is neither sensible nor intelligible. In contrast to Heidegger, for Derrida the abyss (*Abgrund*) is not "the bottomless depth (*Ungrund*) of some hidden base." The play of the world arises, he insists, because "there is *more than one* ground."[178] Twenty years after *Of Grammatology*, Derrida described Heidegger's notion of "the play of the world" in *Of Spirit: Heidegger and the Question* (1987) as a concentric "becoming-world of world" that always tends toward a limited "collecting together" (*Versammlung*).[179] Derrida also implies that Heidegger's use of world remained tied to the assumption of a "clear difference between the open and the closed."[180]

### Heidegger, the Animal and the World

In 1961–1962 Derrida delivered five as yet unpublished lectures at the Sorbonne for a seminar devoted to "Le monde chez Heidegger."[181] Derrida's 1964–1965 seminar, *Heidegger: La question de l'Être et l'histoire*—which he briefly considered publishing as a book in 1965—is soon to be published.[182] When these works appear we will no doubt know more about Derrida's early critical reading of Heidegger's concept of world. As Heidegger observes when he first introduces world in *Being and Time*, world gives Dasein an understanding of its own being and access to entities "whose character of Being is other than that of Dasein."[183] World therefore opens the relation of Dasein to entities or beings who do not take their own existence as a question of Being. As we have seen, Heidegger returns to this use of world to think of Dasein and its others in his 1929–1930 lectures, *The Fundamental Concepts of Metaphysics*. Over an eighteen-year period from 1985 to 2003 Derrida offered a series of readings of Heidegger's 1929–1930 seminar.[184] These readings constitute by far and away Derrida's most explicit engagement with the concept of world.

At the same time, at least in *Of Spirit* (1987) and in *The Animal That Therefore I Am* (1997), Derrida raises the question of world very much in relation to his reading of Heidegger. As we shall see, it is only in his final seminar in 2003 that he gestures to a concept of world in his own name. "What do we call the world?" he asks in *Of Spirit* and then answers his question by quoting Heidegger from *Introduction to Metaphysics*, "Reply: 'The world is always a *spiritual* world.'"[185] In 1935, he notes, Heidegger insists that when it comes to the spiritual world, human Dasein has no others: the animal has no world. However, Derrida points out, five years earlier in his 1929–1930 seminar, Heidegger had generated a more equivocal concept of world. In contrast to the stone (which simply has no world), the animal has a world and yet is deprived of the world.[186] It is on this problem of world as Dasein's relation to others and of the animal that both "*has* and *does not have* a world" that Derrida will focus his most sustained reading of Heidegger's seminar sixteen years later in the 2002–2003 sessions of the seminar on *The Beast and the Sovereign*.[187] Derrida's sustained interest in world is focused on the equivocal or shifting differences in Heidegger's own attempt to account for the other of human Dasein.

In contrast to the many twists and turns that he analyses in Heidegger's treatment of the world from 1925 to 1936, there is a remarkable consistency in Derrida's own analysis of Heidegger's seminar over these eighteen years. In this sense, one cannot read Derrida as he reads Heidegger. In his lectures on the animal in 1997, Derrida asks once again in his reading of Heidegger, "What is the world? What does one call 'world'?"[188] Situating this question in Heidegger's 1929–1930 distinction between Dasein as world-forming (*welt-bildend*) and "the animal that is poor in world" (*weltarm*), Derrida outlines a long tradition in the history of philosophy of treating the animal as a general singularity that can be juxtaposed to the individual differentiation of human beings. In this sense, the limitation or confinement of the animal has also determined the unique possibilities of the human.

In his 1997 lectures, Derrida only manages to offer some brief but very concise remarks on *The Fundamental Concepts of Metaphysics*. In these re-corded comments, he challenges Heidegger's key argument that in contrast to Dasein the animal merely lives and has no existence.[189] Dasein is aware of its mortality and can self-register or self-display its existence—*as such* and *as a whole*—as a being-in-the-world. Dasein, being and world therefore rely on defining the general essence of animals as merely living.[190] For Derrida, this raises the attendant question of a *life* that is not determined by its relation to world—as it is in Husserl and Heidegger—and the customary definitions of life and death in the history of philosophy.

In the later *The Beast and the Sovereign* seminars (2001–2003), Derrida challenges Heidegger's emphatic distinctions between human and animal by addressing the shared conditions of living and dying and "the world as world of life-death."[191] In a 1975 seminar Derrida had already challenged the traditional boundaries between life and death with the concept of life-death (*la-vie-la-mort*) as a living on or living over of life in death and of death in life.[192] As Derrida himself notes, his emphasis on the determinations and ide-alizations of life started with his early critique of Husserl's use of the "living present" (*lebendige Gegenwart*) as the "ultimate form of ideality."[193] Husserl's philosophy is then primarily a "philosophy of life" and of the "living voice," Derrida argues, because life always "escapes the transcendental reduction."[194] Derrida also questioned Heidegger's need to found the world of human Dasein—the world *as such and as a whole*—on the denial that animals have access to death.[195] In his 1929–1930 seminar, Heidegger "comes to the assertion that only man dies, whereas the animal for its part does not die, but simply ceases to live."[196] For Derrida, this is yet one more instance of a philosophical tradition that insists on speaking of "the relation to death *as such*."[197]

Derrida brought attention to the valorisation of the "as such" (*comme tel*) in the work of Heidegger as early as 1963.[198] Fifty years later in his last seminar in 2003, he once again argues that the authority of the *as such* founds "every philosophy and justifies every ontology as well as every phenomenology."[199] As we have seen, the *as such* is the privilege of opening and manifesting, of making manifest, of making *the other* manifest.[200] Heidegger treats world as the exclusive manifestation of being as such for human *Dasein*, a manifestation that the animal cannot access but which defines—and confines—the animal in a discrete world-like sphere.[201]

Derrida also emphasizes in his remarks in 1997 that Heidegger has taken three different approaches to the problem of the world: being-in-the-world, the historical world and the comparative world. He suggests that these three approaches lead to an impasse. Heidegger not only recognizes that the animal has a world and does not have a world but also offers differing accounts of the animal's relation to death.[202] Heidegger must acknowledge in the midst of this third approach, "We don't finally know what world is!"[203] As Heidegger attempts to distinguish mere animal living from Dasein's existing, he cannot avoid a series of uncanny moments of circularity and vertigo. As Derrida remarks, in this context "it's the concept of world itself that becomes problematic and fragile."[204]

Derrida is cautious about declaring that the Heideggerian world is simply without animals because the "comparative examination" leads not only to moments of conceptual fragility but also to the larger question of privation (*Entbehrung*). For Heidegger, the animal is for the most part not without world but poor in the world: the animal has world and is deprived of world. Derrida asks how the feeling of such a deprivation is possible if the animal has no access to the human facility of self-display, of taking the world *as such*.[205] For Derrida, the "deconstructive strategy" here is to move beyond the *opposition* of human self-display or the capability of the apophantic logos and "a nonapophantic marking" (Derrida replacing logos here with a trace).[206] He concludes by asking whether the human Dasein does indeed have this capacity to take the world—everything in the midst of which we find our-selves—as a mediated or calibrated assertion of self-display.[207]

Ten years earlier in *Of Spirit*, Derrida had described Heidegger's assertion of the absolute differences between the stone, the animal and man in rela-tion to the world as an example of "the profoundest metaphysical human-ism."[208] Heidegger may have avoided the metaphysical world that Kant first challenged in the *Critique of Pure Reason*, but he did not avoid metaphysical humanism. Heidegger's difficulty in reformulating a truly new concept of world in the history of philosophy could be taken as a warning: perhaps one cannot establish a viable concept of world without, ultimately, succumbing to "the profoundest metaphysical humanism."

Derrida's aim in his 1997 lectures is to "reproblematise" the motif of world not to offer an alternative notion of world.[209] At the same time, the legacy of the fantasy of a world without animals in the history of philosophy inextri-cably links the question of the merely living animal to the concept of world. As Derrida asks, "Is being-with-the-animal a fundamental and irreducible structure of being-in-the-world, so much so that the idea of a world without animals could not even function as a methodological fiction?"[210] Nonethe-less, Derrida does not explain in 1997 what a world *with* animals would mean, and he only touches on this issue almost in passing at the end of his 2003 seminar. If anything, Derrida resists the temptation to add yet another con-cept of world to the many worlds in the history of philosophy.

In *The Beast and the Sovereign*, volume 2 (2002–2003), in what would be his final seminar, Derrida offers an extended reading of Heidegger's analysis of the comparative world in *The Fundamental Concepts of Metaphysics* in con-junction with an account of Daniel Defoe's *Robinson Crusoe* (1719). Derrida argues that the concept of world is critically important because it indicates a domain in which animals and humans live and die together.[211] This un-avoidable *cohabitation* allows us to rethink the attempts to place the human, the animal, life and death in discrete *world-like* spheres. As Derrida remarks, "They co-habit the world that is the same."[212] This world is the same but it is not identical. As Derrida first argued in 1964, this means that we can take the world as a concept that "does not enclose the other."[213] Animals and humans live and die together in the world, and this should make us rethink the idealization of the concept of world in the history of philosophy. Cohabi-tation challenges the tradition of understanding the concept of world as a *discrete* domain, realm or sphere.

Derrida's extended reading of Heidegger takes us from the limitations of the comparative world to the possibilities of the cohabiting world. The cohabiting world is a concept of "the world in which one-lives-one-dies."

In other words, world registers "a place of common habitat" where one can no longer rely on the traditional boundaries and limitations between what is living and what is dead.[214] Derrida also makes it very clear that living and dying *in* this cohabitation "does not have here the sense of a container."[215] We are in the world but we are no longer operating within the logic of containment. As we have seen, Derrida treats the ethical relation to the other as truly other and the alterity of the death of the other as the only vantage point of the "origin" and "end" of the world as a whole. In contrast to Heidegger, it is evident that both animals and humans share this relation to death *as* the end of the world.

Warning against the temptation to treat this cohabiting world as a simple unity or loss of difference, Derrida insists that one cannot truly establish that "the world is one and the same thing" for two human beings let alone animals and humans.[216] Within the cohabiting world, Derrida will argue, there is *always more than one world*. We must recognize two possibilities at once. On the one hand, "there really must be a certain *presumed, anticipated* unity of the world even in order discursively to sustain within it multiplicity, untranslatable and un-gatherable, the dissemination of possible worlds."[217] On the other hand, beyond this virtual and even quasi-fictional unity and the recognition of a multiplicity of disseminating worlds, there is the possibility that there is *no world*.

The cohabiting world must contend with the "infinite anxiety" that "nothing is less certain than the world itself." As Derrida points out, the very possibility of a multiplicity of worlds suggests the "absence of a common world." Derrida is specifically talking about the possibility of the shared and differentiated world of animals and humans, but one can extend this "infinite anxiety" to the concept of world itself. As Derrida says, "Perhaps there is no world."[218] This is of course a possibility that has haunted the history of philosophy since Kant and can be found in Hegel, Husserl and Heidegger. For Derrida, if we examine the persistent and unbridgeable differences between ourselves and those to whom we are closest, there is always "the abyssal unshareable."[219] This radical separation and isolation reinforces that "there is no world, not even a world, not even one and the same world, no world that is one: *the* world, *a* world, a world that is *one*."[220]

This profound absence of one world cannot be excluded from thinking the cohabiting world. Faced with the need to think at once the shared and the unshareable world, Derrida returns to his reading of the fictions of the Kantian regulative world. Alluding in part to *Robinson Crusoe*, he argues that if we are confronted by "the insularity of islands that are not even in the world, the same world, or on a world map," this absence of any "common world" or even of a "life-world" must lead us to "pretend" that there is a cohabiting world.[221] For Derrida, relying on no more than a "fragile convention," in the end one must act *as if* there is a shared world.[222] At the same time, this fiction is no more than a kind of "life insurance," an "animal ruse of life."[223] This fiction of world is an inescapable part of life and death, of animals and humans living together and dying together. There is always the possibility that there is no world, but the world remains a necessary fiction.

# CHAPTER SIX

# World, Fiction and Earth

## 1. Literature and the Impossibility of World

Having examined the concept of world in the history of philosophy from Kant to Derrida, in this final chapter I would like to turn to other related problems that we have touched on in previous chapters: the question of the fiction of world, the relation between the concepts of world and earth and the possibility of a philosophy without world. Initially, I will focus on a number of influential twentieth-century readings of Hegel's *Phenomenology of Spirit* to explore how philosophy invents its own worlds and how the tradition of the philosophical concept of world can be challenged by rethinking the fictional worlds of literature. I will then turn to some recent critical ecological or earth-oriented readings of Derrida's work to examine how the possibilities of the concept of world are limited by a valorisation of the earth as its ideal and absolute other. Finally, I will conclude by briefly addressing the impasses in advocating a philosophy without world. In the history of philosophy since Kant, there has always been the possibility that there is no world, but an emphatic declaration of its end only reflects the desire to escape philosophy itself.

### Kojève, Hyppolite and Blanchot

As we have seen, like Kant before him, Hegel was unable to start the *Phenomenology* with a concept of world. In the first sections of the *Phenomenology*, there is the sense, perception and understanding of things, but there is no explicit discussion of world itself. Kant himself only turns to the world itself in the *Critique of Pure Reason* in the Transcendental Dialectic when world is no longer a possible object of experience and becomes a problem of the systematic unity of the ideas of reason. In the *Phenomenology*, Hegel marks the emergence of the supersensible world and its antagonistic relation to actuality in his account of self-consciousness and reason, but it is only when consciousness rises to the stage of spirit that one can speak of the actual world *as* the world of spirit. It is then that we understand retrospectively that it is these spiritual worlds that have given the discrete shapes, domains and spheres of each developing stage of the *Phenomenology*. It is only when we come to spirit that we realize that we were never without world.

One could argue that in their influential readings of Hegel, Alexandre Kojève and Jean Hyppolite both produce their own fictional worlds by attempting to read this absent world *into* the earlier sections of the *Phenomenology*. This creation of a fictional world in the midst of Hegel's text is compounded by their interest in Hegel's *apparent* discussion of literary writers and literature in general in the final stages of consciousness's journey through reason. Kojève and Hyppolite's works on Hegel appeared in 1946–1947 and are both cited by Maurice Blanchot in his ostensible review of their books, "Literature and the Right to Death" (1947–1948). This forty-page article not only raises the question of the relation between Hegelian philosophy, the world and literature but also suggests that the relation between literature, language and death can frustrate the attempt to think of either philosophical concepts of world (as the possibility of discrete spheres, domains or realms) or fictional worlds (as perfect, hermetically sealed virtual worlds). In contrast to the seemingly unavoidable fictional and self-evident worlds that Kojève and Hyppolite generate in their philosophical work, Blanchot's elusive intertwining of the literary and the philosophical suggests a space of literature that renders a discrete or hermetic—and even heuristic—concept of world impossible.

Blanchot first published "Literature and the Right to Death" in two separate essays in the journal *Critique*.[1] The first part, under the title "Le règne animal de l'esprit," appeared in November 1947. This title is a translation of part of the title of the opening of the third and final section of Hegel's long chapter on reason in the *Phenomenology*. The full title is "The Spiritual Animal Kingdom and Deceit, or the 'Matter in Hand' Itself" (*Der geistige Tierreich und der Betrug, oder die Sache selbst*).[2] Blanchot himself would remove this incomplete citation or partial title from the final version of his essay when it was published as a single essay in 1949 in *The Work of Fire*.[3]

In one of the two footnotes to "Le règne animal de l'esprit," Blanchot warns his reader not to take his work as a close reading of Hegel: "It should be understood that the remarks which follow are quite remote [*restent fort loin*] from the text of the *Phenomenology* and make no attempt to illuminate it [*ne cherchent pas à l'éclairer*]."[4] Given his initial choice of title for his article, Blanchot's denial of reading the *Phenomenology* describes a complex geneal-ogy of denegation that cannot be separated from the interpretations of Hegel by Kojève and Hyppolite and the relation between "The Spiritual Animal Kingdom," world and literary fiction.

As Andrzej Warminski has suggested, Blanchot's denial of reading the *Phenomenology* raises questions about how one reads Hegel.[5] Can one still read Hegel "*fort loin*" *du texte*? Lydia Davis translates this as "quite remote from the text," which diminishes the distance of *loin*, of "far or long away from," but also the emphatic nature of this distance, *fort loin*, "largely, greatly or very far away." If one could read the *Phenomenology* "*fort loin*" *du texte*, what kind of reading of the text would this be if it also "*ne cherchent pas à l'éclairer*"? One could argue, despite his denials, Blanchot offers the possibility of a new way of reading Hegel. This new way of reading Hegel is found in thinking of both philosophy and literature.

Blanchot's denial of reading Hegel is not straightforward. This is the case not least because the reference in the text to this footnote on reading Hegel is preceded by the phrase "*dit à peu près Hegel*," which can be variously translated as "Hegel just about says" or "Hegel says near enough" or "Hegel virtually says," as Lydia Davis translates the passage.[6] One could say that Blanchot's new reading of Hegel provides us with a virtual or even a quasi-fictional Hegel, a Hegel that should not be read too closely so that one can explore literature as a question of language and also think of literature as the impossibility of the philosophical concept of world.

Blanchot informs us that "*le règne animal de l'esprit*" refers to Hegel's ac-count of "all the ways in which someone who has chosen to be a man of letters [*un littérateur*] condemns himself."[7] He appears to be following Kojève, Hyppolite and Georges Bataille here, all of whom take this section of the *Phenomenology* as a direct commentary on literature or the so-called literary man.[8] Leslie Hill has also argued that Blanchot's reading of Hegel follows Kojève, an interpretation that I would dispute.[9] If we take a naïve reading of Hegel, and keep in mind that he is using a series of metaphors to describe a particular stage or world-like discrete sphere in consciousness's development of its reasoning, it is not obvious why this section of the *Phenomenology* has any relation to the question of literature.

Judith Butler has used Hegel's reliance on metaphor and figure to desig-nate the distinct phases of the *Phenomenology* in her own reading of Hegel. She argues that throughout the *Phenomenology*, "figures emerge to describe a state that has not yet achieved a stable logical status; indeed, the figure marks the instability of logical relations. Conversely, though, every logical relation assumes a shape or an appearance that is figural."[10] Butler goes on to describe the different stages of the *Phenomenology* as both "instructive fictions" and "particular configurations of the world." According to Butler, these "instructive fictions" are limited "ways of organizing the world."[11] However, the distinction between figurative and literal designations is itself a problematic way of interpreting Hegel, not least because we are only dealing with the experience of consciousness in the *Phenomenology*. Butler has also conflated "fiction" and "world"—terms that Hegel keeps quite distinct and which Blanchot implies are often erroneously confused by Hegelians.

Kojève and Hyppolite say a great deal about literature, its fictions and fictional worlds within a larger philosophical framework on the basis of assuming that Hegel is talking about the literary character and men of letters in this section of the *Phenomenology*. In his summary of the *Phenomenology* in his *Introduction to the Reading of Hegel* (1947), Kojève assumes that there is an entirely formed or given concept of world from the outset. He argues that the first three divisions of the *Phenomenology*—Consciousness, Self-Consciousness and Reason—can be summarised as "A.—Man opposes the World . . . B.—Man is conscious of his *opposition* to the world . . . C.—Man becomes aware of his interaction with the world, he realizes self-consciousness *in* the World."[12]

In his reading of Hegel, Kojève readily evokes the world as a critical but undefined concept. For example, at one point he observes, "Man is real only to the extent that he lives in a natural world. This world is, to be sure, 'foreign' to him; he must 'deny' it, transform it, fight it, in order to realize himself in it. But without this world, outside of this world, man is nothing."[13] The "world" here is the absolute measure of man: he must live "in a natural world" and he must transform this world, but he must also never step "outside of this world" or he "is nothing." The difference between "the natural world" and "the technical world" in turn provides the framework for transcending the limitations of the animal kingdom.[14] As Kojève remarks, "Work creates a real objective World, which is a non-natural World, a cultural, historical, human World. And it is only in this World that man lives an essentially different life from that of animals (and 'primitive' man) in the bosom of Nature."[15]

This same easy assumption about the status of world is found in Kojève's description of the literary in the third division of reason in the *Phenomenology*, which he entitles "The Man of Letters" (*L'homme de lettres*). This section is then broken down into three different parts: "the *idea* which the Man of Letters has of himself," "the creation of a work of literature" and "the existential *experience* of the Man of Letters."[16] Kojève's summary of "The Spiritual Animal Kingdom" or what he calls "the *idea* which the Man of Letters has of himself" is short and to the point: "The Individual, who, without *acting*, is content to *speak* about the World [parler *du Monde*] and who pretends to serve 'eternal values': the 'Republic of Letters' and the *imposture* of 'objectivity.'"[17] Kojève's reading here reinforces his overall Marxist polemic about the social and political inactivity of the literary man and the need for "action in the world."[18] For Kojève, action is primarily concerned with the "transformation of the world."[19] His interest in political and social action leads him to construct a concept of world that is, significantly, not found in this part of Hegel's work. As we have seen, there is no world in the *Phenomenology* until consciousness moves beyond reason and reaches spirit. It is only when one can speak of the world *as* spirit that Hegel refers to the *actual* world.

Kojève's lectures on Hegel were delivered in Paris from 1933 to 1939, and it was in 1939 that Hyppolite published the first part of his translation of the *Phenomenology*, which includes the section on "Le règne animal de l'esprit."[20] As Hyppolite's translation attests, the words "literature," "literary" and even "artist" do not appear in "Le règne animal de l'esprit." Hegel explicitly turns to the status of the artist and to the work of art in his later chapter on religion.[21] In other words, only *after* the appearance of spirit and of the world as spirit. Indeed, it is in this later section that Hegel openly addresses the torturous dialectical relation between the artist and artistic work and its temporary resolution in language—the very trajectory that Blanchot traces and reconfigures in "Literature and the Right to Death."[22] For Hegel, artistic and literary work requires understanding and reason, but it must have spirit.

Blanchot, in contrast to Kojève, appears to challenge the equation of "The Spiritual Animal Kingdom" with a self-evident critique of the social and political utility of the "man of letters." In his note distancing himself from reading Hegel too closely, he makes it clear that in this section of the *Phenomenology*, "Hegel is considering human work in general" (*l'œuvre humaine en général*) and not only literary work.[23] Blanchot here is counteracting a philosophical reading of the Hegelian attitude toward the literary and making the case for a distinctive relation to fiction—and to fictional worlds—in literature.

Following Hyppolite's translation, one can read this section of the *Phenomenology* without any specific reference to literature or literary activity. "The Spiritual Animal Kingdom" is concerned with the development of consciousness as a limited individuality that initially appears "as simple being-in-itself."[24] As an aspect of reason, this simple subjective individuality only reflects itself through a universality that remains *within* a simple individuality.

Hegel describes this as "the same universal animal life." Within such a limited environment, this universal animal life is able to maintain itself as a unity.[25] At this basic stage, the individuality of consciousness enjoys its freedom without attempting to challenge its limitations.[26] This individuality, Hegel stresses, has *not yet* taken on any "*special* capacity, talent, character" (*Fähigkeit, Talent, Charakter*).[27] It is an individuality without distinctive attributes or characteristics. It is only with the arrival of world-forming spirit that this animal-like state will be entirely surpassed.

This simple individuality eventually realises its specific talents and produces works. Kojève's insistence that these works are exclusively literary in nature may be in part an issue of translation as Hyppolite's *l'œuvre* has connotations of artistic and literary production, while Hegel's *das Werke* has a wide range of meanings for the labour that arises from the thoughts and actions of a reasoning individual, including enterprise, production and workmanship, as well as written work, publications and books. These works are taken as subjective reflections until this nascent individuality is differentiated by complex relations and determined by a higher level of reflection. It is the *work* that has been produced and not the individual that then becomes the thing itself (*la Chose même*) or a spiritualized universality that exceeds the claims or deceptions of individuality. This facilitates the eventual synthesis of complex individuality, reality and universality preparing the groundwork for the movement into spirit. The critical point here is that there is as yet no spiritual world, no spiritual world as actuality in this section of the *Phenomenology*. There is therefore no fictional or literary *world* for Kojève's apparent men of letters. There is no fully developed actual world (as spirit) that can be contrasted to an entirely elaborated fictional or literary world. In short, there is *no world* in "The Spiritual Animal Kingdom."

### Faust, Karl Moor, Don Quixote

While Kojève saw man at the heart of the *Phenomenology*, Hyppolite—much like his student Derrida—did not.[28] However, even if Hyppolite resists the anthropological figure or metaphor, he still embraces the *literary figure* in framing this section of Hegel. In this sense, Hyppolite also assumes the operation of a concept of world that is not found in Hegel's work. In his own interpretation of this section of the *Phenomenology*, Hyppolite provides an extended analysis of the repeated failures of rational self-consciousness to *make a world* by situating itself *in* the world (only spirit can do this).[29] In this context, the literary and supposed stance of the literary man appears to be just one of the many failures of reasoning self-consciousness.

Immediately after his translation of the title of this section, "Le règne animal de l'esprit et la tromperie ou la Chose même," Hyppolite refers the reader to a footnote offering an alternative title: "Les animaux intellectuels."[30] He then quotes from Émile Bréhier's *Histoire de la philosophie* (1929–1932).[31] Hyppolite appears to have followed Bréhier's reading of Hegel quite closely in his later commentary *Genesis and Structure of Hegel's* Phenomenology of Spirit (1946), the work that Blanchot obliquely reviews in "Literature and the Right to Death."

Bréhier describes the three stages of the second division of reason, or "the actualization of rational self-consciousness through its own activity," in terms of three *literary figures*: Goethe's Faust, Schiller's Karl Moor and Cervantes's Don Quixote. Bréhier then argues that "The Spiritual Animal Kingdom"—the first stage of the third division of reason—is Hegel's pointed critique of these archetypal literary figures. He writes,

> Over against such ineffectual heroes of Romanticism as Faust, Karl von Moor, or Don Quixote are those who narrow their ideal to a cause they can effectively serve or a limited end they can attain, those whom Hegel facetiously calls "intellectual animals" [*les "animaux intellectuels"*], and whose cause is like the air they must breathe in order to live. Their numbers include all the specialists, professors or artists who arbitrarily attribute an absolute value to their task without noticing that for other individuals it is an alien reality, for which they will try to substitute their own cause.[32]

It is worth pointing out that Bréhier does not directly connect this section of the *Phenomenology* to literature or to the man of letters. Hegel's intellectual animals are "specialists, professors or artists."[33]

In contrast to Kojève, in *Genesis and Structure* Hyppolite emphasizes a positive literary aspect to this trajectory, as if it is only *through* the literary that the individual can ultimately learn about the world as spirit. In this sense, spirit is the *Aufhebung* of the literary. Interestingly, Hyppolite is not entirely happy with Hegel's apparent sequence of literary figures to describe the world-like shapes of the progress of consciousness through reason.[34] As a "series of *concrete figures* borrowed from the age," he notes, the figures of Faust, Karl Moor and Don Quixote seem "rather strange as a sequence."[35]

What is strange about this sequence? Presumably "the age" in question is the Romantic period of the late eighteenth century, as Goethe's *Faust* was first published as a fragment in 1790 and Hegel himself quotes from this work.[36] Schiller's *The Robbers* had already appeared in 1781. The only work well out of this literary period is *Don Quixote*, which was published in two parts from 1605 to 1615.[37] If Hyppolite is concerned with the order of these literary figures, they clearly do not describe an accurate historical chronology as Don Quixote comes after Karl Moor. The literary seems to be out of step with the apparently linear historical progression that shadows Hegel's description of the various internal stages of the development of consciousness. In this sense, the literary abundantly reflects the litany of deceptions, follies and failures of an individuality that lacks a concrete connection to the actual world as spirit.[38] This legacy of using the literary figure to illustrate or to advance the reading of Hegel's text can still be seen in Butler's evocation of Don Quixote in *Subjects of Desire* (1987). "Like Don Quixote," she observes, "Hegel's subject is an impossible identity who pursues reality in systematically mistaken ways."[39]

According to Hyppolite, the flawed, world-like stages of individuality represented by Faust, Karl Moor and Don Quixote lead to the egoistic inactivity of the literary man and, finally, to the detachment of rational virtue which signals the limits of reason for a consciousness on the threshold of spirit.[40] In the midst of this, it is important to note that the concept of world itself is never compromised because—as we later learn—each world-like shape of the *Phenomenology* is *already* "a spiritual world."[41] However, this retrospective authority, which Kojève and Hyppolite both claim, is only apparent to Hegel's *ideal* readers, to the readers who only read very closely *with* Hegel. As we have seen, these quasi-literary stages are finally superseded not by the individual but through the manufactured or created work (*l'œuvre, das Werke*) of the individual. The Hegelian literary man, Hyppolite argues, is *in* the world but this world is not actual for consciousness—there is no wider perspective of the world as a whole—because this is still "the world of individuality."[42] It is this relation between the individual and the work as a *transcendence* of "the world of individuality" that will particularly interest Blanchot.[43]

According to Hyppolite, from the world "as the *work* of self-consciousness" we are taken to the eventual disappearance of "the notion of an opaque and impenetrable thing." This *vanishing thing* will in turn "be replaced by a new notion of objectivity" that will "open" the world *as* spirit.[44] As Hyppolite observes, "At the end point of the dialectic we are studying, the opaque thing of consciousness (*Ding*) which at the level of reason became the world—but the world of acting individuality (*Sache*)—becomes first spiritual essence (*das geistige Wessen*) and then reason which itself is its own world: spirit (*Geist*)."[45] Going beyond the spiritual animal kingdom ensures the disappearance of the world *as* a mere thing. Hyppolite's reading of Hegel suggests that the literary work—and its inadequate fictional worlds—has contributed to the transformation of the world from thing to spirit. As Derrida might say, the ideality of the literary object facilitates the *Aufhebung* of the concept of world.[46] It is in the context of the *Aufhebung* of world as the spiritualization of the thing that we must turn to the opening paragraph of Blanchot's essay.

### Starting with the Thing

Blanchot's opening paragraph to his 1947 essay is remarkable, not least because it begins with a thing, the writer's pen, which is addressed by the writer. It is worth concentrating on this paragraph in some detail. Blanchot writes,

> One can certainly write without asking why one writes. As a writer watches his pen form the letters, does he even have a right to lift it and say to it: "Stop! What do you know about yourself? Why are you moving forward? Why can't you see that your ink isn't making any marks, that although you may be moving ahead freely, you're moving through a void, that the reason you never encounter any obstacles is that you never left your starting place? And yet you write—you write on and on, disclosing to me what I dictate to you, revealing to me what I know; as others read, they enrich you with what they take from you and give you what you teach them. Now you have done what you did not do; what you did not write has been written: you are condemned to be indelible."[47]

Blanchot starts with a writer speaking to a *thing*. This strange scene follows directly after the title, "The Spiritual Animal Kingdom"—a title, as we have seen, that is itself a citation from a section of the *Phenomenology* that describes the disappearance of the perceived thing as the *Aufhebung* of world. If we take Blanchot's opening as a gesture to the *Phenomenology*, he is beginning *before* the *Aufhebung* of the thing and the articulation of world as spirit. There is, as yet, no actual world. This thing, this writer's pen, is an active thing: it appears to have its own activity. It is a question here not of the activity of the literary man, but of the writer's pen itself: "As a writer watches his pen form the letters, does he even have a right to lift it and say to it: 'Stop!'" Blanchot suggests that if the writer is watching the pen as it writes, then we must ask: who is writing—and what is writing?

One could contrast Blanchot's opening paragraph to Heidegger's insistence in *The Fundamental Concepts of Metaphysics* that a working pen has a readiness (*Fertigkeit*) to write, but it does not have in itself the capacity (*Fähigkeit*) to write.[48] In the midst of struggling with the problem of the comparative world of humans and animals—and we can remind ourselves that we are in the midst of Hegel's spiritual *animal* kingdom—Heidegger insists that the readiness of the pen indicates a distinctly human potentiality of "making something ready in and through production." The pen, Heidegger assumes, is always "ready for writing."[49] For Blanchot, on the contrary, the writer's pen appears itself to have a kind of capacity and may also not have a constant readiness for the writer. It is a thing that is not within the control of the consciousness or will of the writer. It is a thing that resists Hegel's narrative from his very first designations of the thing in his opening chapters in the *Phenomenology* on sense certainty and perception to the spiritualization of the thing in the closing sections of reason.

Blanchot begins his essay with an apostrophe to the writer's pen. There is no sense that this pen has been personified or given an anthropocentric mobility. The form of apostrophe suggests not only an address to a personified thing, but also an address to someone who is absent or dead. Blanchot's final title for his essay will be "Literature and the Right to Death," and there is already a relation here to death as the possibility of language, of speaking and writing registering things that are not present before us. This address is also made in the French familiar *tu*: this is a familiar thing, an intimate thing; it is a thing that has already moved through the formality, hierarchy and distance of the *vous*, as if an address to what is absent can only be made in the intimacy of the *tu*.[50]

Of course, the questions addressed to the writer's pen are absurd, and we should not overlook the possibility that the opening of Blanchot's essay is an oblique satire on Kojève. These questions could be taken as a series of ridiculous *philosophical* questions, ridiculous because they are addressed to a thing, to a pen. "What do you know about yourself?" Why don't you see where you are going or what you are doing? The pen does not answer any of these questions. It is silent and yet it writes: "And yet you write—you write on and on."

"Why can't you see that your ink isn't making any marks?" the writer asks. Blanchot links this blind forward momentum to a seemingly futile lesson: "The reason you never encounter any obstacles is that you never left your starting place." This could be taken as a quasi-Hegelian lesson: recognizing the power of the negative is the only way that anything can move, can gain a forward momentum and a teleological assurance. One could counter this Hegelian interpretation of these questions about self-knowledge, orientation and direction with an unconscious, blind writing of a thing that writes *without a world*.

The last part of this opening paragraph offers three condensed stages that echo the discrete world-like spheres of the *Phenomenology*: the relation between the pen and the writer; the relation of the thing to the reader; and, finally, the relation to the published work. Between the pen and the writer there is a relation that could be described as that of master and slave (the section of the *Phenomenology* that Kojève famously privileges), but it is a very equivocal relation: "I dictate," "I know" the writer insists. At the same time, it is only through the actions of the pen that this mastery is possible: "disclosing to me," "revealing to me." The mastery of the writer, of the world that his writing will create, is dependent on the capricious thing-as-pen.

The relation between the thing-as-pen and the reader is also equivocal: "as others read, they enrich you with what they take from you and give you what you teach them." Readers are enriched by the labour of the pen. This enrichment is a form of taking: the readers take and they gain. More enigmatically, they also give something back, but they only give back what the pen has taught them. The reader takes and adds to the labour of the pen and gives back, but only gives what he or she has already received. This contradictory and disorientating sense of taking *as* a giving and giving *as* a receiving indicate that Blanchot is already straining and exceeding the inversions and reversals of the controlled negations that drive the Hegelian dialectic.[51]

If Blanchot begins with a thing that resists the explicit spiritualization of the thing in "The Spiritual Animal Kingdom," the opening of his essay can also be seen as a refusal of the *Aufhebung* of world, of determining the actual world *as* spirit that follows in the *Phenomenology*. If the thing exceeds the philosophical categories of its Hegelian regulation and spiritualization, one can also say the same for the concept of world, for the so-called literary world and the fictional worlds of literature that have been categorized and used *in the name of Hegel* by Kojève and Hyppolite.

In the final stage of this paragraph, which begins with a very Hegelian "now," the writing of the pen has, despite itself, been fixed by the published work: "what you did not write has been written: you are condemned to be indelible." This determination and dispossession of the thing is the equivocal advent of the literary work.[52] Later in his essay, Blanchot will identify "the Thing itself" (*la Chose même*) as a key aspect of the idealization of the literary work. As he observes, for those who follow Hegel, the spiritualization of the thing announces "the spiritual truth" of the literary work and "the World as it is sketched out in the work."[53]

## Literature and Philosophy

After this extraordinary opening paragraph Blanchot goes on to offer what is most likely a critique of Jean-Paul Sartre's insistence that literature must be political and writers must be political agents. For Blanchot, the force of the creative negations of reality that allow language to register what is not actually present and to open "the space of literature" cannot be reduced to bad faith or imposture.[54] This also announces a wider question about the relation between literature and philosophy. Charting the futility of a philosophical reflection that attempts to capture "the element of emptiness" in literature, Blanchot suggests that if philosophy imposes on literature, the unique negativity within the literary will become "a caustic force" that will destroy any project of mastery, both in literature itself and in philosophy.[55]

Hegel himself privileges force (*Kraft*) in the *Phenomenology* in his discussion of force and understanding as the third and last stage of consciousness. Having described how consciousness defines itself and limits itself through the thing in mere perception, Hegel turns to force and understanding to account for consciousness becoming its own measure and object. Force first appears as a perpetual transition, as a unification and dissolution, a centring and de-centring. Finally, as an ex-pression or externalizing dispersal, force drives itself back into itself and facilitates consciousness turning to itself as its *own* object and the arrival of self-consciousness.[56] Blanchot's *force caustique* is somewhat similar to and quite different from Hegelian *Kraft*. It is a reactive force: it reacts against the assertion of philosophy over the literary. But it is also a force that undoes the capacity of literature itself to assume a mastery and to have the freedom to take itself as its own object. As Blanchot observes, "If reflection, imposing as it is, approaches literature, literature becomes a caustic force, capable of destroying the very capacity in itself and in reflection to be imposing."[57]

In contrast to the critical moment of consciousness superseding the perceived thing and starting along the road to self-consciousness, literature's reaction to philosophy results in the loss of its own ability to master itself. The relation between literature and philosophy is obviously combative but is also the possibility of a necessary transformation of the literary. Without philosophy, or without its reaction to the withdrawal or distancing (*éloignement*) of philosophy, literature could easily claim its own, deceptive "empire." It is precisely the desire for this ideal empire that gives literature a misguided right to supersede "the life of the world."[58] As much as philosophy attempts to dictate to the literary, without its reaction against philosophy, literature believes that it can bypass or disregard "the life of the world." In other words, according to Blanchot, literature falls into the very trap that Kojève discerns in the inactivity of the men of letters: it merely constructs its own, perfect fictional worlds.

Nonetheless, the violent reaction of philosophy to the caustic force of the literary leaves it "penetrated by a corrosive, volatile element."[59] One could read this as a critical commentary on Sartre, but it is perhaps more interesting to take it as a reading of the history of philosophy in general from Plato's *Republic* to Heidegger's lectures on Hölderlin.[60] In challenging the relation between the philosophical concept of world and the fictional worlds of the literary work,

Blanchot is addressing the "ancient quarrel between philosophy and literature" that Plato himself inherited and reacted against in the *Republic*.[61]

It is worth noting here a very different but predominant legacy of the "ancient quarrel" between literature and philosophy. Paul Ricoeur has argued that in the literary there is always "the world of the text" and the "world of the reader."[62] Literary works, Ricoeur suggests, are distinguished by an expansive "power of reference" that is not only descriptive but also metaphorical and symbolic. In this unique literary context, world is understood as "the ensemble of references opened up by every kind of text, descriptive or poetic, that we have read, understood, and loved." For Ricoeur, literature and its fictions *make a world* for us from the surrounding world: "to understand a text is to interpolate among the predicates of our situation all the significations which make a *Welt* out of our *Umwelt*."[63] As Mikel Dufrenne has observed, in this world-centred perspective the aesthetic object is "in the world and contains its own world."[64]

One of the problems with this compelling explanation for what a good novel does for the engrossed reader is that it assumes that this fictional world is a *discrete* domain, realm or sphere that also provides a vantage point of this world *as a whole*. At the very least, when we read our attention is porous and shifting as it moves back and forth between the page and our immediate surroundings. In other words, if we follow Ricoeur's account, the apparent worlds created by fiction are comparable with—and most likely taken from— the concept of world in the history of philosophy. This reliance on seemingly self-evident philosophical concepts of world generates the idealized notion of hermetically sealed fictional or virtual worlds in the literary work.

### The Impossibility of World
Blanchot offers a very different analysis of world when it is placed between philosophy and literature. He argues in "Literature and the Right to Death" that literary work is constituted and tormented by two sliding slopes (*versants*), one that is sliding toward an "ideal absence" and one that is sliding toward a "physical presence."[65] Both of these movements rely on a relation to "the amazing power of the negative" but offer no Hegelian *Aufhebung* or ultimate moment of synthesis.[66] Perpetually sliding toward a goal that they will never attain, as day leads to night and night leads to day, these two persistent temptations of literature cannot avoid sliding into one another.[67] Literature strains to either hold on to a purely fictional and ideal domain or to grasp once and for all the true sphere of things as they are in reality. Poised between spirit and matter, literature perpetually oscillates between these two elusive determinations.

For Blanchot, the slide of literature toward an ideal absence is founded on treating death as the possibility of language. Words and names for living, mortal things that will one day die or be destroyed register the inherent absence in all speech and writing that allows language to record what is no longer present.[68] This absence is then given an ideal or spiritual status when the literary work believes it can dispense altogether with the negations of reality that have constituted language. The slide of literature toward a physical presence, on the other hand, searches for an underlying tangible and material existence before essence or being. This attempt to use literature to find a primary reality encounters the mute inexpressibility of things beyond language. Blanchot suggests that literature undergoes an unending ordeal as it tries to establish its *own* worlds—the literary world of spirit and the literary world of things—through a self-defeating and impossible *Aufhebung* of language.

It is in the context of the always hoped for and always failing *discrete worlds* of literature that we can begin to think of the literary experience as the impossibility of world. At a banal level, one can find this inability to form a hermetically sealed sphere, domain or realm in the constant small interruptions of reading that force one to be at once "in the book" and "in reality." Contrary to Ricoeur, neither of these shifting, mobile states can be described as the *world* of the text or the *world* of the reader.

As Derrida pointed out in his final seminar on *The Beast and the Sovereign*, this emphasis on the *impossibility* of world is also part of Blanchot's pointed critique of Heidegger and the description of *Dasein*'s being-toward-death as the possibility *of* impossibility.[69] For Blanchot, the assertions of an ideal literary absence are frustrated by the volatile relation to death as the possibility of language that never stops announcing its own impossibility. The claims for the authority of words-things or a senseless and fundamental materiality are equally frustrated by the nothingness of existence that disenables both language and being as possibility.[70]

Blanchot's account of literature as the heightened relation to language and death also allows us to think of the impossibility of the philosophical concept of world.[71] Sliding toward an ideal absence, which also includes an attempt to efface or negate language itself, literature projects itself as "an idea inscribed in the world as though it were the absolute perspective of the world in its totality."[72] This describes the persistent attempts in the history of philosophy to use world to establish a unique world-like vantage point of the world *as a whole*. Literature, Blanchot observes, takes "an idea inscribed in the world" *as* "the absolute perspective of the world." In other words, it is not merely found *in* the world so it can speak *of* the world as a whole. In this sense, the literary aspires to an elusive world that produces an "unreal" and "*imaginary*" whole.[73] This world is the dream of a literature gazing toward an idealized absence. While it is easy to treat this literary spiritual world as a fiction, one can also extend this fictionality to the history of philosophy and to the many fictions that it has generated in constructing nuanced concepts to support a vantage point somewhere beyond or above the world. This is perhaps the most fictional world in the history of the concept of world.

Blanchot himself does not reach such an emphatic conclusion, or at least he sees a utility in this fiction of a complete world. As "the work of the negative in the world and for the world," he writes, this literary work "represents the world for us, it teaches us to discover the total being being of the world."[74] At the same time, he reminds us that this search for "the total of the world" is itself also the attempt to foreclose the tangible and material existence before essence as the impossibility of death. The evocation of death *as* possibility, as the end of being, always creates its *own* illusory world: "there is world, because we can destroy things and suspend existence."[75] In this sense, Heidegger's being-in-the-world "as such and as a whole" is a fictional world.[76]

If literature as spirit or idea lends itself to seeking out the world as "total being," literature as primal thing is equally misguided in its attempts to reach underneath the concept of world and to establish an exclusively earthly domain. We must avoid treating the earth as the absolute or transcendental other of world. As Blanchot remarks, this movement "is not beyond the world, but neither is it in the world itself: it is the presence of things before the *world* exists, their perseverance after the world has disappeared, the stubbornness of what remains when everything vanishes and the dumbfoundedness of what appears when nothing exists."[77] Literature attempts to align itself "with everything in the world that seems to perpetuate the refusal to come into the world."[78] Relying on a quasi-Kantian fictional *as if* to ground its rejection of the idea of world, within this perspective literature is only interested "in what things and beings would be if there were no world."[79]

Blanchot's point is that neither of these positions—literature as spirit claiming the world as a whole or literature as things seeking the perfect other of world in a primal material reality—are possible as determined and fully realized positions. As fully realized positions, both generate illusory fictions. The first sliding slope requires an "*imaginary*" whole, and with the second slope one can equally imagine but not represent things without world, without names, without either collective or singular nouns. One of Blanchot's profound insights is that it is *language* that makes our concepts of world possible. If we were immersed in the midst of the inexhaustible particularity of everything without language and there were no discrete designations—no names for things or proper nouns—we would be unable to orient ourselves and there would be no discrete spheres, domains or realms. There would be no world.

For Blanchot, literature can neither fully claim world as its possibility nor can it entirely disregard world as its possibility, and this impossibility alters our traditional understanding of the concept of world. Literature in search of things as they are slides toward the "strangeness of that existence which being has rejected" and can only register "a world sapped by crude existence."[80] Literature becomes "the very impossibility of emerging from existence."[81] Believing that it can "express the reality of the human world," literature finds itself "deprived of the world."[82]

Turning to its other perpetually sliding slope of ideal absence, literature once again works toward "the advent of the world."[83] However, this unrealized advent is "really the work of death in the world" generating an unavoidable finitude.[84] For Blanchot, the mobility and dislocation of literature and its lack of fixed "place and moment," leaves it again and again "at the edge of the world and as if at the end of time," always already displacing the hoped for "advent of the world."[85] If literature as the attempt to grasp a pure absence finds itself "at the edge of the world," literature as the attempt to grasp a full presence expresses "the world of the end of the world."[86] Subject to a perpetual "slipping back and forth," and despite its own dreams and desires, literature is finally "not really in the world."[87]

"Literature is language turning into ambiguity," Blanchot concludes. This movement announces its "force" not only as a corrosive reaction against philosophy but also as "a force of creative negation."[88] As the force of *creative negation*, the literary and its fictions have always brought ambiguity to the concept of world.[89] Endlessly sliding toward its own deferred goals, literature is neither truly *in* the world, nor able to claim a vantage point of the world *as a whole*. When "the general meaning of language is unclear," Blanchot argues, when "we do not know if it is expressing or representing, if it is a thing or means that thing," literature finds itself "out of sight of the world and out of thought of the world."[90]

For literature and its ambiguous reliance on language, its "right to death," there is no access to world as either a discrete sphere or as a unique vantage point: the literary is a sliding toward *and* a sliding away from the dream of world as a whole.[91] Announcing the impossibility of death, literature never arrives at the concept of world.[92] For Blanchot, this also reinforces the inability of literature to form or maintain a self-enclosed fictional or purely virtual world. The literary work is constituted by "real words and an imaginary story, a world in which everything that happens is borrowed from reality, and this world is inaccessible."[93] It is precisely because there are no comprehensive fictional worlds that literature shows us the "irreducible *double meaning*" of the nothingness that "helps to make the world."[94] In relation to literature as a question of language, world is the impossibility of possibility. Between philosophy and literature, there is no world.

## 2. Derrida and the Eco-Polemicists

In the last few years a highly critical reading of Derrida's work has linked the imperative to respond to climate change and global warming to the designation of the *anthropocene* as "a new geological era" for our times in which "the human species" itself has become "a decisive geological force."[95] Situating human activity as a significant factor in the destruction of the earth's ecosystem, these polemical readings of deconstruction have focused on what they see as Derrida's inability to move beyond thinking about "human institutions" and to address the "effects of non-human agency."[96] These readings argue that in relation to "our global environmental crisis," Derrida's work remains "anthropocentric and blinkered."[97] From this perspective, it appears that Derrida has failed to offer a sufficiently radical vision of the post-human that responds to the perilous state of the earth. I would like to address this reading of Derrida and to suggest that a post-human, earth-centred criticism generates both a limited concept of world and treats the earth as the idealized other of philosophy.

These readings have argued in general terms that Derrida's emphasis, particularly in his more obviously political works, can now be seen as limited to "human on human ills."[98] According to Timothy Clark, this also implies an apparent "perplexing and seemingly expanding absence or even evasion in Derrida's thinking" when it comes to "the material finitude of the planet."[99] Derrida's silence on the urgent state of the planet's changing climate has also led Tom Cohen to a call for an emphatic "*geomorphic turn*" that would allow us to reread Derrida's entire work from the imperative of the era of the anthropocene and to move beyond the project of phenomenology and its deconstruction.[100]

### The World as the Other of the Earth
One can begin to question this reading by turning to the opposition between Derrida's apparent interest only in "human on human" ethical, social and political relations and what Cohen calls "an accelerating set of ex-anthropic vortices" and "*other materialities*" when thinking from the perspective of the anthropocene.[101] From as early as 1964 in his reading of Emmanuel Lévinas in "Violence and Metaphysics," Derrida had highlighted the limitations of

a logic that opposes the same *as* the identical and the other *as* absolutely other. This assumes that the same can be identical with itself (the "human on human") and that the other can only be designated as other by giving it an absolute or pure status (the "ex-anthropic") above and beyond the sphere of the same.[102]

The emphatic "postism" of the post-human and the claims for the anthropocene as a distinct and "new geological era" also seem to overlook the critical cul-de-sac of such postisms, preisms and periodized epochs that Derrida himself warned against in both critical theory and in Heidegger's later philosophy.[103] At the same time, there is an imperative in these recent readings of deconstruction and climate change that is in part a commendable reaction against treating deconstruction as a platform for the easy ethics and politics of the other that are in truth no more than a resurgent form of good conscience. Indeed, contrary to these celebrations of a new ethics, Derrida suggested in his readings of Lévinas that any assertion of a perfectly calibrated ethics or political ethics was already the failure—the inevitable recurring failure—of any profound response to the other, to others. However, the evocation of the post-human or of the anthropocene as a means of radically rethinking theory in the face of the obvious ecological crisis of global warming can be taken as an instance of the emphatic exit, transcendental signified or pure absence that Derrida criticized from his earliest work. It would have been relatively easy for Derrida to find a critical stance beyond the human, but he was far more interested in thinking of the human *and* its many others.[104]

This logic can be extended to the treatment of world and earth in these polemical readings of Derrida's work. The world is always human, and the earth denotes the unassailable ethical imperative for the nonhuman. Part of the problem with this characterisation of the relation between world and earth is that it also repeats a traditional Kantian framework. When confronted with the concept of world as a conditioned series, there is the temptation to use the concept of the earth to establish what is unequivocally outside the series and to describe the unconditioned as a pure or absolute totality.[105] As we have seen, Derrida challenged the relation between the conditioned series and the pure unconditioned by thinking of "the out-of-series-in-the-series."[106] The recent idealizations of the concept of earth as the absolute other of the world has, if anything, reduced the possibilities of the concept of world. Beyond the imperative to recognize the need to rethink our traditional notions of scale, when "trivial" individual actions are directly linked to global catastrophe, it is important to ask why we need to think of the earth *as* the nonhuman.[107]

### *Près de la terre*

Derrida was always cautious around the concepts of world and earth, not least because of their obvious stature in the thought of Husserl and Heidegger. As we have seen in the previous chapter, he spent much of his early work (1953–1967) testing and challenging Husserl's suspension of the natural attitude to the world in *Ideas* 1, as well as the role played by language and the voice in the idealization of the spiritual world in *Ideas* 2 and the later construction of the life-world as the horizon of all horizons. Derrida also devoted nearly twenty years (1985–2003) to a patient and insistent reading of Heidegger's three remarkable concepts of world: being-in-the-world, the historical world and the comparative world. Had he lived after *The Beast and the Sovereign*, which ends with the promise of a future reading of the inherent domination and violence of human Dasein, it is possible that Derrida would have turned to the concept of earth.[108]

When it comes to the concept of earth, Derrida devotes some pages in his earliest work, his introduction to *The Origin of Geometry*, to Husserl's "Foundational Investigations of the Phenomenological Origin of the Spatiality of Nature: The Originary Ark, Earth, Does Not Move" (1934).[109] In this fragment, Husserl offers a dazzling reformulation of Copernican orthodoxies and argues that "all bodies have their place but not the earth itself." "For all of us," he argues, "the earth is the ground and not a body."[110] While Husserl may privilege the ground as an "absolute *here*," Derrida notes, he also questions the treatment of the earth as an *object* of geology, anthropology and psychology and argues that it is by treating the earth as "the ground" that one can have a wider perspective of the earth as a whole.[111]

Some of these recent critiques of Derrida's relation to the concept of earth are most likely inspired by "The Origin of the Work of Art" (1935–1936) and rely on a distinctly Heideggerian framework of marking a clear difference between world and earth.[112] Though Derrida offered some significant passing remarks on the relation between world and earth in his own reading of Heidegger's essay in "Restitutions of the Truth in Pointing" (1978), we can only hope that a more extensive response will appear as Derrida's seminars are published.[113] As Christopher Johnson has noted, Derrida referred to the earth in his early essay "Force and Signification" (1963), warning against the idealization of language by linking the "universal element" of air to speech and of earth to writing. The concept of earth facilitates the "metaphorization" of the solid, the material and the historical.[114] In his 1978 essay, Derrida cautions against taking Heidegger's use of the earth as the advocacy of a fixed ground, but he also notes the assumption of a persistent "solidity" or "reliability" (*Verlässlichkeit*) in the "preoriginary" relation to "the silent call of the earth."[115]

The Heideggerian concept of earth is commonly understood as "an inexhaustible horizon of that which is non-human in the world," and this is a proposition shared by many of today's eco-polemicists.[116] If one takes Heidegger's use of earth as an attempt to find a more radical means for indicating the true *other* of beings, of the truth of being, there is a wide gap between Hans-Georg Gadamer's excitement over Heidegger's introduction of the earth "as a philosophical concept" and Luce Irigaray's later critique of Heidegger's evocation of the earth as "a solid crust."[117] While Gadamer's reading is more faithful to Heidegger's intentions, Irigaray reflects the equivocal nature of opposing *the* earth to the history of the many varied and fluid concepts of world. The registering of the nonhuman as either one philosophical concept among others or as an utterly unique tangible object raises problems about how to encapsulate or contain the earth in the history of philosophy.

In "The Origin of the Work of Art," Heidegger makes an emphatic assertion: the work of art is that which has the unique capacity "to transform all familiar relations to world and to earth."[118] For Gadamer, this transformation entailed using the earth as a concept to indicate a "referential field" that was no longer "related solely to human beings."[119] John Sallis has argued that Heidegger's concept of earth is "not something within the world."[120] In this sense, the concept of earth is not so much radically transformed by Heidegger as used to occupy the need—already found in his previous works—for a vantage point or wider perspective of what is beyond and above the world (the worldhood of world, world as transcendence, world "as such and as a whole").

As the opening of "The Origin of the Work of Art" demonstrates, Heidegger is clearly trying to extricate the concepts of world and earth from their metaphysical determinations. Noting that the Kantian thing in itself does not appear but still supports "the world as a totality," Heidegger warns against the metaphysical and theological interpretation of the thing based on "the viewing of the world in terms of matter and form."[121] If it is possible to go beyond the Aristotelian tradition of opposing matter and form, Heidegger suggests that we should be able to think "the clod of earth" *with* the "essence of the thing."[122]

However, as is often the case with Heidegger, this quite revolutionary opening is progressively narrowed and enclosed in a strict framework. As Derrida describes it, there is a detachment followed by a reattachment.[123] Beyond the traditional subject-oriented relation to the work of art as a represented object, Heidegger insists that there is "truth's setting-itself-to-work."[124] One could argue here that in trying to move beyond the subject-object opposition, Heidegger also reinforces its authority by insisting that it is the only alternative to his new way of thinking of the work of art. If we are deaf to the truth of the work of art, Heidegger implies that we have no choice but to find ourselves as an assured subject before a compromised object and in the midst of the most naïve subjectivity.[125] He then gives us his well-known account of "a pair of peasant shoes" found in a series of paintings by Van Gogh. It is the proximity of these shoes to the earth that interests Heidegger. He writes, "Under the soles slides the loneliness of the field-path as evening falls. The shoes vibrate with the silent call of the earth [*Zuruf der Erde*], its silent gift of the ripening grain, its unexplained self-refusal in the wintry field."[126] *On* the earth (*auf die Erde*), these shoes with their "dark opening" are no longer merely *in* the world.

As Derrida suggests, the implications of this movement were already apparent in Heidegger's 1929–1930 seminars on the comparative world. Because stones, plants and animals have no language, they have "no openness"—unlike the peasant shoes in Van Gogh's paintings—and without this they are unable to register, struggle with or preserve the earth.[127] As Heidegger had already said in 1935 in the *Introduction to Metaphysics*, animals have no spiritual world. They also have no concept of earth. One can contrast the animals that have now lost both world and earth to the poets who, uniquely for Heidegger, have the power in the "projective saying" of their poetry to articulate the apparently new relation between world and earth. Poetry preserves the earth "as that which remains closed" and "brings the unsayable as such to the world."[128] The earth speaks the "unsayable" through the poetic works of art, while animals, plants and stones can say nothing.

Beyond this problematic concept of the earth that itself relies on world-like exclusionary discrete spheres and domains, Heidegger's essay also increasingly limits the remarkable concepts of world that he delineated in *Being and Time*, "On the Essence of Ground" and *The Fundamental Concepts of Metaphysics*. Returning to Van Gogh's paintings, it is clear that this new relation to earth requires the reassuring self-inertia of the world. Finding "protection in the *world* of the peasant woman," this relation also ensures that she "is certain of her world."[129] In other words, the "silent call of the earth" secures and determines world as the reliable, programmatic *other* of the earth. This delimitation of world also appears to rest on another very familiar assumption: there may be many worlds but there is only one earth.

As much as Heidegger attempts to provide a dynamic account of the "strife" between world and earth as a truthful struggle between revealing and concealing, between showing as mere beholding (Husserlian phenomenology) and showing that is held back and occulted (hermeneutical phenomenology), we remain within the traditional Aristotelian logic of containment.[130] The singular, unique earth always stands in relation to a possible world. When Heidegger remarks that the Greek temple is "a work that cannot be regarded as a work of representational art," he concludes, "Standing there, the temple opens up a world [*eine Welt*] and at the same time, setting this world back onto the earth [*auf die Erde*] which itself first comes forth as homeland."[131] For Heidegger, it is always a question of *the* earth in relation to *a* world.

Within the context of thinking about works of art, Heidegger also suggests that the concept of earth provides the conditions of possibility for the work of art to open and maintain "a world." These conditions of possibility include shelter and protection and a gathering back or re-collection. As Derrida often said, this describes Heidegger's persistent logocentrism or privileging of a movement that gathers itself back into itself as a unity.[132] If Heidegger's earth moves, it only moves to gather, shelter and protect.[133] Once again, one could say this protection as a condition of possibility resolves the problem of the comparative world. The world for human Dasein alone is already protected, and there can be no work of art—as dynamic opening and closing—for animals.[134]

According to Michel Haar, as it has been determined by its primary relation to earth, *a* world registers the restriction of world to the world, while *the* earth announces a "*trans-epochal* determination," a "nonhistorical" liberation that has already broken "with nature as a base or foundation."[135] After challenging the traditional opposition of form and matter, this question of ground is clearly the most radical aspect of Heidegger's essay.[136] Nonetheless, regardless of the fluid state of this mobile or shifting ground or non-ground, Heidegger still needs to remind us in his 1935 paper that "the stone is world-less" even as he affirms that the "rocky ground" of the Greek temple provides "unstructured yet unforced support."[137] The earth may not be the "idea of a mass of matter," but it *supports* the idea of world *as* the non-stone, non-plant and non-animal.[138]

It is only after Heidegger describes the rather conventional threat of the "art industry" to the work of art that he turns to the nonrepresentational example of the Greek temple and the "unstructured" support of the earth.[139] The concept of earth provides Heidegger with a classical vantage point beyond what is merely *in* the world. The earth rises above stones, plants and animals, re-collects and protects the work against the "art industry." In an almost Hegelian gesture, Heidegger then returns the rocks and stones *to* the earth, but only *through* the work of art that has created "a world."[140] The work *as* a discrete world-like domain or realm "moves the earth into the open of a world and holds it there," a world that has in turn been gathered, sheltered and protected by the earth.[141] It is only this predetermined earth-centred world that can then hold on to the unique impenetrability of the earth.[142] The world of "The Origin of the Work of Art" is a truly contained world.[143]

Heidegger's momentary gesture of reversal at the start of his essay—of insisting on taking a world opened by the work of art *before* the appearance of "men and animals, plants and things"—can be read as a very Aristotelian gesture.[144] For Aristotle, though particulars come first in fact, universals in truth always come first.[145] The placing of world in relation to earth recalls not the "modern meaning of placing," as Heidegger argues, but the oldest.[146] It was also Aristotle who used the seemingly absolute or clear difference between world and earth to define place as an untouched structure of containment.[147] However one characterizes the work of art as a "fixing in place of truth," for Heidegger this placing "frees" the earth "to be, *for the first time, itself.*"[148] World will always be contained by the earth *itself.*

Given his later emphasis on the cohabitation of the world of living and dying animals and humans, it is of course hardly fortuitous that when Derrida touches on the relation between world and earth in Heidegger's thought in his 1990 conversation with Maurizio Ferraris, he refers to an animal. Though he is responding to Heidegger's later *Identity and Difference* (1957) and criticising the Heideggerian assumption of always arriving at an assured destination, his use of "the poematic hedgehog" that is related to the earth and placed somewhere between the animal, the poet and *tekhnē* can be taken as a reading of "The Origin of the Work of Art."[149]

Turning to the relation between world and earth, Derrida highlights Heidegger's reliance on the anthropocentric, theological and political coordinates of the closed and the open and the low and the high. The "poematic hedgehog," he argues, indicates "something of the earth [*de la terre*] that does not open" *and* something that is "close to the earth" (*près de la terre*).[150] It is at once *of* the earth and *close to* the earth (not of the earth). One could read Derrida's double relation to the earth—that which is at once *of* the earth and *close to* the earth—as an unavoidable mixing of the *anthropos* and the *geo*. This is, once again, a very human problem. For Derrida, the *près de la terre* is also the problem of a world that humans and animals cohabit.[151]

## Geo-Logocentrism

In the name of an urgent ethical ecology, the eco-polemical readings of Derrida's work reinhabit a familiar Heideggerian framework in which the human world is defined by its relation to the nonhuman earth. The earth becomes the symmetrical other of the world as an exclusively human domain. As much as Heidegger's world opens or reveals the concealment of earth and the struggle between world and earth offers a radical alterative to the history of aesthetics, it is a world that is contained by its seamless and constant relation to the earth as its singular other. The evocation of earth limits the possibilities—and comparative equivocations that are so important for Derrida—of world.

In these readings, there is the temptation to use the earth—as a concept or object or idealized other of world—to find the perfect exit from both Derrida's version of deconstruction and from the history of philosophy. Derrida is most compelling when he is patiently reading the history of philosophy, and beyond the evident dangers of the Hegelian history of philosophy and philosophy of history, this interest in history is always apparent in Derrida's work. One could describe this turn to an earth-centred form of critical thought, with its pre-Copernican great silent nonhuman other at the centre, as a kind of geo-logocentrism.

As Derrida suggested, one cannot just dismiss the temptation to grasp an absolute presence, plenitude or alterity. The era of the anthropocence as a framework for thinking the absolute other of world and of all the so-called human worlds in the history of philosophy takes us to a seemingly endless variation on the geo: the geo-logical, the geo-graphical, the geo-temporal, the geo-spatial and the geo-historical.[152] Some thirty years ago in *Time and Narrative*, volume 1 (1983), Paul Ricoeur offered in the work of Fernand Braudel a brief but compelling account of a "geohistory" that illustrated this inherently metaphysical temptation.[153]

The first 350 pages of Braudel's remarkable *The Mediterranean and the Mediterranean World in the Age of Phillip II* (1949) are devoted to "The Role of the Environment."[154] Braudel's slightly awkward title—*The Mediterranean and the Mediterranean World*—captures an important distinction between the Mediterranean and the Mediterranean *as* a world.[155] In his preface, Braudel suggests that he has tried to write a history of "the sea itself," which he calls "the greatest document" of the Mediterranean's "past existence." This emphasis on the "sea itself," which one can juxtapose to the Mediterranean world, suggests not only the possibility of reaching out to something that is tangible and fluid but also to something that is *uncontained*.

Pre-human or post-human, the earth and its seas are uncontained, while the human world is always contained. Despite the eventual emphasis on human habitation and cultivation, Braudel begins his magisterial work with the vistas—the vantage points and perspectives—of the *sea itself*: "its character is complex, awkward, and unique. It cannot be contained within our measurements and classifications. No simple biography beginning with a date of birth can be written of this sea; no simple narrative of how things happened would be appropriate to its history."[156]

If we have not yet arrived or are no longer in the world, where are we? For Braudel, the demarcation of this environment *without world* is primarily a question of time, of a "geographical time."[157] Writing some sixty years ago, Braudel evokes a new kind of temporality in historical writing that addresses "man in relationship to the environment."[158] He defines this historical work as the story of "geographical time" in contrast to a narrative of social and individual time.[159] Geographical time is informed by "the slow unfolding of structural realities."[160] The tempo of this structural diachrony could be easily dismissed today, but it also captures some of the contemporary lure or magnetism of the *geo*, of the pull to the "sea itself" or even to Heidegger's "silent call of the earth."[161] As Ricoeur notes, Braudel's *longue durée* could be taken as an index of "durable equilibrium" and "stability within change." However, Ricoeur argues, Braudel's geohistory is not anchronological and atemporal. Like the sea itself, there is the promise of the tangible and the fluid, of a "varying duration" over the centuries and millennia, of slow *and* fast changes on a scale that always exceeds the measure of social and individual time.[162] Geohistory and geographical time undulate outside human time.

There is something very attractive about this seemingly discrete non-human time, even in the midst of global ecological crisis, but it is quite different from the *accélération affolante* or "an alarming rate of acceleration" that Derrida discerns in *The Animal That Therefore I Am* in the shifting relations between humans and animals over the last two hundred years.[163] These mad, crazy *differantial* speeds are part of human-animal history, of history as an incessant departure from any hoped for totality.[164] If Derrida's work does not lend itself to evoking the "silent call of the earth," the "sea itself" or all the nonhuman geos of the eco-polemicists, it is precisely to combat the valorisation of the earth as yet another transcendental signified and the determination of world as no more than a "human on human" domain. The apparent absence of the earth—as a concept or object—from Derrida's work is a reminder that one must be vigilant about using the earth as the sublime other of philosophy itself. The eco-polemical readings of Derrida operate within sight of this absolute terminus, this silent, suffering, deadly other.

## Posthumous Contemporary

It has been argued that the termination of the human project and the radical transformation of planet earth marks "an event whose scale, complexity and incalculability is such as to resist representation or being conceptualized."[165] The scale of this event may well or may well not be like this—a gradual diminishing, a quick suffocation or a violent conflict over dwindling leftovers—but this does not necessarily require that it resists representation or conceptualization or offers us the singular and unequivocally universal instance of the unrepresentable or nonconceptual. It is relatively easy to think of catastrophe.

When confronted by the definition of the human in the anthropocentric era as "a dominant species that accelerated its own disappearance by consuming and altering its planet," it is of course hard not to think of more traditional apocalyptic narratives.[166] The claim the anthropocene and the ethics of the post-human are the only way to think about the future and to refashion the past brings to mind another historical moment when there was an equally pressing call for radical global readjustment. As Arnaldo Momigliano notes, with the rise of the Christian era in the fourth century, pagan historiography was confronted with the formidable task of writing history for the first time with a future.[167] As the Church Fathers argued over the timescale from Adam to the end of days, history became inextricably intertwined with eschatology. Thinking climate change, global warming, the era of the anthropocene and ecological ethics after Derrida may allow for more circumspection over the demarcations between natural and cultural catastrophe as well as some caution in embracing a rhetoric of apocalypse, but it cannot claim to evade the theological heritage of a profound eschatological narrative.[168]

Rather than using climate change to move beyond the human, we perhaps need today to continue to think about the very human formulations of the concepts of world and earth. Can we be absolutely confident, as David Wood has argued, that Derrida's reference to world in *Specters of Marx* (1993) only "means the human project"?[169] Why should we think of the concept of world in the history of philosophy—which includes, to cite only a few examples, the metaphysical, regulative and categorical worlds of Kant; the very different spiritual worlds of Hegel and Husserl; the phenomenological life-world; being-in-the-world and the comparative world of Heidegger—as exclusively and uniquely human? As we have seen, Derrida himself argues that Heidegger's equivocal containments and exclusions of animals from being-in-the-world should be seen as an unavoidable moment of thinking world and *différance*.

Almost ten years after the death of Jacques Derrida, Derrida studies finds itself in the strange temporality of the posthumous publications, of waiting for the forty years of seminars and lectures to appear. Looking backward into a steadily receding and fixed period, these works are hardly contemporary, but they will no doubt be given a contemporary status or be equally condemned for their lack of relevance or acuity for the pressing issues of the day. As Gadamer notes in *Truth and Method* (1960), the very process of making the past contemporary is closely tied to the nineteenth-century interest in *Bildung* as a "break with the immediate" that preserves the past and enhances the present.[170] In this sense, a "green deconstruction" that is exclusively for today might be nothing more than another Hegelian *Aufhebung* in a long history of *Aufhebungs*.

On the other hand, one only has to think of the volatile atmosphere that marked the tenth anniversary of the death of Heidegger in 1987 to treat the posthumous contemporary as a period of diverging reassessment and even critical liberation. Without challenging the need to think about our evident contribution to global warming and the current changes to the earth's ecosystem, I believe that Derrida's work stands as a testament to a critical caution that is never less than urgent. In the face of the apparent absolute philosophical, political or ethical demand of the moment, Derrida asks us to think and think again about the conditions of possibility and the irreplaceable assumptions of an ethical ecology or even a "green deconstruction." This is not a negation but the rigorous demand for a better affirmation. Derrida was not a *soixante-huitard*, and this resistance to joining the heady enthusiasm or sudden, unavoidable moral imperatives of the day make his work, if anything, starkly contemporary.[171]

## 3. The Lure of the *Sans Monde*

In writing this book, I have been tempted on a number of occasions to conclude by offering an extended account of my own concept of world.[172] This "new" concept would use world to register *the midst as the uncontained*. The *midst* would not be the middle, as a subject-orienting ground or position, but *in media res*, a finding oneself in the midst, in the middle of a relation to an indefinite and ungraspable beginning and end. The midst as the *uncontained* would challenge the long tradition of using the concept of world within a classical logic of containment, of insisting that the uncontained inaugurates a history of containment. The midst as the uncontained would also offer no wider perspective or superior vantage point on the world. There would be no opposition or clear difference between being merely *in* the world and speaking of the world *as a whole*. The uncontained would not facilitate the Kantian unconditioned, Hegelian spirit, Husserlian suspension, Heideggerian being or Derridean alterity. The uncontained would be without containment.

However tempting this formulation of yet another concept of world is, I hope that this book has already alerted the reader to its inevitable limitations. This "new" concept of world, this fiction of Tlön, would still rely on a subject-centred framework: I am always *finding* myself in the excessive midst as the uncontained (even if this self is something other, something surprising that finds me).[173] As we have seen, it also invites a problematic comparison with the treatment of the earth as a unique instance of the uncontained. The evocation of a sublime, absolute and assured uncontainment always risks becoming yet another quasi-theological concept. This "new" world would be no more than a grand metaphysical gesture against metaphysics.

A more profound response to the history of concept of world is to ask whether there can be a philosophy without world. In other words, beyond the limitations of the uncontained-contained opposition would be a more disturbing hypothesis: *there is no world*. Despite all its rich intricacy, the history of the concept of world would be no more than the history of a mere technical mechanism for designating discrete spheres and secure vantage points. More radically, what we have always called world would be no more than a metaphysical fiction, a series of idealized demarcations that have no heuristic value. I have also been tempted by this conclusion. World can teach us nothing because there is no world. While it has let go of God and the self, Continental philosophy still keeps this old metaphysical friend alive. It cannot let the world go.

The problem with this emphatic declaration of the end of the concept of world is that it denies the history of philosophy and its designation of world as something distinct (one can say the same for God and the self). Clearly, the concept of world does make a difference. This very tempting announcement of the nonexistence or pure fictionality of world also denies the obvious efficacy of structures of containment, even if they are tempered, differentiated or porous. There is nothing new about denying the world or announcing its end. These gestures also assume that *there is already a world*. Whether it is from the natural philosophy of the pre-Socratics or from the incalculable influence of the book of Genesis, the history of philosophy has always responded to the world as something that already exists.

This assumption is found in Emmanuel Lévinas's audacious account of the "without world" (*sans monde*) and his attempt to refute Heidegger's being-in-the-world.[174] For Lévinas, there is an elemental existence that precedes being-in-the-world.[175] The "anonymous rustling" of existence without world is a relentless and disturbing insistence prior to and beyond being, the substantive and consciousness.[176] Lévinas can only announce this antecedent and more authentic existence by first recognizing the world and its disappearance. As he observes, "The being which we become aware of when the world disappears is not a person or a thing, or the sum total of persons and things; it is the fact that one is, the fact that *there is*."[177] Registered *as* without world, the "*there is*" (*il y a*) is always reliant on the world. Lévinas goes on to offer his own concept of world in which a distinctly phenomenological world shaped by "intention and light" is amalgamated with a quasi-elemental world of desire, nourishment and enjoyment.[178]

One can also see this inadvertent preservation of world in the recent work of Jean-Luc Nancy. In his reading of Hegel, Nancy argues that world does not enhance but disperses the subject.[179] He declares "the end of the world" as *kósmos*, as an ordered whole.[180] In its place, Nancy describes a "sense of the world" which relies on a sharp distinction between what is in the world and the impossibility of being beyond the world.[181] In place of the cosmos as a classical Greek concept and a theological determination, there is an opening or coming into this world as the "dawn of bodies" and "the world of bodies."[182] This world registers itself as a radical "spacing."[183] As Ian James has remarked, "Nancy is trying to find a postphenomological language to express the way in which, through our bodily senses, the world is always already there for us."[184] Even if this sense or excess of the world, or "nonworld" (*immonde*) as Nancy calls it, is no longer subject-oriented, confined by the traditional categories of sensible and intelligible, immanent and transcendent and open to the nonnatural prosthetic or "ecotechnical," it still declares the birth of one world in the name of the death of another world.[185] For Lévinas and Nancy, the *sans monde* is always *with* the world.

If neither the reinvention nor the stark dismissal of the concept of world can provide an effective alternative to the history of this concept, we are still left with the question of the relation between world and language. Blanchot was no doubt right to suggest that we could have no world either in fiction, philosophy or reality without language.[186] One only has to look at the objects around us at any given moment to understand how difficult it would be to orient oneself in the world without nouns and proper names. Language gives an essential coherence and continuity to the world. One might even describe it as the possibility of world. Of course, as Derrida argues in his critique of the *imperium* of linguistics, language does not necessarily have the ordering, unity and transparency that would give us a homogenous and exact concept of world.[187] Blanchot himself speaks of the possibility of a "language that does not have the world to say."[188]

As Ludwig Wittgenstein argues in the *Philosophical Investigations* (1953), language allows us to take a vague concept such as "stand over there" as a clear statement that we can understand and act upon.[189] Language also allows us to take world not as a metaphysical concept, which aligns it in perpetuity with the unreachable heights of the soul and God, but as an *everyday blurred concept*.[190] Such a concept is structured not by the old Platonic conceit of a singular and universal form or essence but by its "family resemblances."[191] Language allows us to "stand over there" with an understanding that lies somewhere *between* the related concepts of *the* world, *my* world and world as the *possibility* of a discrete domain, sphere or realm. This compelling recognition of the link between language and different concepts of world also suggests that the call for a philosophy without world would fulfil yet another profoundly metaphysical temptation: the yearning for a pure experience without language.

What is world? In the history of philosophy, it is a concept that attempts—and repeatedly fails—to balance a sense of authentic immersion and necessary transcendence. It is a concept that exceeds the common boundaries of objects and things but also requires a range that is beyond the capacities of the subject. As much as everyday language may expose the porous nature of concepts of world, we must always keep open the *possibility* that there is no world. This is the only way we can avoid returning world to the subject. In my own experience, I can still say that I don't know what it means to declare that "I have a world" or to refer to "Stendhal's world," as if "world" designates some kind of mobile or discrete sphere with tangible boundaries. This seems to be no more than a highly subjective notion of "personal space," the frail claims of memory and the pleasant fictions of subject-oriented reconstructions of the past. The question of world as a domain of privacy or of public rights in political theory is of course something quite different.

As a problem in the history of philosophy since Kant, world is a remarkable concept that has constantly sought to place itself beyond the reach of both the object and the subject. However, since the classical period, world has also evoked a resilient logic of containment. Faced in twentieth-century philosophy with the alternative to enforce a series of increasingly dubious restrictions or to embrace the dream of the entirely uncontained, one can perhaps do no better than say that world is a concept that describes distinct spheres, realms or domains that are always slightly uncontained. *There are worlds and they are always less than a world.* At the same time, if contemporary philosophy can treat the concept of world as the quasi-uncontained, as something more flexible, dynamic and open, it still cannot move beyond the tradition of world as both the need for immersion and the search for transcendence.

# Notes

## Preface

1. Jean-Luc Nancy, *The Sense of the World*, trans. Jeffrey S. Librett (Minneapolis: University of Minnesota Press, 1993). See also Alain Badiou, *The Logic of Worlds: Being and Event II*, trans. Alberto Toscano (London: Continuum, 2009). For a good broad overview of Nancy and Badiou see Ian James, *The New French Philosophy* (Cambridge: Polity, 2012).

2. While there are of course some articles on the problem of world in individual philosophers, beyond wider studies of Heidegger's being-in-the-world and Husserl's life-world, there are hardly any monographs on world itself in the thought of a particular philosopher. One of the very few general studies on the concept of world in the last fifty years, Joseph Kocklemans's, *The World in Science and Philosophy* (Milwaukee, WI: Bruce Publishing Company, 1969) is heavily indebted to Heidegger's treatment of world.

3. Neil Turnbull, "The Ontological Consequences of Copernicus: Global Being in the Planetary World," *Theory, Culture & Society* 23 (2006): 125–39.

## Chapter 1. The Kantian World

1. William Blake, "The Book of Urizen," in *The Complete Poetry and Prose of William Blake*, ed. David V. Erdman, comm. Harold Bloom, rev. ed. (New York: Anchor Books, 1988), 83, plate 28, line 23.

2. Immanuel Kant, *Critique of Pure Reason*, trans. Paul Guyer (Cambridge: Cambridge University Press, 1998), B xxii. A refers to the first edition of 1781 and B to the second edition of 1787.

3. *Critique of Pure Reason*, B xvi.

4. *Critique of Pure Reason*, B xiv.

5. Arthur Schopenhauer, *The World as Will and Representation: Volume 1*, ed. and trans. Judith Norman, Alistair Welchman and Christopher Janaway (Cambridge: Cambridge University Press, 2010), 8. See in this volume "Critique of the Kantian Philosophy," 441–565. See also *The World as Will and Representation: Volume 2*, trans. E. F. Payne (New York: Dover, 1966). Rejecting Kant's insistence that things in themselves remain inaccessible, Schopenhauer argued that there is a dynamic relation between "the will as thing in itself and its appearance, i.e., between the world as will and the world as representation," *The World as Will and Representation: Volume 1*, 144. See also Christopher Janaway, *Self and World in Schopenhauer's Philosophy* (Oxford: Oxford University Press, 1999).

6. Georg Wilhelm Friedrich Hegel, *The Science of Logic*, trans. George di Giovanni (Cambridge: Cambridge University Press, 2010), 158, 201, 527; G. W. F Hegel, *Phenomenology of Spirit*, trans. A. V. Miller (Oxford: Oxford University Press, 1977), § 295, § 438, § 441, § 492; Schopenhauer, *The World as Will and Representation: Volume 1*, 448, 454–55, 457–58, 481. On Nietzsche, see chapter 5 of this book and R. Kevin Hill, *Nietzsche's Critiques: The Kantian Foundations of His Thought* (Oxford: Oxford University Press, 2003).

7. Edmund Husserl, *The Crisis of European Sciences and Transcendental Phenomenology: An Introduction to Phenomenological Philosophy*, trans. and intro. David Carr (Evanston, IL: Northwestern University Press, 1970), 97.

8. Martin Heidegger, *Phenomenological Interpretation of Kant's Critique of Pure Reason*, trans. Parvis Emad and Kenneth Maly (Bloomington: Indiana University Press, 1997), 14. See also Michaël Foessel, *Kant et l'équivoque du monde* (Paris: CNRS, 2008).

9. *Critique of Pure Reason*, A 671/B 699.

10. Gilles Deleuze, *The Logic of Sense*, ed. Constantin V. Boundas, trans. Mark Lester and Charles Stivale (New York: Continuum, 2004), 201.

11. Immanuel Kant, *Lectures on Metaphysics*, ed. and trans. K. Americks and S. Naragon (Cambridge: Cambridge University Press, 1997), 206–45, 341–43, 358–70; 475–79.

12. *Critique of Pure Reason*, 406 n. 20 (737). See Alexander Gottlieb Baumgarten, *Metaphysick*, trans. Georg Friedrich Meier, ed. Johann August Eberhard (Jena: Dietrich Scheglmann Reprints, 2004 [1783]), 73–110.

13. Baumgarten, *Metaphysick*, 217 (§ 651). See also Christian Wolff, *Theologia Naturalis: Methodo Scientifica Pertractata* (Verona: Dionisio Ramnanzini, 1738), 132. See also Lewis White Beck, *Early German Philosophy: Kant and His Predecessors* (Cambridge: Belknap, 1969), 269–71, 283–86.

14. Plato, *Gorgias*, trans. Robin Waterfield (Oxford: Oxford University Press, 1994), 507e–508a; Plato, *Lysis, Symposium, Gorgias*, trans. W. R. M. Lamb (Cambridge, MA: Harvard University Press, 1925).

15. Diogenes Laertius, *Lives of Eminent Philosophers*, trans. R. D. Hicks, 2 vols. (Cambridge, MA: Harvard University Press, 1980), vol. 1, 8:48–49.

16. Aristotle, *The Metaphysics*, intro. and trans. Hugh Lawson-Tancred (London: Penguin, 2004), 1030b. I have also consulted Aristotle, *Metaphysics*, trans. Hugh Tredennick, 2 vols. (Cambridge, MA: Harvard University Press, 1975).

17. *The Metaphysics*, 1030a, 1031b.

18. *The Metaphysics*, 1029a–b.

19. *The Metaphysics*, 1069a, 1072a.

20. *The Metaphysics*, 1072a, 1072b.

21. *The Metaphysics*, 1075b, 1074a.

22. David Hume, *Dialogues Concerning Natural Religion and Other Writings*, ed. Dorothy Coleman (Cambridge: Cambridge University Press, 2007), 32. For Hume, the world did not so much resemble an animal as a vegetable (48). Philo calls it "the great vegetable" (53).

23. *The Metaphysics*, 1033b, 1030a.

24. Aristotle, *Physics*, trans. Robin Waterfield, intro. David Bostock (Oxford: Oxford University Press, 1996), 211b 10–13, 212b 7–12. See also Aristotle, *The Physics*, trans. Philip H. Wicksteed and Francis M. Cornford, 2 vols. (London: Heinemann, 1929).

25. Plato, *Timaeus*, in *Timaeus, Critias, Cleitophon, Menexenus, Epistles*, trans. R. G. Bury (Cambridge, MA: Harvard University Press, 1925), 30c–d. See also John Sallis, *Chorology: On Beginnings in Plato's* Tiameus (Bloomington: Indiana University Press, 1999).

26. Kant, *Lectures on Metaphysics*, 3.

27. Kant, *Lectures on Metaphysics*, 206.

28. Kant, *Lectures on Metaphysics*, 208–9.

29. Kant, *Lectures on Metaphysics*, 208.

30. Kant, *Lectures on Metaphysics*, 209.

31. Kant, *Lectures on Metaphysics*, 341.

32. Kant, *Lectures on Metaphysics*, 341. See also Immanuel Kant, *Prolegomena to Any Future Metaphysics That Will Be Able to Come Forward as Science*, in *Theoretical Philosophy after 1781*, ed. Henry Allison and Peter Heath, trans. Gary Hatfield (Cambridge: Cambridge University Press, 2002), 109.

33. Kant, *Lectures on Metaphysics*, 341–42.

34. Kant, *Lectures on Metaphysics*, 213.

35. Immanuel Kant, "To Marcus Herz, February 21 1772," in *Correspondence*, ed. and trans. Arnluf Zweig (Cambridge: Cambridge University Press, 1999), 134–35. See also "To Marcus Herz, May 1st 1781," 179.

36. Immanuel Kant, "To Johann Benouilli, November 16 1781," in *Correspondence*, ed. and trans. Arnluf Zweig (Cambridge: Cambridge University Press, 1999), 186.

37. Immanuel Kant, *On the Form and Principle of the Sensible and Intelligible World*, in *Theoretical Philosophy 1755–1770*, ed. and trans. David Walford and Ralf Meerbote (Cambridge: Cambridge University Press, 1992), 377.

38. *On the Form and Principle of the Sensible and Intelligible World*, 380.

39. *On the Form and Principle of the Sensible and Intelligible World*, 381, 401.

40. *On the Form and Principle of the Sensible and Intelligible World*, 391.
41. *On the Form and Principle of the Sensible and Intelligible World*, 391.
42. *Critique of Pure Reason*, A 20–26.
43. *Critique of Pure Reason*, A 45/B 63.
44. *Critique of Pure Reason*, A 114; A 125–27. Note that these passages were taken out of the second edition.
45. *Critique of Pure Reason*, B xxxix–xli.
46. *Critique of Pure Reason*, A 375.
47. *Critique of Pure Reason*, A 26/B 42.
48. *Critique of Pure Reason*, A 80/B 106; B 137–38; A 237/B 296.
49. *Critique of Pure Reason*, A 249. See Paul Guyer and Allen W. Wood, introduction to *Critique of Pure Reason*, by Immanuel Kant, trans. Paul Guyer (Cambridge: Cambridge University Press, 1998), 12–13.
50. *Critique of Pure Reason*, A 249–54; A 433/B 461; A 438/B 466.
51. *Critique of Pure Reason*, A 270/B 326.
52. *Critique of Pure Reason*, A 289/B 345.
53. G. W. Leibniz, *Discourse on Metaphysics*, in *Philosophical Texts*, trans. Richard Francks and R. S. Woolhouse, intro. R. S. Woolhouse (Oxford: Oxford University Press, 1998), 61 (§ 9).
54. G. W. Leibniz, *Specimen Dynamicum: An Essay in Dynamics*, in *Philosophical Texts*, trans. Richard Francks and R. S. Woolhouse, intro. R. S. Woolhouse (Oxford: Oxford University Press, 1998), 154–56; G. W. Leibniz, *Monadology*, in *Philosophical Texts*, 268, 270.
55. *Critique of Pure Reason*, A 255/B 310–11; A 259/B 315.
56. *Critique of Pure Reason*, A 257/B 312.
57. *Critique of Pure Reason*, A 249–50.
58. *Critique of Pure Reason*, A 255/B 311.
59. *Critique of Pure Reason*, A 334/B 391.
60. *Critique of Pure Reason*, A 257/B 312.
61. *Critique of Pure Reason*, A 520/B 548.
62. *Critique of Pure Reason*, A 489/B 518.
63. *Critique of Pure Reason*, A 302/B 358; A 305/B 361.
64. *Critique of Pure Reason*, A 296–98/B 353–54; A 339/B 397.
65. *Critique of Pure Reason*, A 297/B 353.
66. *Critique of Pure Reason*, A 307–9/B 364–66.
67. *Critique of Pure Reason*, A 309/B 365.
68. *Critique of Pure Reason*, A 322/B 379.
69. *Critique of Pure Reason*, A 326/B 383.
70. *Critique of Pure Reason*, A 326/B 383; B xiv, B xxx–xxxi.
71. *Critique of Pure Reason*, A 334–35/B 391–92.
72. *Critique of Pure Reason*, A 334/B 391.
73. *Critique of Pure Reason*, A 334/B 391.
74. *Critique of Pure Reason*, A 591/B 619; A 605/B 633.

75. *Critique of Pure Reason*, A 605/B 633; A 614–15/B 642–43. See also *Prolegomena to Any Future Metaphysics*, 129, 137.

76. *Critique of Pure Reason*, A 408/B 435.

77. *Kritik der reinen Vernunft*, ed. Jens Timmermann (Hamburg: Felix Meiner, 1998), A 490/B 517.

78. *Critique of Pure Reason*, A 408/B 434.

79. *Critique of Pure Reason*, A 420/B 447.

80. On the question of the interests of reason, see Gilles Deleuze, *Kant's Critical Philosophy: The Doctrine of the Faculties*, trans. Hugh Tomlinson and Barbara Habberjam (London: Athlone, 1995); Jacques Derrida, "The 'World' of the Enlightenment to Come," in *Rogues: Two Essays on Reason*, trans. Pascale-Anne Brault and Michael Naas (Stanford, CA: Stanford University Press, 2005), 117–59.

81. *Critique of Pure Reason*, A 409–15/B 436–42.

82. *Critique of Pure Reason*, A 417/B 444.

83. *Critique of Pure Reason*, A 451–59/B 477–87.

84. *Critique of Pure Reason*, A 420–24/B 448–51.

85. *Critique of Pure Reason*, B xxxi, A 184/B 227, A 228/B 280, B 426.

86. *Critique of Pure Reason*, A 451/B 479.

87. *Critique of Pure Reason*, A 453/B 481; A 459/B 487.

88. *Critique of Pure Reason*, A 453/B 481.

89. *Critique of Pure Reason*, A 459/B 487.

90. *Critique of Pure Reason*, A 455/B 483; A 457/B 485.

91. *Critique of Pure Reason*, A 455/B 483.

92. *Critique of Pure Reason*, A 484/B 512.

93. *Critique of Pure Reason*, A 482/B 510. See also A 479/B 507.

94. *Critique of Pure Reason*, A 484/B 512.

95. *Critique of Pure Reason*, A 464–65/B 492–93.

96. *Critique of Pure Reason*, A 483/B 511.

97. *Critique of Pure Reason*, A 483–84/B 511–12.

98. *Critique of Pure Reason*, A 620/B 648.

99. *Critique of Pure Reason*, A 466/B 494; A 521/B 549.

100. *Critique of Pure Reason*, A 498/B 526. See also A 500/B 528.

101. *Critique of Pure Reason*, A 500–501/ B 528–29, A 505 /B 533.

102. *Critique of Pure Reason*, A 508–10/B 536–38.

103. *Critique of Pure Reason*, A 643/B 671.

104. *Critique of Pure Reason*, A 644–45/B 672–73; A 669–74/B 697–701.

105. *Critique of Pure Reason*, A 552–53/B 580–81; A 557/B 585.

106. *Critique of Pure Reason*, A 564–65/B 592–93.

107. *Critique of Pure Reason*, A 520/B 548; A 523–24/B 551–52.

108. *Critique of Pure Reason*, A 530–31/B 558–59.

109. *Critique of Pure Reason*, A 537/B 565.

110. *Critique of Pure Reason*, A 537–47/B 565–77.

111. *Critique of Pure Reason*, A 546/B 574.

112. *Critique of Pure Reason*, A 547/B 575.

113. Aristotle, *The Metaphysics*, 987b.

114. P. F. Strawson, *The Bounds of Sense: An Essay on Kant's* Critique of Pure Reason (London: Routledge, 1975 [1966]), 15.

115. *Critique of Pure Reason*, A 622/B 650.

116. Henry E. Allison, *Kant's Transcendental Idealism: An Interpretation and Defense*, revised ed. (New Haven, CT: Yale University Press, 2004), xv, 12. For a critical response to Allison, see Paul Guyer, *Kant and the Claims of Knowledge* (Cambridge: Cambridge University Press, 1987), 337–42.

117. *Kant's Transcendental Idealism*, 11, 14, 16.

118. *Kant's Transcendental Idealism*, 11, 30.

119. *Kant's Transcendental Idealism*, 21, 38, 59.

120. *Critique of Pure Reason*, A 845/B 873.

121. *Critique of Pure Reason*, A 247/B 303.

122. *Kant's Transcendental Idealism*, 46–47.

123. *Critique of Pure Reason*, A 845/B 873. See also A 498/B 526. Allison uses this latter passage to illustrate Kant's critique of the world as ontologically given (*gegeben*) in itself. See *Kant's Transcendental Idealism*, 385, 391.

124. *Critique of Pure Reason*, A 560/ B 588, A 564/B 592. See also A 579/B 607.

125. *Critique of Pure Reason*, A 632/B 660; A 609–15/B 637–43.

126. *Critique of Pure Reason*, A 616–17/B 644–45. See also *Prolegomena to Any Future Metaphysics*, 146–50.

127. *Critique of Pure Reason*, A 677–78/B 705–6; A 670/B 698.

128. *Critique of Pure Reason*, A 672/B 700.

129. *Critique of Pure Reason*, A 672/B 700.

130. Friedrich Schiller, *Philosophical Writings*, trans. Caroline Bland, ed. T. J. Reed, in *Immanuel Kant: Critical Assessments*, ed. Ruth F. Chadwick, 4 vols. (London: Routledge, 1992), 1:7.

131. *Critique of Pure Reason*, A 79–82/B 105–7. Kant writes, "Following Aristotle we will call these concepts *categories*, for our aim is basically identical with his although very distant from it in execution."

132. Martin Heidegger, *Hölderlin's Hymn "The Ister,"* trans. William McNeill and Julia Davis (Bloomington: Indiana University Press, 1996), 23–24. See also Martin Heidegger, *The Fundamental Concepts of Metaphysics—World, Finitude, Solitude*, trans. William McNeill and Nicholas Walker (Bloomington: Indiana University Press, 1995), 47.

133. Plato, *The Republic*, trans. G. M. A. Grube and C. D. C. Reeve (Indianapolis, IN: Hackett, 1992), 508b. See also 517 b–c.

134. Aristotle, *Metaphysics*, 1010a 29–30.

135. Plotinus, *The Enneads*, ed. John Dillon, trans. Stephen Mackenna (London: Penguin, 1991), 25 [2.3.1], 94–95 [2.4.4], 115 [2.9.6].

136. Aristotle, *Categories and De Interpretatione*, ed. and trans. J. L. Ackrill (Oxford: Oxford University Press, 1963), 6a 11–18.

137. *Critique of Pure Reason*, A 409/B 435–36. See Aristotle, *Metaphysics*, 1069a 18–23.

138. *Critique of Pure Reason*, A 79–81/B 104–6.

139. *Critique of Pure Reason*, A 804/B 832.

140. *Critique of Pure Reason*, A 806/B 834.

141. *Critique of Pure Reason*, A 807/ B 835.

142. Allison, *Kant's Transcendental Idealism*, 48.

143. *Critique of Pure Reason*, A 808/B 836. See Immanuel Kant, *Religion within the Boundaries of Mere Reason*, in *Religion and Rational Theology*, ed. Allen W. Wood, trans. George di Giovanni (Cambridge: Cambridge University Press, 1996), 6:5–6. Kant also speaks here of the "sublime, never fully attainable idea" of the ethical community as an ideal totality or whole (6:96–98, 100).

144. *Critique of Pure Reason*, A 808–10/B 836–38.

145. *Kant's Transcendental Idealism*, xvi.

146. Nietzsche writes of Kant, "The 'categorical imperative' crept into his heart and made him stray back to 'God,' 'soul,' 'freedom,' 'immortality,' like a fox who strays back into his cage. Yet it had been *his* strength and cleverness that had *broken open* the cage!" Friedrich Nietzsche, *The Gay Science*, ed. Bernard Williams, trans. Josefine Nauckhoff and Adrian Del Caro (Cambridge: Cambridge University Press, 2001), 188 (§ 335).

147. *Critique of Pure Reason*, A 811/B 839.

148. *Critique of Pure Reason*, A 812/B 840.

149. G. W. Leibniz, *Principles of Nature and Grace, Based on Reason*, in *Philosophical Texts*, trans. Richard Francks and R. S. Woolhouse, intro. R. S. Woolhouse (Oxford: Oxford University Press, 1998), 258–66. See also *Critique of Pure Reason*, A 812/B 840 n. 30 and 31 (754).

150. *Critique of Pure Reason*, A 813–16/B 841–44.

151. See Immanuel Kant, *Groundwork of the Metaphysics of Morals*, in *Practical Philosophy*, ed. and trans. Mary J. Gregor, intro. Allen Wood (Cambridge: Cambridge University Press, 1999), 4:438; 4:452; 4:457–63.

152. *Groundwork of the Metaphysics of Morals*, 4:457–58.

153. *Groundwork of the Metaphysics of Morals*, 4:458.

154. *Religion within the Boundaries of Mere Reason*, 6:60.

155. Immanuel Kant, *Critique of Practical Reason*, in *Practical Philosophy*, ed. and trans. Mary J. Gregor, intro. Allen Wood (Cambridge: Cambridge University Press, 1999), 5:43. See also 5:42–50, 5:65, 5:87, 5:114–15. In the *Critique of Pure Reason*, Kant uses the difference between ectype and archetype to mark the stage at which we can begin to learn to philosophize (A 838/B 866).

156. *Critique of Practical Reason*, 5:47–49, 5:70. See also 5:133.

157. *Critique of Practical Reason*, 5:94.

158. *Critique of Practical Reason*, 5:105.

159. *Critique of Pure Reason*, A 841/B 869.

160. *Critique of Pure Reason*, A 845/B 873.

161. *Critique of Pure Reason*, A 850/B 878.

162. *Critique of Pure Reason*, A 832–33/B 860–61.

163. Immanuel Kant, *Critique of the Power of Judgement*, ed. Paul Guyer, trans. Paul Guyer and Eric Matthews (Cambridge: Cambridge University Press, 2000), 5:175–76.

164. Elisabeth Ellis, *Kant's Politics: Provisional Theory for an Uncertain World* (New Haven, CT: Yale University Press, 2005), 4.

165. Immanuel Kant, *Toward Perpetual Peace*, in *Practical Philosophy*, ed. and trans. Mary J. Gregor, intro. Allen Wood (Cambridge: Cambridge University Press, 1999), 8:367. See also 8:373.

166. *Toward Perpetual Peace*, 8:344, 8:357, 8:360.

167. *Toward Perpetual Peace*, 8:349, 8:358.

168. Pauline Kleingeld, *Kant and Cosmopolitanism: The Philosophical Ideal of World Citizenship* (Cambridge: Cambridge University Press, 2012).

169. Immanuel Kant, *An Answer to the Question: What Is Enlightenment?* in *Practical Philosophy*, ed. and trans. Mary J. Gregor, intro. Allen Wood (Cambridge: Cambridge University Press, 1999), 8:37.

170. *Toward Perpetual Peace*, 8:350, 8:353, 8:360, 8:376, 8:378.

171. Immanuel Kant, *Anthropology from a Pragmatic Point of View*, ed. and trans. Robert B. Louden, intro. Manfred Kuehn (Cambridge: Cambridge University Press, 2006), 3. See also Martin Heidegger, *Kant and the Problem of Metaphysics*, trans. Richard Taft, 5th ed. (Bloomington: Indiana University Press, 1997), 144–53.

172. *Anthropology from a Pragmatic Point of View*, 3. See David L. Clark, "Kant's Aliens: The *Anthropology* and Its Others," *New Centennial Review* 1, no. 2 (2001): 213.

173. *Anthropology from a Pragmatic Point of View*, 15.

174. *Anthropology from a Pragmatic Point of View*, 238.

175. *Anthropology from a Pragmatic Point of View*, 18.

176. *Anthropology from a Pragmatic Point of View*, 3; Michel Foucault, *Introduction to Kant's Anthropology*, ed. Roberto Nigro, trans. Roberto Nigro and Kate Briggs (Los Angeles: Semiotext(e), 2008), 32. See also 53–55.

177. Immanuel Kant, *Of the Different Races of Human Beings*, in *Anthropology, History and Education*, ed. Günter Zöller and Robert B. Louden, trans. Holly Wilson and Günter Zöller (Cambridge: Cambridge University Press, 2007), 97.

178. Foucault, *Introduction to Kant's Anthropology*, 33. See *Anthropology from a Pragmatic Point of View*, 238. At the same time, Foucault later argues that "the structure of the relationship between the given and the *a priori* in the *Anthropology* is the opposite of that revealed in the *Critique*" (68).

179. For Foucault, Kant's "citizen of the world" (*Weltbürger*) belongs to a concrete legal and juridical "realm" which distinguishes the pragmatic from the practical (42). See also 102.

180. *Critique of Pure Reason*, A 759/B 787. See also 614. See also Geoffrey Bennington, *Frontiers: Kant, Hegel, Wittgenstein* (e-book, 2003).

181. *Critique of Pure Reason*, A 758/B 787.

182. *Critique of Pure Reason*, A 762/B 790.

183. Martin Heidegger, "Kant's Thesis about Being," in *Pathmarks*, ed. William McNeill, trans. Ted E. Klein Jr. and William E. Pohl (Cambridge: Cambridge University Press, 1998), 340.

184. Jacques Derrida, *Edmund Husserl's* Origin of Geometry: *An Introduction*, trans. John P. Leavey Jr. (Lincoln: University of Nebraska Press, 1989), 153. See also 135–42.

185. Emmanuel Lévinas, "Heidegger, Gagarin and Us," in *Difficult Freedom: Essays on Judaism*, trans. Seán Hand (Baltimore, MD: Johns Hopkins University Press, 1990), 233.

186. Maurice Blanchot, "The Conquest of Space," in *Maurice Blanchot: Political Writings, 1953–1993*, trans. and intro. Zakir Paul, foreword Kevin Hart (New York: Fordham University Press, 2010), 70.

187. "The Conquest of Space," 71.

188. See Schopenhauer on Kepler and Kant, *The World as Will and Representation: Volume 1*, 92–93.

189. See the recently published collection Immanuel Kant, *Natural Science*, ed. Eric Watkins (Cambridge: Cambridge University Press, 2012). See also Michael Friedman, *Kant and the Exact Sciences* (Cambridge, MA: Harvard University Press, 1992).

190. Immanuel Kant, *Opus Postumum*, ed. and intro. Eckart Förster, trans. Eckart Förster and Michael Rosen (Cambridge: Cambridge University Press, 1993), 238. See also 228, 235.

191. See Eckart Förster, *Kant's Final Synthesis: An Essay on the* Opus Postumum (Cambridge, MA: Harvard University Press, 1995), 115. See also Immanuel Kant, *Metaphysical Foundations of the Natural Sciences*, in *Theoretical Philosophy after 1781*, ed. Henry Allison and Peter Heath, trans. Michael Friedman (Cambridge: Cambridge University Press, 2002), 171–270.

192. *Opus Postumum*, 222.

193. *Opus Postumum*, 231. See also 224.

194. *Opus Postumum*, 230, 231, 235, 239, 245.

195. *Opus Postumum*, 227. See also 228, 235, 245.

196. *Opus Postumum*, 228.

197. *Opus Postumum*, 222.

198. See Schopenhauer's remarks, *The World as Will and Representation: Volume 1*, 443–44.

199. Edmund Husserl, *The Origin of Geometry*, in *The Crisis of European Sciences and Transcendental Phenomenology: An Introduction to Phenomenological Philosophy*, trans. and intro. David Carr (Evanston, IL: Northwestern University Press, 1970), 353–78.

## Chapter 2. Hegel and the World as Spirit

1. Jean Hyppolite, *Genesis and Structure of Hegel's* Phenomenology of Spirit, trans. Samuel Cherniak and John Heckman (Evanston, IL: Northwestern University Press, 1974), 4.

2. On the post-Kantian context, see Terry Pinkard, *German Philosophy 1760–1860: The Legacy of Idealism* (Cambridge: Cambridge University Press, 2002).

3. *Genesis and Structure*, 8.

4. *Phenomenology of Spirit* §137.

5. *Phenomenology of Spirit* §139.

6. *Phenomenology of Spirit* §142.

7. *Phenomenology of Spirit* §143.

8. *Phenomenology of Spirit* §143.

9. *Phenomenology of Spirit* §144.

10. Terry Pinkard, *Hegel's Phenomenology: The Sociality of Reason* (Cambridge: Cambridge University Press, 1994), 42–43.

11. G. W. F. Hegel, *Phänomenologie des Geistes*, ed. Johannes Hoffmeister (Hamburg: Felix Meiner, 1952), 111. Hegel writes, "Schließt sich erst über der *sinnlichen* als der *erscheinenden Welt* nunmehr eine *übersinnliche* als die *wahre* Welt auf, über dem verschwindenden *Diesseits* das bleibende *Jenseits*."

12. *Phenomenology of Spirit* §146; *Phänomenologie des Geistes*, 112.

13. *Phenomenology of Spirit* §147.

14. *Phenomenology of Spirit* §149; *Phänomenologie des Geistes*, 114–15.

15. G. W. F. Hegel, *Philosophy of Mind*, trans. W. Wallace and A. V. Miller, rev. and intro. Michael Inwood (Oxford: Clarendon Press, 2007), 5.

16. *Phenomenology of Spirit* § 157, 159.

17. *Phenomenology of Spirit* §160; *Phänomenologie des Geistes*, 124.

18. *Phenomenology of Spirit* §158; *Phänomenologie des Geistes*, 122. See also Hans-Georg Gadamer, "Hegel's 'Inverted World,'" in *G. W. F. Hegel: Critical Assessments*, vol. 3, *Hegel's Phenomenology and Logic*, ed. Robert Stern (London: Routledge, 1993), 131–47; Joseph C. Flay, "Hegel's Inverted World," *Review of Metaphysics* 23, no. 4 (1970): 662–78.

19. *Phenomenology of Spirit* §160.

20. *Phenomenology of Spirit* §159–62.

21. Pinkard, *Hegel's Phenomenology*, 44.

22. *Hegel's Phenomenology*, 44.

23. *Phenomenology of Spirit* §232.

24. *Phenomenology of Spirit* §232; *Phänomenologie des Geistes*, 176.

25. *Phenomenology of Spirit* §232; *Phänomenologie des Geistes*, 176. Translation modified.

26. *Phenomenology of Spirit* §232.

27. *Phenomenology of Spirit* §238.

28. *Phenomenology of Spirit* §240.

29. *Phenomenology of Spirit* §240; *Phänomenologie des Geistes*, 183.

30. *Phenomenology of Spirit* §302; *Phänomenologie des Geistes*, 223.

31. *Phenomenology of Spirit* §302; *Phänomenologie des Geistes*, 223. Translation modified.

32. *Phenomenology of Spirit* §308. Translation modified. The references to world in this passage have been introduced by the translator. See *Phänomenologie des Geistes*, 227.

33. *Phenomenology of Spirit* §339; *Phänomenologie des Geistes*, 249.

34. *Phenomenology of Spirit* §347, 381; *Phänomenologie des Geistes*, 255, 274.

35. *Phenomenology of Spirit* §354, 356; *Phänomenologie des Geistes*, 258–59.

36. *Phenomenology of Spirit* §379; *Phänomenologie des Geistes*, 273. Despite his critique of *actualitas* in Hegel's philosophy, one could even take Heidegger's continual insistence on the world *as a whole* as an instance of "the show of an unchanging course," of the concept of world on its course, its natural course. See Martin Heidegger, "Hegel's Concept of Experience," in *Off the Beaten Track*, ed. and trans. Julian Young and Kenneth Haynes (Cambridge: Cambridge University Press, 2002), 116.

37. *Phenomenology of Spirit* §386, 389; *Phänomenologie des Geistes*, 278, 279.

38. *Phenomenology of Spirit* §436.

39. *Phenomenology of Spirit* §438; *Phänomenologie des Geistes*, 313.

40. *Phenomenology of Spirit* §441; *Phänomenologie des Geistes*, 315.

41. *Phenomenology of Spirit* 443; *Phänomenologie des Geistes*, 316.

42. *Phenomenology of Spirit* §492; *Phänomenologie des Geistes*, 353.

43. *Phenomenology of Spirit* §525, 581. See also §604.

44. *Phenomenology of Spirit* §633. See also §658.

45. Hegel, *The Science of Logic*, 29.

46. *The Science of Logic*, 29.

47. *The Science of Logic*, 37.

48. *The Science of Logic*, 42.

49. *The Science of Logic*, 158.

50. *The Science of Logic*, 201.

51. Michael Baur, "From Kant's Highest Good to Hegel's Absolute Knowing," in *A Companion to Hegel*, ed. Stephen Houlgate and Michael Baur (Oxford: Wiley-Blackwell, 2011), 464–65.

52. *The Science of Logic*, 734. See also 696, 729.

53. *The Science of Logic*, 418–19, 438.

54. *The Science of Logic*, 439–42.

55. *The Science of Logic*, 448.

56. *The Science of Logic*, 444.

57. *The Science of Logic*, 444.

58. *The Science of Logic*, 445.

59. *The Science of Logic*, 445.

60. *The Science of Logic*, 445–46.

61. *The Science of Logic*, 671.

62. G. W. F. Hegel, *Philosophy of Nature, Part Two of the Encyclopaedia of the Philosophical Sciences (1830)*, trans. A. V. Miller, foreword J. N. Findlay (Oxford: Clarendon Press, 1970), 308.

63. *Philosophy of Nature*, 308.

64. *Philosophy of Nature*, 351.

65. *Philosophy of Nature*, 352.

66. *Philosophy of Nature*, 353–55.

67. *Philosophy of Nature*, 373.

68. *Philosophy of Nature*, 378.

69. *Philosophy of Nature*, 403.

70. *Philosophy of Nature*, 381.

71. *Philosophy of Nature*, 406–10.

72. Werner Hamacher, *Pleroma—Reading in Hegel*, trans. Nicholas Walker and Simon Jarvis (Stanford, CA: Stanford University Press, 1998), 206–97. See *Philosophy of Nature*, 395–406, 442–45. See also *Philosophy of Mind*, 29–30.

73. *Philosophy of Nature*, 443.

74. G. W. F. Hegel, *The Encyclopaedia Logic, Part 1 of the Encyclopaedia of Philosophical Sciences with the* Zuzsätze, trans. T. F. Geraets, W. A. Suchting and H. S. Harris (Indianapolis, IN: Hackett, 1991), 85.

75. Michael Inwood, introduction to *Philosophy of Mind*, by G. W. F. Hegel, trans. W. Wallace and A. V. Miller, rev. and intro. Michael Inwood (Oxford: Clarendon Press, 2007), xiv.

76. *Philosophy of Mind*, 26.

77. *Philosophy of Mind*, 26.

78. *Philosophy of Mind*, 27.

79. *Philosophy of Mind*, 35.

80. *Philosophy of Mind*, 35.

81. *Philosophy of Mind*, 36.

82. *Philosophy of Mind*, 36.

83. *Philosophy of Mind*, 37.

84. *Philosophy of Mind*, 53.

85. *Philosophy of Mind*, 57.

86. *Philosophy of Mind*, 53.

87. William Wordsworth, *The Prelude: The Four Texts (1798, 1799, 1805, 1850)*, ed. Jonathan Wordsworth (London: Penguin, 1995).

88. *Philosophy of Mind*, 57, 58.

89. *Philosophy of Mind*, 59, 60.

90. *Philosophy of Mind*, 61.

91. Karl Marx, *Writings of the Young Marx on Philosophy and Society*, ed. and trans. Lloyd D. Easton and Kurt H. Guddat (New York: Anchor, 1967), 51–66; Alexandre Kojève, *Introduction to the Reading of Hegel: Lectures on the* Phenomenology of Spirit, ed. Raymond Queneau and Alan Bloom, trans. James H. Nichols (Ithaca, NY: Cornell University Press, 1991).

92. G. W. F. Hegel, *Elements of the Philosophy of Right*, ed. Allen W. Wood, trans. H. B. Nisbet (Cambridge: Cambridge University Press, 1991).

93. *Philosophy of Mind*, 86.

94. *Philosophy of Mind*, 88, 86.

95. *Philosophy of Mind*, 140.

96. *Philosophy of Mind*, 57.

97. *Phenomenology of Spirit* §757; *Phänomenologie des Geistes*, 527.

98. *Philosophy of Mind*, 42.

99. Rodolphe Gasché, *Europe, or the Infinite Task: A Study of a Philosophical Concept* (Stanford, CA: Stanford University Press, 2009).

100. *Philosophy of Mind*, 43–44.

101. G. W. F. Hegel, *Lectures on the Philosophy of World History*, vol. 1, *Manuscript of the Introduction and the Lectures of 1822–3*, ed. and trans. Robert F. Brown and Peter C. Hodgson, with William G. Geuss (Oxford: Clarendon Press, 2011).

102. *Lectures on the Philosophy of World History*, 134.

103. *Lectures on the Philosophy of World History*, 136–37.

104. *Lectures on the Philosophy of World History*, 140.

105. *Lectures on the Philosophy of World History*, 140–41.

106. *Philosophy of Mind*, 44–45.

107. See Lydia L. Moland, *Hegel on Political Identity: Patriotism, Nationalism and Cosmopolitanism* (Evanston, IL: Northwestern University Press, 2011).

108. Terry Pinkard, *Hegel: A Biography* (Cambridge: Cambridge University Press, 2000), 491–92.

109. Karl Marx, *The German Ideology*, in *The Marx-Engels Reader*, ed. Robert C. Tucker (New York: W. W. Norton, 1978), 163–64.

110. *Philosophy of Mind*, 45; *Elements of the Philosophy of Right*, §345.

## Chapter 3. Husserl and the Phenomenological World

1. Edmund Husserl, *Ideas Pertaining to a Pure Phenomenology and to a Phenomenological Philosophy: First Book—General Introduction to a Pure Phenomenology*, trans. F. Kersten (The Hague: Martinus Nijhoff, 1983), 1:xvii (hereafter cited as *Ideas 1*).

2. *Ideas* 1:xvii.

3. *Ideas* 1:5.

4. *Ideas* 1:xviii–xix.

5. *Ideas* 1:xix.

6. *Ideas* 1:xx.

7. *Ideas* 1:11, 43–44, 72, 159–60, 223.

8. *Ideas* 1:6.

9. *Ideas* 1:8.

10. *Ideas* 1:8–9, 37.

11. *Ideas* 1:13–14.

12. *Ideas* 1:8–10.

13. Edmund Husserl, *Cartesian Meditations: An Introduction to Phenomenology*, trans. Dorian Cairns (Dordrecht: Kluwer, 1999), 39–40.

14. Edmund Husserl, *The Phenomenology of Internal Time Consciousness*, ed. Martin Heidegger, intro. Calvin O. Schrag, trans. James S. Churchill (The Hague: Martinus Nijhoff, 1964).

15. *Cartesian Meditations*, 45.

16. *Ideas* 1:16. On the relation between the "fictional world" and the "actual world," see Edmund Husserl, *Ideas Pertaining to a Pure Phenomenology and to a Phenomenological Philosophy: Second Book—Studies in the Phenomenology of Constitution*, trans. R. Rojcewicz and A. Schuwer (Dordrecht: Kluwer, 1989), 2:127 (hereafter cited as *Ideas 2*). See also 274.

17. *The Crisis of European Sciences*, 181.

18. *Ideas* 1:51.

19. *Ideas* 1:52.

20. *Ideas* 1:53.

21. *Ideas* 1:53–54.

22. *Ideas* 1:55–56.

23. See *Ideas* 1:27–28. 31, 88, 171.

24. *Ideas* 1:17.

25. *Ideas* 1:57–58.

26. *Ideas* 1:61.

27. *Ideas* 1:63.

28. *Ideas* 1:71–72.

29. *Ideas* 1:73, 75–76.

30. *Ideas* 1:73, 76–77.

31. *Ideas* 1:81, 78.

32. *Ideas* 1:82.

33. *Ideas* 1:87, 95.

34. Klaus Held, "Husserl's Phenomenological Method," in *The New Husserl: A Critical Reader*, ed. Donn Welton, trans. Lanei Rodemeyer (Bloomington: Indiana University Press, 2003), 19–20.

35. Klaus Held, "Husserl's Phenomenology of the Life-World," in *The New Husserl: A Critical Reader*, ed. Donn Welton, trans. Lanei Rodemeyer (Bloomington: Indiana University Press, 2003), 52–57. See also Maurice Merleau-Ponty, *Phenomenology of Perception*, trans. Colin Smith (London and New York: Routledge, 2002), 385.

36. *The Crisis of European Sciences*, 164.

37. *Ideas* 1:109–12.

38. *Ideas* 1:102–3.

39. *Ideas* 1:104.

40. Held, "Husserl's Phenomenological Method," 24.

41. *Ideas* 1:106.

42. *Ideas* 1:110.

43. Karsten Harries, "Descartes and the Labyrinth of the World," *International Journal of Philosophical Studies* 6 (1998): 307–30.

44. Held, "Husserl's Phenomenological Method," 21–22.

45. Paul Ricoeur, *Husserl: An Analysis of His Phenomenology*, trans. Edward G. Ballard and Lester E. Embree, intro. David Carr (Evanston, IL: Northwestern University Press, 2007), 36.

46. Edmund Husserl, "Phenomenology," in *Deconstruction in Context: Literature and Philosophy*, ed. Mark C. Taylor (Chicago: University of Chicago Press, 1986), 123.

47. Edmund Husserl, "Author's Preface to the English Edition," in *Ideas: General Introduction to Pure Phenomenology*, trans. W. R. Boyce Gibson (New York: Collier, 1962 [1931]), 14. See also Dagfinn Føllesdal, "The *Lebenswelt* in Husserl," in *Science and the Life-World: Essays on Husserl's Crisis of European Sciences*, ed. David Hyder and Hans-Jörg Rheinberger (Stanford, CA: Stanford University Press, 2009), 32–33. I have followed Føllesdal's revised translation of this passage.

48. *Ideas* 1:112, 116.

49. *Ideas* 1:114.

50. *Ideas* 1:113.

51. *Ideas* 1:190–91.

52. Merleau-Ponty, *Phenomenology of Perception*, xv.

53. *Ideas* 2:183.

54. Ricoeur, *Husserl: An Analysis of His Phenomenology*, 37.

55. Held, "Husserl's Phenomenology of the Life-World," 36.

56. Ricoeur, *Husserl: An Analysis of His Phenomenology*, 38.

57. *Ideas* 2:65. See Merleau-Ponty, *Phenomenology of Perception*; and *The Visible and the Invisible*, ed. Claude Lefort, trans. Alphonso Lingis (Evanston, IL: Northwestern University Press, 1968). See also Joseph Duchêne, "The Concept of 'World' and the Problem of Rationality in Merleau-Ponty's *Phénoménologie de la perception*," *International Philosophical Quarterly* 17 (1977): 393–413.

58. *Ideas* 2:39–41.

59. *Ideas* 2:61, 70.

60. *Ideas* 2:74.

61. *Ideas* 2:61, 72–73, 78, 80.

62. *Ideas* 2:78.

63. Ricoeur, *Husserl: An Analysis of His Phenomenology*, 52. See also 46–48.

64. *Ideas* 2:82–83.

65. *Ideas* 2:86–87.

66. *Ideas* 2:87.

67. *Ideas* 2:88.

68. Derrida, *Edmund Husserl's* Origin of Geometry, 132–33.

69. *Ideas* 2:88.

70. *Ideas* 2:89, 91–92.

71. Ricoeur, *Husserl: An Analysis of His Phenomenology*, 51, 57, 63–64.

72. *Ideas* 2:101.

73. *Ideas* 2:102, 116–17.

74. *Ideas* 2:103, 109, 113.

75. Ricoeur, *Husserl: An Analysis of His Phenomenology*, 52.

76. *Ideas* 2:119.

77. *Ideas* 2:120.

78. *Ideas* 2:136–37, 139–40.

79. *Ideas* 2:188.
80. *Ideas* 2:141.
81. *Ideas* 2:144–46, 176.
82. *Ideas* 2:147, 150.
83. *Ideas* 2:172.
84. *Ideas* 2:174.
85. *Ideas* 2:175.
86. *Ideas* 2:181.
87. *Ideas* 2:183, 311.
88. *Ideas* 2:188.
89. *Ideas* 2:189.
90. *Ideas* 2:189.
91. *Ideas* 2:189.
92. *Ideas* 2:192.
93. *Ideas* 2:193.
94. *Ideas* 2:195–96.
95. *Ideas* 2:199.
96. *Ideas* 2:196, 199.
97. *Ideas* 2:230.
98. *Ideas* 2:201, 203.
99. *Ideas* 2:203–4.
100. *Ideas* 2:207.
101. *Ideas* 2:205.
102. *Ideas* 2:206–7.
103. *Ideas* 2:213.
104. *Ideas* 2:215, 219.
105. *Ideas* 2:294–95.
106. *Ideas* 2:251. See also Ricoeur's critical comments on Husserl's concept of spirit, *Husserl: An Analysis of His Phenomenology*, 79–80. He suggests that "*Geist* is nothing other than the ego of phenomenology, but without the light of the phenomenological reduction" (80).
107. *Ideas* 2:221. See also 253–56.
108. René Descartes, *Meditations on First Philosophy*, vol. 1 of *The Philosophical Writings of Descartes*, trans. John Cottingham, Robert Stoothoff and Dugald Murdoch (Cambridge: Cambridge University Press, 1986), 16.
109. *Meditations on First Philosophy*, 11.
110. *Cartesian Meditations*, 4.
111. *Cartesian Meditations*, 7, 14.
112. *Cartesian Meditations*, 79.
113. Føllesdal, "The *Lebenswelt* in Husserl," 38–45. For a brief account of the life-world, see Dan Zahavi, *Husserl's Phenomenology* (Stanford, CA: Stanford University Press, 2003), 125–32; Held, "Husserl's Phenomenology of the Life-World," 57–61.
114. *Cartesian Meditations*, 17.

115. *Cartesian Meditations*, 18.

116. *Cartesian Meditations*, 20.

117. *The Crisis of European Sciences*, 137. See also 148.

118. *The Crisis of European Sciences*, 172.

119. *Cartesian Meditations*, 20.

120. *Cartesian Meditations*, 3.

121. *Cartesian Meditations*, 25, 31.

122. *Cartesian Meditations*, 26.

123. *Cartesian Meditations*, 26.

124. *Cartesian Meditations*, 26.

125. *Cartesian Meditations*, 28, 30.

126. *Cartesian Meditations*, 86; *The Crisis of European Sciences*, 182–86.

127. *Cartesian Meditations*, 30, 91. See 89–157.

128. *Cartesian Meditations*, 91.

129. *Cartesian Meditations*, 106–8, 125–26, 130. On the cultural world, 132–36.

130. See also Ricoeur, *Husserl: An Analysis of His Philosophy*, 115–42.

131. *Cartesian Meditations*, 108. See Emmanuel Lévinas, *Discovering Existence with Husserl*, trans. Richard A. Cohen and Michael B. Smith (Evanston, IL: Northwestern University Press, 1998); *Time and the Other*, trans. Richard A. Cohen (Pittsburgh, PA: Duquesne University Press, 1987); *Totality and Infinity: An Essay on Exteriority*, trans. Alphonso Lingis (Pittsburgh, PA: Duquesne University Press, 1969).

132. *Cartesian Meditations*, 109–20.

133. *Cartesian Meditations*, 123.

134. *Cartesian Meditations*, 31. My emphasis.

135. *Cartesian Meditations*, 33. Husserl also refers to "an actuality-phenomenon" to emphasize that the reality of perceived objects have not changed, only their self-evident status.

136. *Cartesian Meditations*, 33.

137. I have addressed the history of this term in *Derrida and Disinterest* (London: Continuum, 2006).

138. *Cartesian Meditations*, 35.

139. *Cartesian Meditations*, 37.

140. *Cartesian Meditations*, 36.

141. *Cartesian Meditations*, 37.

142. *Cartesian Meditations*, 151.

143. *The Crisis of European Sciences*, 9.

144. *The Crisis of European Sciences*, 13.

145. *The Crisis of European Sciences*, 22.

146. *The Crisis of European Sciences*, 23–25.

147. *The Crisis of European Sciences*, 26, 28, 31, 33.

148. *The Crisis of European Sciences*, 35.

149. *The Crisis of European Sciences*, 34.

150. Held, "Husserl's Phenomenology of the Life-World," 57–58.

151. *The Crisis of European Sciences*, 39.

152. *The Crisis of European Sciences*, 48–49.

153. *The Crisis of European Sciences*, 50.

154. *The Crisis of European Sciences*, 50.

155. *The Crisis of European Sciences*, 51.

156. *The Crisis of European Sciences*, 51.

157. *The Crisis of European Sciences*, 54–55.

158. *The Crisis of European Sciences*, 139–40.

159. *The Crisis of European Sciences*, 56. See also 71–73.

160. *The Crisis of European Sciences*, 60.

161. *The Crisis of European Sciences*, 60.

162. *The Crisis of European Sciences*, 62.

163. *The Crisis of European Sciences*, 62.

164. *The Crisis of European Sciences*, 65–70.

165. *The Crisis of European Sciences*, 65, 73.

166. *The Crisis of European Sciences*, 76.

167. *The Crisis of European Sciences*, 78.

168. *The Crisis of European Sciences*, 79.

169. *The Crisis of European Sciences*, 80.

170. *The Crisis of European Sciences*, 82.

171. *The Crisis of European Sciences*, 87–88, 93. See also David Hume, *A Treatise of Human Nature*, ed. David Fate Norton and Mary J. Norton (Oxford: Oxford University Press, 2001), 129–38.

172. *The Crisis of European Sciences*, 95.

173. *The Crisis of European Sciences*, 96–97.

174. *The Crisis of European Sciences*, 155, 159, 170. See Leonard Lawlor, *Derrida and Husserl: The Basic Problem of Phenomenology* (Bloomington: Indiana University Press, 2002), 112–15, 139; Gasché, *Europe, or the Infinite Task*, 303–38. See also Jacques Derrida, *Voice and Phenomenon: Introduction to the Problem of the Sign in Husserl's Philosophy*, trans. Leonard Lawlor (Evanston, IL: Northwestern University Press, 2011), 9.

175. *The Crisis of European Sciences*, 142.

176. *The Crisis of European Sciences*, 95.

177. *The Crisis of European Sciences*, 95.

178. *The Crisis of European Sciences*, 99.

179. *The Crisis of European Sciences*, 106–7.

180. *The Crisis of European Sciences*, 107–8.

181. *The Crisis of European Sciences*, 58, 70, 98, 112–13.

182. *The Crisis of European Sciences*, 119.

183. *The Crisis of European Sciences*, 144, 149.

184. *The Crisis of European Sciences*, 150. See Donn Welton, *The Other Husserl: The Other Horizons of Transcendental Phenomenology* (Bloomington: Indiana State University Press, 2000), 335.

185. *The Crisis of European Sciences*, 151–52.

186. *The Crisis of European Sciences*, 152.

187. *Ideas* 2:292.

188. *Cartesian Meditations*, 77, 83–85.

189. *The Crisis of European Sciences*, 143.

## Chapter 4. Heidegger and the Problem of World

1. Martin Heidegger, *Being and Time*, trans. John Macquarrie and Edward Robinson (Oxford: Blackwell, 1962), 13. The pages cited in this work refer to the page numbers cited in the margins.

2. *Being and Time*, 12.

3. *Being and Time*, 13.

4. *Being and Time*, 75.

5. *Being and Time*, 54, 69, 88.

6. *Being and Time*, 276.

7. *Being and Time*, 15–16.

8. *Being and Time*, 17.

9. *Being and Time*, 15–16.

10. *Being and Time*, 21.

11. *Being and Time*, 21–22.

12. *Being and Time*, 25.

13. *The Fundamental Concepts of Metaphysics*, 176–77.

14. *The Fundamental Concepts of Metaphysics*, 177.

15. *The Fundamental Concepts of Metaphysics*, 177.

16. *Being and Time*, 28–29.

17. *The Fundamental Concepts of Metaphysics*, 177.

18. *Being and Time*, 37.

19. *Being and Time*, 137.

20. *Being and Time*, 137.

21. *Being and Time*, 35.

22. *Being and Time*, 36.

23. *Being and Time*, 38.

24. *Being and Time*, 41.

25. *Being and Time*, 41.

26. *Being and Time*, 181.

27. *Being and Time*, 53.

28. *Being and Time*, 52.

29. *Being and Time*, 43.

30. *Being and Time*, 54.

31. *Being and Time*, 55; Hubert L. Dreyfus, *Being-in-the-World: A Commentary on Heidegger's* Being and Time, Division I (Cambridge, MA: MIT Press, 1991), xi.

32. *Being and Time*, 55.

33. *Being and Time*, 55.

34. *Being and Time*, 57.

35. *Being and Time*, 62.

36. *Being-in-the-World*, 58.

37. Martin Heidegger, *History of the Concept of Time: Prolegomena*, trans. Theodore Kisiel (Bloomington: Indiana University Press, 1985), 15.

38. *Being-in-the-World*, 58.

39. *Being-in-the-World*, 50–54.

40. *Being-in-the-World*, 17, 23, 88, 95–96.

41. *Being and Time*, 125. Dreyfus's own need for the priority of a determining public domain is also apparent in his criticisms of Heidegger's account of the spatiality of being-in-the-world. For Dreyfus, this is a private space that should become public, as if the only alternative to propriety is the public sphere. See *Being-in-the-World*, 132–36, 143–45. One could contrast this to Derrida's critique of Heideggerian spatiality as a predicate of proximity, whether it is close to the private or to the public. See Jacques Derrida, *Spurs: Nietzsche's Styles/Éperons: Les styles de Nietzsche*, trans. Barbara Harlow, intro. Stefano Agosti (Chicago: University of Chicago Press, 1979).

42. *Being and Time*, 206.

43. *Being and Time*, 205.

44. *Being and Time*, 63.

45. *Being and Time*, 63.

46. *Being and Time*, 63.

47. *Being and Time*, 63–64.

48. *Being and Time*, 98–100.

49. *Being and Time*, 64–65.

50. *Being and Time*, 66.

51. *Being and Time*, 66.

52. *Being-in-the-World*, 61–62.

53. *Being and Time*, 66–68, 71.

54. *Being and Time*, 72.

55. *Being and Time*, 72.

56. *Being and Time*, 185–88.

57. *Being and Time*, 72.

58. *Being and Time*, 72.

59. *Being and Time*, 73.

60. *Being and Time*, 74.

61. *Being and Time*, 75.

62. *Being and Time*, 79–80.

63. *Being and Time*, 84.

64. *Being and Time*, 41.

65. Martin Heidegger, *Introduction to Metaphysics*, trans. Gregory Fried and Richard Polt (New Haven, CT: Yale University Press, 2000), 11. See Martin Heidegger,

*The Basic Problems of Phenomenology*, trans. Albert Hofstader, rev. ed. (Bloomington: Indiana University Press, 1982), 4–10; "The Age of the World Picture," in *Off the Beaten Track*, ed. and trans. Julian Young and Kenneth Haynes (Cambridge: Cambridge University Press, 2002), 57–72.

66. *Being and Time*, 113.
67. *Being and Time*, 75.
68. *Being and Time*, 75.
69. *Being and Time*, 83.
70. *Being and Time*, 86.
71. *Being and Time*, 86.
72. *Being and Time*, 87.
73. *Being and Time*, 98–100, 101–2.
74. *Being and Time*, 103.
75. *Being and Time*, 103.
76. *Being and Time*, 120.
77. *Being and Time*, 105–6; *Being and Time*, trans. Joan Stambaugh and Dennis J. Schmidt (Albany: State University of New York Press, 2010).
78. *Being and Time*, 108.
79. *Being and Time*, 106.
80. *Being and Time*, 108–9.
81. *Being and Time*, 107–8.
82. *Being and Time*, 112.
83. *Being and Time*, 110.
84. *Being and Time*, 128.
85. *Being and Time*, 130.
86. *Being and Time*, 130.
87. *Being and Time*, 130.
88. *Being and Time*, 131.
89. *Being and Time*, 133, 135.
90. *Being and Time*, 137.
91. *Being and Time*, 138.
92. *Being and Time*, 191.
93. *Being and Time*, 192.
94. *Being and Time*, 236, 259, 262–64, 297.
95. *Being and Time*, 350.
96. *Being and Time*, 360.
97. *Being and Time*, 365.
98. *Being and Time*, 138.
99. *Being and Time*, 146.
100. *Being and Time*, 158. See also Husserl, *Ideas* 1:22.
101. *Being and Time*, 158.
102. *Kant and the Problem of Metaphysics*, 167. Heidegger later describes this hermeneutical relation in a paper from 1950 as "a presence sheltered in absence." Martin

Heidegger, "Language," in *Poetry, Language, Thought*, trans. Albert Hofstadter (New York: Harper & Row, 1975), 199.

103. *Being and Time*, 219.

104. *Being and Time*, 33.

105. *Being and Time*, 34, 149.

106. *Being and Time*, 359–60.

107. *Being and Time*, 187.

108. *Being and Time*, 188.

109. *Being and Time*, 151.

110. *Being and Time*, 188–89.

111. *Being and Time*, 189.

112. *Being and Time*, 189.

113. *Being and Time*, 251, 266, 276–78.

114. *Being and Time*, 265. See also Alphonso Lingis, "The World as a Whole," *Research in Phenomenology* 25 (1995): 142–59.

115. *Being and Time*, 189.

116. *Being and Time*, 152.

117. Martin Heidegger, "On the Essence of Ground," in *Pathmarks*, ed. and trans. William McNeill (Cambridge: Cambridge University Press, 1998), 97.

118. *The Fundamental Concepts of Metaphysics*, 177.

119. *History of the Concept of Time*, 6.

120. *The Fundamental Concepts of Metaphysics*, 177.

121. *The Fundamental Concepts of Metaphysics*, 177.

122. "On the Essence of Ground," 121.

123. "On the Essence of Ground," 120.

124. *The Fundamental Concepts of Metaphysics*, 177.

125. "On the Essence of Ground," 110.

126. Martin Heidegger, *The Principle of Reason*, trans. Reginald Lilly (Bloomington: Indiana University Press, 1996).

127. "On the Essence of Ground," 102.

128. "On the Essence of Ground," 103.

129. "On the Essence of Ground," 110. Heidegger had already noted in *Being and Time* that "the world is transcendent" when it is grounded in the unified horizon of temporality (366).

130. "On the Essence of Ground," 110.

131. "On the Essence of Ground," 120.

132. "On the Essence of Ground," 111–12.

133. "On the Essence of Ground," 112–13. For a different account of Christianity and world see Jean-Yves Lacoste, *Experience and the Absolute: Disputed Questions on the Humanity of Man*, trans. Mark Raftery-Skehan (New York: Fordham University Press, 2004).

134. "On the Essence of Ground," 115.

135. *Being and Time*, 208.

136. *Phenomenological Interpretation of Kant's* Critique of Pure Reason, 14.

137. *Being and Time*, 203.

138. "On the Essence of Ground," 119.

139. "On the Essence of Ground," 116.

140. "On the Essence of Ground," 116–18.

141. "On the Essence of Ground," 118.

142. "On the Essence of Ground," 117.

143. "On the Essence of Ground," 118.

144. "On the Essence of Ground," 119.

145. "On the Essence of Ground," 119–20.

146. "On the Essence of Ground," 121.

147. "On the Essence of Ground," 119; Kant, *Anthropology*, 3.

148. "On the Essence of Ground," 122–23.

149. "On the Essence of Ground," 127.

150. "On the Essence of Ground," 123.

151. "On the Essence of Ground," 125.

152. "On the Essence of Ground," 125–26.

153. "On the Essence of Ground," 126.

154. "On the Essence of Ground," 126; Martin Heidegger, "Vom Wesen des Grundes," in *Wegmarken* (Frankfurt am Main: Victor Klostermann, 1976), 164.

155. "On the Essence of Ground," 127.

156. "On the Essence of Ground," 128.

157. "On the Essence of Ground," 128.

158. "On the Essence of Ground," 128–29.

159. "On the Essence of Ground," 129.

160. "On the Essence of Ground," 129.

161. "On the Essence of Ground," 129.

162. "On the Essence of Ground," 130.

163. "On the Essence of Ground," 130.

164. "On the Essence of Ground," 130, 132.

165. "On the Essence of Ground," 130.

166. Husserl, *Ideas* 1:181. See also "On the Essence of Ground," 131.

167. "On the Essence of Ground," 132.

168. "On the Essence of Ground," 134–35.

169. Jeff Malpas, *Heidegger's Topology: Being, Place, World* (Cambridge, MA: MIT Press, 2006), 164, 169–70, 185, 189.

170. Jacques Derrida, *The Animal That Therefore I Am*, ed. Marie-Louis Mallet, trans. David Wills (New York: Fordham University Press, 2008), 151.

171. *The Fundamental Concepts of Metaphysics*, 178.

172. *The Fundamental Concepts of Metaphysics*, 9.

173. *The Fundamental Concepts of Metaphysics*, 24. Heidegger discusses the relation between *Begriff* and *Inbegriff* in his later *Contributions to Philosophy (From Enowning)*, trans. Parvis Emad and Kenneth Maly (Bloomington: Indiana University Press,

1999), 44–45 (§ 27). See also Richard Polt, *The Emergency of Being: On Heidegger's Contributions to Philosophy* (Ithaca, NY: Cornell University Press, 2006), 115–28.

174. *The Fundamental Concepts of Metaphysics*, 3.

175. *The Fundamental Concepts of Metaphysics*, 24–25. See also Martin Heidegger, "On the Essence of Truth," in *Pathmarks*, ed. William McNeill, trans. John Sallis (Cambridge: Cambridge University Press, 1998), 136–54.

176. *The Fundamental Concepts of Metaphysics*, 5.

177. *The Fundamental Concepts of Metaphysics*, 5.

178. See also Jacques Derrida, "The Double Session," in *Dissemination*, trans. Barbara Johnson (Chicago: University of Chicago Press, 1981), 173–285.

179. *The Fundamental Concepts of Metaphysics*, 6.

180. *The Fundamental Concepts of Metaphysics*, 6.

181. *The Fundamental Concepts of Metaphysics*, 9.

182. *The Fundamental Concepts of Metaphysics*, 19.

183. *The Fundamental Concepts of Metaphysics*, 177. For an extensive overview of Heidegger's account of animals see William McNeill, "Life beyond the Organism: Animal Being in Heidegger's Freiburg Lectures, 1929–1930," in *Animal Others: On Ethics, Ontology, and Animal Life*, ed. H. Peter Steeves, foreword Tom Regan (Albany: State University of New York Press, 1999), 197–248. See also Brett Buchanan, *Onto-Ethologies: The Animal Environments of Uexküll, Heidegger, Merleau-Ponty* (Albany: State University of New York Press, 2008), 65–114; Matthew Calarco, *Zoographies: The Question of the Animal from Heidegger to Derrida* (New York: Columbia University Press, 2008), 15–54.

184. *The Fundamental Concepts of Metaphysics*, 35, 39.

185. *The Fundamental Concepts of Metaphysics*, 44.

186. *The Fundamental Concepts of Metaphysics*, 44–45.

187. *The Fundamental Concepts of Metaphysics*, 47.

188. *The Fundamental Concepts of Metaphysics*, 54–55.

189. *The Fundamental Concepts of Metaphysics*, 37–40.

190. *The Fundamental Concepts of Metaphysics*, 26.

191. *The Fundamental Concepts of Metaphysics*, 34.

192. *The Fundamental Concepts of Metaphysics*, 26–30.

193. *The Fundamental Concepts of Metaphysics*, 28.

194. *The Fundamental Concepts of Metaphysics*, 62.

195. *The Fundamental Concepts of Metaphysics*, 62.

196. *The Fundamental Concepts of Metaphysics*, 66, 63, 88–89.

197. *The Fundamental Concepts of Metaphysics*, 61.

198. *The Fundamental Concepts of Metaphysics*, 64.

199. *The Fundamental Concepts of Metaphysics*, 89.

200. *The Fundamental Concepts of Metaphysics*, 101, 105.

201. *The Fundamental Concepts of Metaphysics*, 128.

202. *The Fundamental Concepts of Metaphysics*, 137.

203. *The Fundamental Concepts of Metaphysics*, 138.

204. *The Fundamental Concepts of Metaphysics*, 140.

205. *The Fundamental Concepts of Metaphysics*, 139.

206. *The Fundamental Concepts of Metaphysics*, 143.

207. *The Fundamental Concepts of Metaphysics*, 143.

208. *The Fundamental Concepts of Metaphysics*, 147.

209. *The Fundamental Concepts of Metaphysics*, 147.

210. *The Fundamental Concepts of Metaphysics*, 147.

211. *The Fundamental Concepts of Metaphysics*, 147. See also *Being and Time*, 364–66.

212. *The Fundamental Concepts of Metaphysics*, 169.

213. *The Fundamental Concepts of Metaphysics*, 177.

214. *The Fundamental Concepts of Metaphysics*, 177.

215. *The Fundamental Concepts of Metaphysics*, 178.

216. *The Fundamental Concepts of Metaphysics*, 179.

217. *The Fundamental Concepts of Metaphysics*, 267.

218. *The Fundamental Concepts of Metaphysics*, 185, 186.

219. Hannah Arendt, "'What Remains? The Language Remains': A Conversation with Günter Gaus," in *The Portable Hannah Arendt*, ed. and intro. Peter Baehr (London: Penguin, 2000), 16–17. See also Hannah Arendt, *The Human Condition* (Chicago: University of Chicago Press, 1999).

220. *The Fundamental Concepts of Metaphysics*, 185–86, 193.

221. *The Fundamental Concepts of Metaphysics*, 187.

222. *The Fundamental Concepts of Metaphysics*, 180.

223. *The Fundamental Concepts of Metaphysics*, 186, 188.

224. *The Fundamental Concepts of Metaphysics*, 193.

225. *The Fundamental Concepts of Metaphysics*, 193.

226. *The Fundamental Concepts of Metaphysics*, 193.

227. *The Fundamental Concepts of Metaphysics*, 194.

228. *The Fundamental Concepts of Metaphysics*, 194.

229. *The Fundamental Concepts of Metaphysics*, 195.

230. *The Fundamental Concepts of Metaphysics*, 195.

231. *The Fundamental Concepts of Metaphysics*, 195.

232. *The Fundamental Concepts of Metaphysics*, 196.

233. *The Fundamental Concepts of Metaphysics*, 196.

234. *The Fundamental Concepts of Metaphysics*, 197.

235. *The Fundamental Concepts of Metaphysics*, 197–98.

236. *The Fundamental Concepts of Metaphysics*, 198–99.

237. *The Fundamental Concepts of Metaphysics*, 199.

238. *The Fundamental Concepts of Metaphysics*, 199.

239. *The Fundamental Concepts of Metaphysics*, 227–28.

240. *The Fundamental Concepts of Metaphysics*, 237–38.

241. *The Fundamental Concepts of Metaphysics*, 240.

242. *The Fundamental Concepts of Metaphysics*, 239.

243. Heidegger is of course also responding to the work of Uexküll. See Jakob von Uexküll, *A Foray into the World of Animals and Humans, with a Theory of Meaning*, trans. Joseph D. O'Neil (Minneapolis: Minnesota University Press, 2010).

244. *The Fundamental Concepts of Metaphysics*, 241–42.

245. *The Fundamental Concepts of Metaphysics*, 247.

246. *The Fundamental Concepts of Metaphysics*, 243.

247. *The Fundamental Concepts of Metaphysics*, 247.

248. *The Fundamental Concepts of Metaphysics*, 268–69.

249. *The Fundamental Concepts of Metaphysics*, 269.

250. *The Fundamental Concepts of Metaphysics*, 271, 273.

251. *The Fundamental Concepts of Metaphysics*, 253.

252. *The Fundamental Concepts of Metaphysics*, 255.

253. *The Fundamental Concepts of Metaphysics*, 260.

254. *The Fundamental Concepts of Metaphysics*, 264.

255. *The Fundamental Concepts of Metaphysics*, 269.

256. *The Fundamental Concepts of Metaphysics*, 270.

257. *The Fundamental Concepts of Metaphysics*, 274.

258. *The Fundamental Concepts of Metaphysics*, 280, 284.

259. *The Fundamental Concepts of Metaphysics*, 288. For Heidegger, the logical assertion a *is* b or a *as* b as true or false is already a *metaphysical* statement or a manifestation of the relation between truth and being (290).

260. *The Fundamental Concepts of Metaphysics*, 309–10.

261. *The Fundamental Concepts of Metaphysics*, 312, 314, 322.

262. *The Fundamental Concepts of Metaphysics*, 316; Aristotle, *On Interpretation*, trans. H. P. Cooke (Cambridge, MA: Harvard University Press, 2002), 16 a 13.

263. *The Fundamental Concepts of Metaphysics*, 367–69. See also Martin Heidegger and Eugen Fink, *Heraclitus Seminar*, trans. Charles H. Seibert (Evanston, IL: Northwestern University Press, 1993). See chapter 5 of this book for a discussion of Fink's work.

264. *The Fundamental Concepts of Metaphysics*, 306–7.

265. *The Fundamental Concepts of Metaphysics*, 323.

266. *The Fundamental Concepts of Metaphysics*, 344.

267. *The Fundamental Concepts of Metaphysics*, 32.

268. *The Fundamental Concepts of Metaphysics*, 351, 355.

269. Martin Heidegger, "Letter on 'Humanism,'" in *Pathmarks*, ed. William McNeill, trans. Frank A. Capuzzi (Cambridge: Cambridge University Press, 1998), 266.

270. *The Fundamental Concepts of Metaphysics*, 361–62.

271. *The Fundamental Concepts of Metaphysics*, 334–35, 341–43, 350.

272. *The Fundamental Concepts of Metaphysics*, 347, 366.

273. *The Fundamental Concepts of Metaphysics*, 347.

274. *The Fundamental Concepts of Metaphysics*, 356.

275. *The Fundamental Concepts of Metaphysics*, 357.

276. *Introduction to Metaphysics*, 4, 20.

277. *Introduction to Metaphysics*, 40.

278. *Introduction to Metaphysics*, 41, 44.

279. *Introduction to Metaphysics*, 47. See also Jacques Derrida, *Of Spirit: Heidegger and the Question*, trans. Geoffrey Bennington and Rachel Bowlby (Chicago: University of Chicago Press, 1989); Philippe Lacoue-Labarthe, *Heidegger, Art and Politics: The Fiction of the Political*, trans. Chris Turner (Oxford: Blackwell, 1990).

280. *Introduction to Metaphysics*, 48.

281. *Introduction to Metaphysics*, 52.

282. One can also already note the relatively minor role given to world in the account of fundamental ontology in 1929 at the end of *Kant and the Problem of Metaphysics*.

283. Martin Heidegger, "The Origin of the Work of Art," in *Off the Beaten Track*, ed. and trans. Julian Young and Kenneth Haynes (Cambridge: Cambridge University Press, 2002), 37, 43.

284. "The Origin of the Work of Art," 26–27.

285. "The Origin of the Work of Art," 24, 26. See also 32.

286. Hans-Georg Gadamer, "Being Spirit God," in *Heidegger's Ways*, trans. John W. Stanley, intro. Dennis J. Schmidt (Albany: State University of New York Press, 1994), 190; Michel Haar, *The Song of the Earth: Heidegger and the Grounds of the History of Being*, trans. Reginald Lilly (Bloomington: Indiana University Press, 1993). See also Luce Irigaray, *The Forgetting of the Air in Martin Heidegger*, trans. Mary Beth Mader (Austin: University of Texas Press, 1999).

287. See Husserl, *Cartesian Meditations*, 48; Martin Heidegger, *Aristotle's Metaphysics Θ 1–3: On the Essence and Actuality of Force*, trans. Walter Brogan and Peter Warnek (Bloomington: Indiana University Press, 1995). On Husserl and Heidegger see Pierre Keller, *Husserl and Heidegger on Human Experience* (Cambridge: Cambridge University Press, 1999); Lilian Alweiss, *The World Unclaimed: A Challenge to Heidegger's Critique of Husserl* (Athens: Ohio University Press, 2003); Søren Overgaard, *Husserl and Heidegger on Being in the World* (Dordrecht: Kluwer, 2004).

# Chapter 5. Derrida and the End of the World

1. Everett Fox, ed. and trans., *The Five Books of Moses* (London: Harvill, 1995), *Genesis* 6:4; Harold Fisch, ed. and trans., *The Holy Scriptures* (Jerusalem: Koren, 1992), *Bereshit* 6:4.

2. *The Five Books of Moses*, *Bereshit* 1:1.

3. *Phenomenology of Spirit*, § 32.

4. Eugen Fink, "The Phenomenological Philosophy of Edmund Husserl and Contemporary Criticism," in *The Phenomenology of Husserl: Selected Critical Readings*, ed. and trans. R. O. Elveton (Chicago: Quadrangle, 1970), 95–100; Ronald Bruzina, *Edmund Husserl and Eugen Fink: Beginnings and Ends in Phenomenology, 1928–1938* (New Haven, CT: Yale University Press, 2004), 174–223, 370–71, 442–43; Joshua Kates, *Essential History: Jacques Derrida and the Development of Deconstruction* (Evanston, IL: Northwestern University Press, 2005), 107–11.

5. Jacques Derrida, *The Work of Mourning*, trans. Pascale-Anne Brault and Michael Naas (Chicago: University of Chicago Press, 2001), 115.

6. Jacques Derrida, *The Problem of Genesis in Husserl's Philosophy*, trans. Marian Hobson (Chicago: University of Chicago Press, 2003), 71.

7. *The Problem of Genesis*, 72.

8. *Ideas* 1:102–3.

9. *Ideas* 1:104.

10. *Ideas* 1:110.

11. *Ideas* 1:112. See Jacques Derrida, "Rams: Uninterrupted Dialogue—Between Two Infinities, the Poem," in *Sovereignties in Question: The Poetics of Paul Celan*, ed. Thomas Dutoit and Outi Pasanen (New York: Fordham University Press, 2005), 160; Derrida, *Edmund Husserl's* Origin of Geometry, 95–96; *The Problem of Genesis*, 79.

12. Jacques Derrida, "Différance," in *Margins of Philosophy*, trans. Alan Bass (Chicago: University of Chicago Press, 1982), 8.

13. Derrida, *Voice and Phenomenon*, 74–75.

14. *Voice and Phenomenon*, 14. See also 11–12, 29, 67, 70.

15. Jacques Derrida, "The Pit and the Pyramid: Introduction to Hegel's Semiology," in *Margins of Philosophy*, trans. Alan Bass (Chicago: University of Chicago Press, 1982), 71; Hegel, *The Science of Logic*, 647. Note that I am not following Miller's translation which is used in the English translation of Derrida's essay. See also Jacques Derrida, *Of Grammatology*, trans. Gayatri Chakravorty Spivak (Baltimore, MD: Johns Hopkins University Press, 1976), 3–73.

16. *Ideas* 2:181.

17. *Phenomenology of Spirit* §312–18.

18. *Phenomenology of Spirit* §508.

19. *Phenomenology of Spirit* §65, 666.

20. "The Pit and the Pyramid," 87 n. 15. Derrida cites G. W. F. Hegel, *Philosophische Propädeutik*, in *Sämtliche Werke*, vol. 3, ed. Hermann Glockner (Stuttgart: Frommans, 1949), 210.

21. "The Pit and the Pyramid," 73.

22. *Voice and Phenomenon*, 12.

23. *Voice and Phenomenon*, 26; "The Pit and the Pyramid," 73.

24. *Voice and Phenomenon*, 27–28. See also 45.

25. *Voice and Phenomenon*, 29, 34.

26. *Voice and Phenomenon*, 65.

27. *Voice and Phenomenon*, 68.

28. *Voice and Phenomenon*, 6.

29. See Jacques Derrida, *The Beast and the Sovereign*, vol. 2, ed. Michel Lisse, Marie-Louise Mallet and Ginette Michaud, trans. Geoffrey Bennington (Chicago: University of Chicago Press, 2011), 266.

30. Husserl, *Ideas* 1:109. See also Jacques Derrida, "No Apocalypse, Not Now: Full Speed Ahead, Seven Missiles, Seven Missives," in *Psyche: Inventions of the Other*, vol.

1, ed. Peggy Kamuf and Elizabeth Rottenberg (Stanford, CA: Stanford University Press, 2007), 387–419.

31. *Edmund Husserl's* Origin of Geometry, 25–26.

32. *Edmund Husserl's* Origin of Geometry, 82–83.

33. *Edmund Husserl's* Origin of Geometry, 92.

34. *Edmund Husserl's* Origin of Geometry, 94. See also Paola Marrati, *Genesis and Trace: Derrida Reading Husserl and Heidegger*, trans. Simon Sparks (Stanford, CA: Stanford University Press, 2005), 47.

35. *Edmund Husserl's* Origin of Geometry, 94–95, 96.

36. *Edmund Husserl's* Origin of Geometry, 94.

37. "Rams," 141.

38. "Rams," 140.

39. Jacques Derrida, *Chaque fois unique, la fin du monde*, ed. Pascale-Anne Brault and Michael Naas (Paris: Galilée, 2003), 9. My translation. An earlier, shorter version of this collection was published as Jacques Derrida, *The Work of Mourning*, trans. Pascale-Anne Brault and Michael Naas (Chicago: University of Chicago Press, 2001).

40. *Chaque fois unique*, 9.

41. *The Work of Mourning*, 95.

42. Jacques Derrida, *Aporias: Dying—Awaiting (One Another at) the "Limits of Truth,"* trans. Thomas Dutoit (Stanford, CA: Stanford University Press, 1993), 75.

43. "Rams," 140.

44. Jacques Derrida, "The University without Condition," in *Without Alibi*, trans. Peggy Kamuf (Stanford, CA: Stanford University Press, 2002), 211.

45. See *Of Grammatology*, 46–48, 61–65, 70–73.

46. Jacques Derrida, "Cogito and the History of Madness," in *Writing and Difference*, trans. Alan Bass (Chicago: University of Chicago Press, 1978), 56.

47. "Rams," 160.

48. *Chaque fois unique*, 11.

49. "Rams," 153, 158.

50. "Rams," 160.

51. "Rams," 158.

52. "Cogito and the History of Madness," 57.

53. Hayim Nahman Bialik and Yehoshua Hana Ravnitzky, *The Book of Legends—Sefer Ha-Aggadah: Legends from the Talmud and Midrash*, trans. William G. Braude (New York: Schocken, 1992), 682, par. 385.

54. "Rams," 160–63. See also Derrida, *Of Spirit*, 48–57; Heidegger, "The Origin of the Work of Art," 23.

55. Jacques Derrida, *Glas*, trans. John P. Leavey Jr. and Richard Rand (Lincoln: University of Nebraska Press, 1986), 47a, 76a–79a.

56. Jacques Derrida, "Violence and Metaphysics: An Essay on the Thought of Emmanuel Lévinas," in *Writing and Difference*, trans. Alan Bass (Chicago: University of Chicago Press, 1978), 124, 125. See 103–7, 131.

57. "Rams," 161. Husserl, *Cartesian Meditations*, 89–151.

58. Ricoeur, *Husserl: An Analysis of His Phenomenology*, 72.

59. Derrida devoted a still as yet unpublished seminar to the fifth *Cartesian Media-tions* in 1962–1963. See www.derridaseminars.org.

60. Jacques Derrida, *On Touching—Jean-Luc Nancy*, trans. Christine Irizarry (Stanford, CA: Stanford University Press, 2005), 3.

61. Merleau-Ponty, *The Visible and the Invisible*, 143. See Derrida's highly critical reading of Merleau-Ponty in *On Touching*, 186–215. See also Ricoeur, *Husserl: An Analysis of His Phenomenology*, 61–62.

62. *On Touching—Jean-Luc Nancy*, 41.

63. *On Touching—Jean-Luc Nancy*, 306.

64. *Edmund Husserl's* Origin of Geometry, 138–41.

65. See *The Problem of Genesis; Of Grammatology; Voice and Phenomenon*.

66. *On Touching—Jean-Luc Nancy*, 306.

67. Jacques Derrida and Jean-Luc Marion, "On the Gift: A Discussion between Jacques Derrida and Jean-Luc Marion. Moderated by Richard Kearney," in *God, the Gift, and Postmodernism*, ed. John D. Caputo and Michael J. Scanlon (Bloomington: Indiana University Press, 1999), 71, 75–76.

68. "Rams," 161.

69. Derrida and Marion, "On the Gift," 75–76.

70. Jacques Derrida, "Before the Law," in *Acts of Literature*, ed. Derek Attridge, trans. Avital Ronell and Christine Roulston (London: Routledge, 1992), 190.

71. There are also more general references to the "as if" in *Of Grammatology*, 199, 267.

72. *Critique of Pure Reason*, A 685/ B 713.

73. *Critique of Pure Reason*, A 680/ B 708.

74. Jacques Derrida, "Provocation: Forewords," in *Without Alibi*, trans. Peggy Ka-muf (Stanford, CA: Stanford University Press, 2002), xxxiv.

75. "The University without Condition," 224.

76. Jean-Luc Nancy, *The Creation of the World or Globalization*, trans. and intro. François Raffoul and David Pettigrew (Albany: State University of New York Press, 2007), 27–28. Derrida obliquely discusses Nancy's use of world and his emphasis on *le sens du monde* in *On Touching—Jean-Luc Nancy*, 27–29, 52–59. I have briefly al-luded to this in "Derrida and the End of the World," *New Literary History* 42, no. 3 (2011): 512–14.

77. "The University without Condition," 203.

78. "The University without Condition," 203.

79. "The University without Condition," 203.

80. "The University without Condition," 207.

81. "The University without Condition," 204.

82. "The University without Condition," 203, 206, 236. See also Jacques Derrida, *Who's Afraid of Philosophy: Right to Philosophy*, vol. 1, trans. Jan Plug et al. (Stanford,

CA: Stanford University Press, 2002); *Eyes of the University: Right to Philosophy*, vol. 2, trans. Jan Plug et al. (Stanford, CA: Stanford University Press, 2005).

83. "The University without Condition," 209.

84. "The University without Condition," 233–34.

85. "The 'World' of the Enlightenment to Come," 144. See also Claude Romano, *Event and World*, trans. Shane Mackinlay (New York: Fordham University Press, 2009).

86. "The University without Condition," 211.

87. "The University without Condition," 211.

88. *Critique of the Power of Judgement*, 185; "The University without Condition," 213.

89. "The University without Condition," 235.

90. "The University without Condition," 231–32.

91. "The University without Condition," 235.

92. "The University without Condition," 223.

93. "The University without Condition," 223–24.

94. "The University without Condition," 224.

95. "The University without Condition," 226.

96. "The University without Condition," 224.

97. "The University without Condition," 224–25. Jacques Derrida, "Faith and Knowledge: The Two Sources of 'Religion' at the Limits of Reason Alone," in *Acts of Religion*, ed. and intro. Gil Anidjar, trans. Samuel Weber (London: Routledge, 2002), 40–101. See also Michael Naas, *Miracle and Machine: Jacques Derrida and the Two Sources of Religion, Science, and the Media* (New York: Fordham University Press, 2012).

98. F. W. J. Schelling, *The Grounding of Positive Philosophy: The Berlin Lectures*, trans. and intro. Bruce Matthews (Albany: State University of New York Press, 2007), 123–24, 147. See also Hans Vaihinger, *The Philosophy of "As If": A System of the Theoretical, Practical and Religious Fictions of Mankind*, trans. Charles Kay Ogden (London: Routledge, 2000 [1911]). On Samuel Taylor Coleridge's reaction to Kant, Rei Terada has noted, "Kant unwittingly encourages fantasies of aberrant perception that might escape his strictures and hence his recommended path to world-acceptance." Rei Terada, *Looking Away: Phenomenality and Dissatisfaction, Kant to Adorno* (Cambridge, MA: Harvard University Press, 2009), 6. On the virtual worlds of the Romantic period, see Peter Otto's important work *Multiplying Worlds: Romanticism, Modernity and the Emergence of Virtual Reality* (Oxford: Oxford University Press, 2011).

99. "The University without Condition," 224.

100. "The 'World' of the Enlightenment to Come," 119.

101. "The 'World' of the Enlightenment to Come," 133.

102. "The 'World' of the Enlightenment to Come," 120–21.

103. "The 'World' of the Enlightenment to Come," 121.

104. "The 'World' of the Enlightenment to Come," 155.

105. "The 'World' of the Enlightenment to Come," 155.

106. Gasché, *Europe, or the Infinite Task*, 313–14.

107. *Europe, or the Infinite Task*, 316, 321. See also Derrida, "The University without Condition," 227.

108. Jacques Derrida, "The Reason of the Strongest," in *Rogues: Two Essays on Reason*, trans. Pascale-Anne Brault and Michael Naas (Stanford, CA: Stanford University Press, 2005), 18.

109. See also Derrida's comments on the Kantian regulative world in "The Reason of the Strongest," 85–86.

110. On Derrida's reading of Hegel see Stuart Barnett, ed., *Hegel after Derrida* (London: Routledge, 1998).

111. *Glas*, 37a.

112. *Glas*, 39a.

113. *Glas*, 43a.

114. *Glas*, 44a; Jacques Derrida, *Glas* (Paris: Galilée, 1995 [1974]), 54a.

115. "The 'World' of the Enlightenment to Come," 123.

116. "The 'World' of the Enlightenment to Come," 123.

117. Immanuel Kant, "On a Recently Prominent Tone of Superiority in Philosophy," in *Theoretical Philosophy after 1781*, ed. and trans. Henry Allison (Cambridge: Cambridge University Press, 2002), 425–46. See also Peter Fenves, *Raising the Tone of Philosophy: Late Essays by Immanuel Kant, Transformative Critique by Jacques Derrida* (Baltimore, MD: Johns Hopkins University Press, 1998).

118. Jacques Derrida, "Of an Apocalyptic Tone Recently Adopted in Philosophy," *Oxford Literary Review* 6, no. 2 (1984): 14.

119. "Of an Apocalyptic Tone," 24, 28. See also Jacques Derrida, "The Law of Genre," in *Parages*, ed. John P. Leavey Jr., trans. Avital Ronell (Stanford, CA: Stanford University Press, 2011), 217–50.

120. *Critique of Pure Reason*, A 673/B 701.

121. "The 'World' of the Enlightenment to Come," 125–27.

122. "The 'World' of the Enlightenment to Come," 130. Husserl, *The Crisis of European Sciences*, 299.

123. "The 'World' of the Enlightenment to Come," 134.

124. "The 'World' of the Enlightenment to Come," 137–38.

125. "The 'World' of the Enlightenment to Come," 143.

126. "The 'World' of the Enlightenment to Come," 144.

127. "The 'World' of the Enlightenment to Come," 144.

128. Jacques Derrida, "Tympan," in *Margins of Philosophy*, trans. Alan Bass (Chicago: University of Chicago Press, 1982), x.

129. Jacques Derrida, *The Truth in Painting*, trans. Geoffrey Bennington and Ian McLeod (Chicago: University of Chicago Press, 1987); Jacques Derrida, "Economimesis," trans. Richard Klein, *Diacritics* 11 (1981): 3–25; Jacques Derrida, "Mochlos, or the Conflict of the Faculties," in *Eyes of the University: Right to Philosophy*, vol. 2, trans. Richard Rand and Amy Wygant (Stanford, CA: Stanford University Press, 2004), 83–112.

130. Jacques Derrida, "Cartouches," in *The Truth in Painting*, trans. Geoffrey Bennington and Ian McLeod (Chicago: University of Chicago Press, 1987), 210.

131. *Physics*, 209a 31–209b 1.

132. It is a question here of *the same time*. Aristotle adds a second and third clause to his example: "You are now in the world, because you are in the air and the air is in the world; and you are in the air because you are on the earth; and by the same token you are on the earth because you are in this particular place, which contains nothing more than you." I am in the world and therefore in the air but I am *also* on the earth and therefore in the air. One could take this as a simple addition of a "here" to support the "now" of the first clause: I am here and now, *hic et nunc*. But it does seem that the middle term, the air—despite Irigaray's reading of air as an alternative to Heidegger's earth—is a possibility of finding myself both in world (a shared place) and on earth (a particular place). If there is a difference between the place that can share an "in" and an "on" in the *same place*, it appears to be a difference between the many and the one that *finds* itself "in the air." At the very least, Aristotle's example also suggests that you cannot simply find yourself "in this particular place, which contains nothing more than you" in the world: you must also be "on the earth."

133. Derrida, "Différance," 8; *Of Grammatology*, 145.

134. Jacques Derrida, *Dissemination*, trans. Barbara Johnson (Chicago: University of Chicago Press, 1981), 213, 257, 311. See also Jacques Derrida, *Limited Inc.*, ed. Gerald Graff, trans. Samuel Weber and Alan Bass (Evanston, IL: Northwestern University Press, 1988); Jacques Derrida, "Typewriter Ribbon: Limited Ink (2)," in *Without Alibi*, ed. and trans. Peggy Kamuf (Stanford, CA: Stanford University Press, 2002), 71–160; "The 'World' of the Enlightenment to Come," 135, 143–44, 148, 152–53.

135. Heidegger, *Introduction to Metaphysics*, 69–70.

136. Jacques Derrida, "Plato's Pharmacy," in *Dissemination*, trans. Barbara Johnson (Chicago: University of Chicago Press, 1981), 159–60. See also Jacques Derrida, "Khōra," in *On the Name*, ed. Thomas Dutoit, trans. Ian McLeod (Stanford, CA: Stanford University Press, 1995), 89–127. For a wider discussion of place, see Edward S. Casey, *The Fate of Place: A Philosophical History* (Berkeley: University of California Press, 1998); and Malpas, *Heidegger's Topology*.

137. *Physics*, 209b 22–28.

138. *Physics*, 209b 28.

139. *Physics*, 211b 10.

140. *On Touching—Jean-Luc Nancy*, 295–96. It is perhaps not surprising that in *Being and Time* Heidegger makes "something like a 'world'" the *possibility* of touching. He writes, "An entity present-at-hand within the world can be touched by another entity only if by its very nature the latter entity has Being-in as its own kind of Being—only if, with its Being-there [Da-sein], something like the world is already revealed to it, so that from out of that world another entity can manifest itself in touching, and thus become accessible in its Being-present-at-hand" (H 55). He goes on to observe, "When two entities are present-at-hand within the world, and furthermore are *worldless* in themselves, they can never "touch" each other, nor can either of

them '*be*' '*alongside*' the other" (H 55). Without world, there is no touching or being touched, no limit or container between the tangible and the intangible.

141. See, for example, Stengers's definition of cosmos as that which registers the "unknown" and "corresponds to no condition," Isabelle Stengers, *Cosmopolitics II*, trans. Robert Bononno (Minneapolis: Minnesota University Press, 2011), 356.

142. "The 'World' of the Enlightenment to Come," 150.

143. "The 'World' of the Enlightenment to Come," 150.

144. "The 'World' of the Enlightenment to Come," 150.

145. See *Edmund Husserl's* Origin of Geometry.

146. *The Problem of Genesis*, 105, 110. See also Edmund Husserl, *Experience and Judgement*, trans. Ludwig Landgrebe (Evanston, IL: Northwestern University Press, 1973).

147. *The Problem of Genesis*, 110.

148. *The Problem of Genesis*, 110. See also Patrick O'Connor, *Derrida: Profanations* (London: Continuum, 2010), 12–36.

149. *The Problem of Genesis*, 110–11.

150. *The Problem of Genesis*, 111–12.

151. *Of Grammatology*, 7–8.

152. *Voice and Phenomenon*, 12.

153. *Of Grammatology*, 67.

154. *Of Grammatology*, 20.

155. *Of Grammatology*, 50; *De la grammatologie* (Paris: Minuit, 1967), 73.

156. *Of Grammatology*, 65, 47.

157. Jacques Derrida, "Structure, Sign and Play in the Discourse of the Human Sciences," in *Writing and Difference*, trans. Alan Bass (Chicago: University of Chicago Press, 1978), 292.

158. Friedrich Nietzsche, *On the Genealogy of Morality*, ed. Keith Ansell-Pearson, trans. Carol Diethe (Cambridge: Cambridge University Press, 2007), 5, 58, 159; Friedrich Nietzsche, *Beyond Good and Evil*, ed. Rolf-Peter Horstmann and Judith Norman (Cambridge: Cambridge University Press, 2002), 7, 85; *The Gay Science*, 131, 201, 204, 249.

159. Gilles Deleuze, *Nietzsche and Philosophy*, trans. Hugh Tomlinson (London: Continuum, 2006), 139.

160. Friedrich Nietzsche, *The Pre-Platonic Philosophers*, ed. and trans. Greg Whitlock (Champaign: University of Illinois Press, 2000), 70–74. See Friedrich Nietzsche, *The Birth of Tragedy and Other Writings*, ed. Raymond Geuss and Ronald Speirs (Cambridge: Cambridge University Press, 1999), 114; *Writings from the Late Notebooks*, ed. Rüdiger Bittner, trans. Kate Sturge (Cambridge: Cambridge University Press, 2003), 38; *Ecce Homo*, in *Basic Writings of Nietzsche*, ed. and trans. Walter Kaufmann (New York: Modern Library, 1968), 729; *On the Genealogy of Morality*, 58. See also Deleuze, *Nietzsche and Philosophy*, 22–23.

161. *The Pre-Platonic Philosophers*, 62.

162. *The Pre-Platonic Philosophers*, 63–64.

163. *The Pre-Platonic Philosophers*, 65–66.

164. *The Pre-Platonic Philosophers*, 71–72.

165. Sarah Kofman, "Nietzsche et l'obscurité d'Héraclite," in *Séductions: De Sartre à Héraclite* (Paris: Galilée, 1990), 91–92, 115.

166. Heraclitus, *Early Greek Philosophy*, ed. and trans. Jonathan Barnes (London: Penguin, 1987), 102. See also Jacques Derrida, "The Theatre of Cruelty and the Closure of Representation," in *Writing and Difference*, trans. Alan Bass (Chicago: University of Chicago Press, 1978), 250, 333 n. 21.

167. *The Pre-Platonic Philosophers*, 70.

168. Friedrich Nietzsche, *Twilight of the Idols*, in *The Anti-Christ, Ecce Homo, Twilight of the Idols, and Other Writings*, ed. Aaron Ridley, trans. Judith Norman (Cambridge: Cambridge University Press, 2005), 171.

169. *Of Grammatology*, 326 n. 14.

170. Eugen Fink, *Nietzsche's Philosophy*, trans. Goetz Richter (London: Continuum, 2003), 172. See also 22–24, 32–35, 62–70, 83–87.

171. Eugen Fink, *Spiel als Weltsymbol* (Stuttgart: W. Kohlhammer, 1960), 18, 23, 29. My translation. See also Stuart Elden, "Eugen Fink and the Question of the World," *Parrhesia* 5 (2008): 48–59.

172. *Spiels als Weltsymbol*, 29, 40, 41.

173. *The Beast and the Sovereign*, 2:278. See also Heidegger, *Introduction to Metaphysics*, 64–66.

174. Heidegger, *The Principle of Reason*, 112–13.

175. Jacques Derrida, *The Ear of the Other*, ed. Christie McDonald, trans. Peggy Kamuf (Lincoln: University of Nebraska Press, 1988), 69. See also Derrida, *Edmund Husserl's Origin of Geometry*, 42 n. 3; Lawlor, *Derrida and Husserl*, 21–22, 28, 226.

176. Ricoeur, *Husserl: An Analysis of His Phenomenology*, 26.

177. *The Ear of the Other*, 6. See Fink, *Spiel als Weltsymbol*, 240–42. Fink uses the subtitle "Die Welt als Spiel ohne Spieler" for these final pages.

178. Jacques Derrida, *The Beast and the Sovereign*, vol. 1, ed. Michel Lisse, Marie-Louise Mallet and Ginette Michaud, trans. Geoffrey Bennington (Chicago: University of Chicago Press, 2009), 334. See also *Of Grammatology*, 163.

179. *Of Spirit*, 52. See also Jacques Derrida, "Heidegger's Ear: Philopolemology (*Geschlecht IV*)," in *Reading Heidegger: Commemorations*, ed. John Sallis, trans. John Leavey Jr. (Bloomington: Indiana University Press, 1992), 187.

180. *Of Spirit*, 54.

181. See www.derridaseminars.org.

182. Jacques Derrida, *Heidegger: La question de l'Être et l'histoire, séminaire de 1964–65 de Jacques Derrida*, edited by Thomas Dutoit (Paris: Galilée, 2013). See also Derrida's interview with Dominique Janicaud, in Dominique Janicaud and Jacques Derrida, "Jacques Derrida," in *Heidegger en France*, 2 vols. (Paris: Hachette, 2005), 2:96.

183. *Being and Time*, 13.

184. See Jacques Derrida, "Heidegger's Hand (*Geschlecht II*)," in *Psyche: Inventions of the Other*, vol. 2, trans. John P. Leavey Jr. and Elizabeth Rottenberg, ed. Peggy Kamuf and Elizabeth Rottenberg (Stanford, CA: Stanford University Press, 2008), 300–301, n. 6.

185. *Of Spirit*, 47.

186. *Of Spirit*, 48–49.

187. *Of Spirit*, 50.

188. *The Animal That Therefore I Am*, 80.

189. *The Animal That Therefore I Am*, 158.

190. *The Animal That Therefore I Am*, 154.

191. *The Beast and the Sovereign*, 2:10, 113–18, 263. See also Michel Henry, *I Am the Truth: Toward a Philosophy of Christianity*, trans. Susan Emanuel (Stanford, CA: Stanford University Press, 2003). As Kevin Hart has pointed out, one can also challenge Husserl's link between "life" and "world" in a reading of phenomenology and Christianity. See Kevin Hart, "'Without World': Eschatology in Michel Henry," in *Phenomenology and Eschatology: Not Yet in the Now*, ed. Neal DeRoo and John Panteleimon Manoussakis (Farnham, UK: Ashgate, 2009), 171, 176, 177.

192. Jacques Derrida, "To Speculate—On 'Freud,'" in *The Post Card: From Socrates to Freud and Beyond*, trans. Alan Bass (Chicago: University of Chicago Press, 1987), 257–409.

193. *Voice and Phenomenon*, 5–6. See also *The Beast and the Sovereign*, 2:124 n. 19.

194. *Voice and Phenomenon*, 9, 12–13.

195. *Aporias*, 35–37.

196. *The Beast and the Sovereign*, 2:115.

197. *Aporias*, 44.

198. "Cogito and the History of Madness," 307 n. 22. See also Derrida's comments on Hegel and the "as such" in "The Pit and the Pyramid," 76.

199. "The University without Condition," 234.

200. *The Beast and the Sovereign*, 2:116–17. As Heidegger observes in *Being and Time*, "The way the Present is rooted in the future and in having been, is the existential-temporal condition for the possibility that what has been projected in circumspective understanding can be brought closer in a making-present, and in such a way that the Present can thus conform itself to what is encountered within the horizon of awaiting and retaining; this means that it must interpret itself in the schema of the as-structure" (360).

201. *The Beast and the Sovereign*, 2:219.

202. *The Animal That Therefore I Am*, 156, 154.

203. *The Animal That Therefore I Am*, 151.

204. *The Animal That Therefore I Am*, 155.

205. *The Animal That Therefore I Am*, 155–56.

206. *The Animal That Therefore I Am*, 156–57, 159.

207. *The Animal That Therefore I Am*, 160.

208. *Of Spirit*, 12.

209. *The Animal That Therefore I Am*, 54.

210. *The Animal That Therefore I Am*, 79. See also Gary Steiner, *Anthropocentrism and Its Discontents: The Moral Status of Animals in the History of Western Philosophy* (Pittsburgh, PA: Pittsburgh University Press, 2005); Leonard Lawlor, *There Is Not*

*Sufficient: An Essay on Animality and Human Nature in Derrida* (New York: Columbia University Press, 2007); Calarco, *Zoographies: The Question of the Animal from Heidegger to Derrida*; Anne-Emmanuelle Berger and Marta Segara, *Demenagaries: Thinking (of) Animals after Derrida* (Amsterdam: Rodopi, 2011).

211. *The Beast and the Sovereign*, 2:263. See also David Farrell Krell, *Derrida and Our Animal Others: Derrida's Final Seminar*, The Beast and the Sovereign (Bloomington: Indiana University Press, 2013).

212. *The Beast and the Sovereign*, 2:264.

213. "Violence and Metaphysics," 152. See also 147, 317 n. 68.

214. *The Beast and the Sovereign*, 2:264.

215. *The Beast and the Sovereign*, 2:264–65. See also *The Animal That Therefore I Am*, 104.

216. *The Beast and the Sovereign*, 2:265.

217. *The Beast and the Sovereign*, 2:265.

218. *The Beast and the Sovereign*, 2:266.

219. *The Beast and the Sovereign*, 2:266.

220. *The Beast and the Sovereign*, 2:266. See also J. Hillis Miller, "'Don't Count Me In': Derrida's Refraining," in *For Derrida* (New York: Fordham University Press, 2009), 174–90.

221. *The Beast and the Sovereign*, 2:267.

222. *The Beast and the Sovereign*, 2:267–68. See also 2:269–75.

223. *The Beast and the Sovereign*, 2:267.

## Chapter 6. World, Fiction and Earth

1. Maurice Blanchot, "Le règne animal de l'esprit," *Critique* 18 (1947): 387–405; "La littérature et le droit à la mort," *Critique* 20 (1948): 30–47.

2. *Phenomenology of Spirit*, § 397; *Phänomenologie des Geistes*, 285.

3. Maurice Blanchot, "La littérature et le droit à la mort," in *La part du feu* (Paris: Gallimard, 1949), 305–45. For general accounts of Blanchot's essay, see Christopher Fynsk, *Language and Relation . . . That There Is Language* (Stanford, CA: Stanford University Press, 1996); Simon Critchley, *Very Little—Almost Nothing: Death*, 2nd ed. (London: Routledge, 2004).

4. Maurice Blanchot, "Literature and the Right to Death," in *The Work of Fire*, trans. Lydia Davis (Stanford, CA: Stanford University Press, 1995), 302; "Le règne animal de l'esprit," 389 n. 1; "La littérature et le droit à la mort," 307 n. 1.

5. Andrzej Warminski, *Readings in Interpretation: Hölderlin, Hegel, Heidegger* (Minneapolis: University of Minnesota Press, 1987), 183–95.

6. "Literature and the Right to Death," 303; "La littérature et le droit à la mort," 307.

7. "Literature and the Right to Death," 302; "La littérature et le droit à la mort," 307.

8. See Georges Bataille, "Lettre à X., chargé d'un cours sur Hegel [6 décembre 1937]," in *Oeuvres complètes* (Paris: Gallimard, 1973), 5:564.

9. Leslie Hill, *Blanchot, Extreme Contemporary* (London: Routledge, 1997), 103–6, 245 n. 3.

10. Judith Butler, *Subjects of Desire: Hegelian Reflections in Twentieth-Century France*, 2nd ed. (New York: Columbia University Press, 1999), xi.

11. *Subjects of Desire*, 21.

12. Alexandre Kojève, *Introduction à la lecture de Hegel: Leçons sur la Phénoménologie de l'esprit professes de 1933 à 1939 à l'École des Hautes Études réunies et publiées par Raymond Queneau* (Paris: Gallimard, 1968 [1947]), 41. The 1969 English translation of Kojève's work by Allan Bloom, *Introduction to the Reading of Hegel*, only translates some 260 pages of the near 600 pages of Kojève's original text. Where only the French text is cited, as in this case, the translations are my own.

13. *Introduction to the Reading of Hegel*, 14.

14. *Introduction to the Reading of Hegel*, 23.

15. *Introduction to the Reading of Hegel*, 26.

16. *Introduction to the Reading of Hegel*, 274; *Introduction à la lecture de Hegel*, 586.

17. *Introduction to the Reading of Hegel*, 273–74; *Introduction à la lecture de Hegel*, 586.

18. *Introduction à la lecture de Hegel*, 91.

19. *Introduction to the Reading of Hegel*, 11.

20. G. W. F. Hegel, *La phénoménologie de l'esprit*, trans. Jean Hyppolite (Paris: Aubier, 1939), 324–43.

21. *La phénoménologie de l'esprit*: 1:324–43.

22. *Phenomenology of Spirit*, §708–10. See also § 713, 729–33.

23. "Literature and the Right to Death," 302; "La littérature et le droit à la mort," 307 n. 1.

24. *La phénoménologie de l'esprit*, 1:325. My translation (as in all further cited references to this work).

25. *La phénoménologie de l'esprit*: 1:325.

26. *La phénoménologie de l'esprit*: 1:326.

27. *La phénoménologie de l'esprit*: 1:326; *Phänomenologie des Geistes*, 287.

28. Jacques Derrida, "The Ends of Man," in *Margins of Philosophy*, trans. Alan Bass (Chicago: University of Chicago Press, 1982), 117.

29. Hyppolite, *Genesis and Structure of Hegel's* Phenomenology of Spirit, 225.

30. *La phénoménologie de l'esprit*, 1:324.

31. Bréhier is described as a "neo-Kantian opponent of Hegel" and relegated to a single footnote in Bruce Baugh, *French Hegel: From Surrealism to Post-Modernism* (London: Routledge, 2003), 183 n. 26. See also Michael S. Roth, *Knowing and History: Appropriations of Hegel in Twentieth-Century France* (Ithaca, NY: Cornell University Press, 1988).

32. Émile Bréhier, *The History of Philosophy*, vol. 6, *The Nineteenth Century: Period of Systems 1800–1850*, trans. Wade Baskin (Chicago: University of Chicago Press, 1968), 166; *Histoire de la philosophie*, ed. Lucien Jerphagnon and Pierre-Maxime

Schuhl (Paris: Presses Universitaires de France, 2004), 1374. I have modified the translation. Baskin omits the phrase "tous les spécialistes" in "tous les spécialistes, professeurs ou artistes qui donnent arbitrairement à leur tâche une valeur absolue."

33. Michael Forster argues contrary to this reading that Hegel is primarily engaging with Herder in *Der geistige Tierreich*. Michael N. Forster, *Hegel's Idea of a Phenomenology of Spirit* (Chicago: University of Chicago Press, 1998), 332–48. See also Gary Shapiro, "Notes on the Animal Kingdom of Spirit," in *The* Phenomenology of Spirit *Reader: Critical and Interpretative Essays*, ed. Jon Stewart (Albany: State University of New York Press, 1998), 225–42; Jon Stewart, *The Unity of Hegel's* Phenomenology of Spirit (Evanston, IL: Northwestern University Press, 2000), 269–77.

34. See also Allen Speight, *Hegel, Literature and the Problem of Agency* (Cambridge: Cambridge University Press, 2001), 20–31.

35. *Genesis and Structure*, 275.

36. *Phenomenology of Spirit*, §360.

37. *Phenomenology of Spirit*, §808.

38. *Genesis and Structure*, 286.

39. *Subjects of Desire*, 23.

40. *Genesis and Structure*, 282–83, 286.

41. *Genesis and Structure*, 280–81.

42. *Genesis and Structure*, 296.

43. *Genesis and Structure*, 306.

44. *Genesis and Structure*, 299.

45. *Genesis and Structure*, 300.

46. Jacques Derrida, "Punctuations: The Time of a Thesis," in *Eyes of the University: Right to Philosophy*, vol. 2, trans. Kathleen McLaughlin (Stanford, CA: Stanford University Press, 2004), 115–16.

47. "Literature and the Right to Death," 300. See also "La littérature et le droit à la mort," 305. The French text from the 1947 article reads,

On peut assurément écrire sans se demander pourquoi l'on écrit. Un écrivain, qui regarde sa plume tracer des lettres, a-t-il même le droit de la suspendre et lui dire: arrête-toi! Que sais-tu sur toi-même? En vue de quoi avances-tu? Pourquoi ne vois-tu pas que ton encre ne laisse pas de traces, que tu vas librement de l'avant, mais dans le vide, que si tu ne rencontres pas d'obstacle, c'est que tu n'as jamais quitté ton point de départ? Et pourtant tu écris: tu écris sans relâche, me découvrant ce que je te dicte et me révélant ce que je sais: les autres, en lisant, t'enrichissent de ce qu'ils te prennent et te donnent ce que tu leur apprends. Maintenant, ce que tu n'as pas fait, tu l'as fait; ce que tu n'as pas écrit est écrit: tu es condamnée à l'ineffaçable ("Le règne animal de l'esprit," 387).

48. *The Fundamental Concepts of Metaphysics*, 220.

49. *The Fundamental Concepts of Metaphysics*, 220–21.

50. See also Jacques Derrida, "Lyotard et *nous*," in *Chaque fois unique, la fin du monde*, edited by Pascale-Anne Brault et Michael Naas (Paris: Galilée, 2003), 259–89.

51. See also Jacques Derrida, *Given Time: 1. Counterfeit Money*, trans. Peggy Kamuf (Chicago: University of Chicago Press, 1992).

52. Blanchot was aware of the equivocal nature of this opening paragraph because he makes a few minor changes to it in the revised version published in 1949. In the 1947 text the writer addresses the pen: "Lui dire: arrête-toi! Que sais-tu sur toi-même? En vue de quoi avances-tu?" In the 1949 text, the capitalisation has been altered: "Lui dire: Arrête-toi! que sais-tu sur toi-même? en vue de quoi avances-tu?" The small revision makes this strange apostrophe a bit clearer and suggests that we should read each of these questions as one voice rather than a series of different voices asking each question. In her English translation, Lydia Davis takes this need for an unequivocal address much further: she places the entire apostrophe from *arrête-toi* until the end of the paragraph in double quotation marks.

53. "Literature and the Right to Death," 308.

54. "Literature and the Right to Death," 300–301. Whether Blanchot's target in this 1947 essay was indeed Sartre and *What Is Literature?* one of its themes is the question of the relation between the writer, the literary work and the social and political or *actual* world. Blanchot compares the argument that *all* literature must be a "literature of action," the position that Sartre advocated, to the revolutionary fervour during the Reign of Terror in 1793–94 (317). Such conditions arise when the writer is no longer content simply to construct an unreal or fictional totality founded on a "global negation." For Blanchot, contrary to Sartre's call for all writers to be politically engaged in both their works and their own lives, this "global negation" in fact "ruins action" *in* the actual world, since it claims an ideal and delusive freedom to imagine "the world as a whole." The writer dreams of a total realised negation of everything in reality, of a permanent idealisation of world that ends in a wholesale negation of self-agency and an unavoidable encounter with the impossibility of death, even of a revolutionary death (315–16, 318, 320–21). For Blanchot, the writer's unique relation to fictional worlds cannot simply be transposed to political action in the real world. See also Maurice Blanchot, *The Space of Literature*, trans. Ann Smock (Lincoln: University of Nebraska Press, 1982).

55. "Literature and the Right to Death," 302.

56. *Phenomenology of Spirit* § 136–37.

57. "Literature and the Right to Death," 302.

58. "Literature and the Right to Death," 302; "La littérature et le droit à la mort," 307. Davis translates *cet empire* as "this vast power."

59. "Literature and the Right to Death," 302.

60. Maurice Blanchot, "The 'Sacred' Speech of Hölderlin," in *The Work of Fire*, trans. Charlotte Mandell (Stanford, CA: Stanford University, 1995), 111–31.

61. Plato, *Republic*, 607b.

62. Paul Ricoeur, "World of the Text, World of the Reader," in *A Ricoeur Reader: Reflection and the Imagination*, ed. Mario J. Valdes (London: Harvester Wheatsheaf, 1991), 492.

63. Paul Ricoeur, "Writing as a Problem for Literary Criticism and Philosophical Hermeneutics," in *A Ricoeur Reader: Reflection and the Imagination*, ed. Mario J. Valdes (London: Harvester Wheatsheaf, 1991), 331; Paul Ricoeur, *Time and Narrative*, vol. 3, trans. Kathleen Blamey and David Pellauer (Chicago: University of Chicago Press, 1988), 157–79.

64. Mikel Dufrenne, *The Phenomenology of Aesthetic Experience*, trans. Edward S. Casey (Evanston, IL: Northwestern University Press, 1973), 198.

65. Blanchot, "Literature and the Right to Death," 330, 341; "La littérature et le droit à la mort," 332.

66. "Literature and the Right to Death," 343. See also Maurice Blanchot, "The Disappearance of Literature," in *The Book to Come*, trans. Charlotte Mandell (Stanford, CA: Stanford University Press, 2003), 195–201.

67. "Literature and the Right to Death," 322. See also Rodolphe Gasché, *Of Minimal Things: Studies on the Notion of Relation* (Stanford, CA: Stanford University Press, 1999).

68. Kevin Hart, *The Dark Gaze: Maurice Blanchot and the Sacred* (Chicago: University of Chicago Press, 2004), 86–87, 111–17.

69. Derrida, *The Beast and the Sovereign*, 2:179–81. See also Derrida, "The University without Condition," 234.

70. "Literature and the Right to Death," 344.

71. "Literature and the Right to Death," 300. Anne-Lise Schulte Nordholt touches on the question of world in *Maurice Blanchot: L'écriture comme expérience du dehors* (Genève: Droz, 1995), 113–15. She equates *le monde* in Blanchot's work with a cultural construct that is exposed to the radical alterity of the outside.

72. "Literature and the Right to Death," 328.

73. "Literature and the Right to Death," 330.

74. "Literature and the Right to Death," 333.

75. "Literature and the Right to Death," 336.

76. Heidegger, *Introduction to Metaphysics*, 4, 20, 52.

77. "Literature and the Right to Death," 328.

78. "Literature and the Right to Death," 330.

79. "Literature and the Right to Death," 333. See Derrida's reading of the Kantian "as if" in "The University without Condition."

80. "Literature and the Right to Death," 340.

81. "Literature and the Right to Death," 322.

82. "Literature and the Right to Death," 334. Blanchot refers to Lévinas. See Emmanuel Lévinas, *Existence and Existents*, trans. A. Lingis (Dordrecht: Kluwer, 1988), 52–64.

83. "Literature and the Right to Death," 338.

84. "Literature and the Right to Death," 338.

85. "Literature and the Right to Death," 338.

86. "Literature and the Right to Death," 335.

87. "Literature and the Right to Death," 339.

88. "Literature and the Right to Death," 341, 308.

89. "Literature and the Right to Death," 341.

90. "Literature and the Right to Death," 341–42.

91. See Emmanuel Lévinas, "On Maurice Blanchot," in *Proper Names*, trans. Michael B. Smith (Stanford, CA: Stanford University Press, 2000), 129, 137.

92. Blanchot, "The Disappearance of Literature," 200. See also Maurice Blanchot, *The Infinite Conversation*, trans. Susan Hanson (Minneapolis: Minnesota University Press, 1993), 167–70.

93. "Literature and the Right to Death," 339.

94. "Literature and the Right to Death," 344.

95. Will Steffen, Paul J. Crutzen and John R. McNeill, "The Anthropocene: Are Humans Now Overwhelming the Great Forces of Nature?" *Ambio* 38 (2007): 614. See Timothy Clark, *Martin Heidegger*, 2nd ed. (London: Routledge, 2011), 166. There was a special issue of the *Oxford Literary Review*, "Deconstruction, Environmentalism and Climate Change," *Oxford Literary Review* 32, no. 1 (2010), edited by Timothy Clark; and there is a recent issue of the *Review*, also edited by Clark, "Deconstruction in the Anthropocene," *Oxford Literary Review* 34, no. 2 (2012). See also the special issue "Limits of the Human," *Angelaki* 16, no. 4 (2011), edited by Debjani Ganguly and Fiona Jenkins.

96. David Wood, "Spectres of Derrida: On the Way to Econstruction," in *Ecospirit: Religions and Philosophies for the Earth*, ed. Laurel Kearns and Catherine Keller (New York: Fordham University Press, 2007), 266; Timothy Clark, "Some Climate Change Ironies: Deconstruction, Environmental Politics and the Closure of Ecocriticism," *Oxford Literary Review* 32, no. 1 (2010): 134–35.

97. David Wood, "On Being Haunted by the Future," *Research in Phenomenology* 36, no. 1 (2006): 287; Timothy Clark, "Climate and Catastrophe: A Lost Opening?" in *Reading Derrida's* Of Grammatology, ed. Sean Gaston and Ian Maclachlan (London: Continuum, 2011), 167.

98. Tom Cohen, "The Geomorphic Fold: Anapocalyptics, Changing Climes and 'Late' Deconstruction," *Oxford Literary Review* 32, no. 1 (2010): 73. This is a response to Derrida's list of the ten "plagues" of the so-called new world order in the *Specters of Marx: The State of the Debt, the Work of Mourning, and the New International*, trans. Peggy Kamuf (London: Routledge, 1994), 81, 86.

99. Clark, "Some Climate Change Ironies," 132, 134.

100. Cohen, "The Geomorphic Fold," 75; Tom Cohen, "Anecographics: Climate Change and 'Late' Deconstruction," in *Impasses of the Post-Global: Theory in the Era of Climate Change*, vol. 2, ed. Henry Sussman (Ann Arbor, MI: Open Humanities Press, 2012), 33.

101. Cohen, "Anecographics," 33. See also 46, 54 n. 14.

102. "Violence and Metaphysics," 152. See also Lévinas, *Totality and Infinity*, 218.

103. Jacques Derrida, "Some Statements and Truisms about Neologisms, Newisms, Postisms, Parasitisms, and Other Small Seismisms," in *The States of "Theory"*:

*History, Art and Critical Discourse*, ed. and intro. David Carroll, trans. Anne Tomiche (New York: Columbia University Press, 1990), 63–94. See also Jacques Derrida, "Envois," in *The Post Card: From Socrates to Freud and Beyond*, trans. Alan Bass (Chicago: University of Chicago Press, 1987), 67; "Envoi," in *Psyche: Inventions of the Other*, vol. 1, ed. Peggy Kamuf and Elizabeth Rottenberg, trans. Peter Caws and Mary Ann Caws (Stanford, CA: Stanford University Press, 2007), 127; *Specters of Marx*, 22, 49; "The 'World' of the Enlightenment to Come," 122.

104. See Jacques Derrida and Elisabeth Roudinesco, *For What Tomorrow . . . Dialogue*, trans. Jeff Fort (Stanford, CA: Stanford University Press, 2004), 152.

105. *Critique of Pure Reason*, A 416–17, 505–6, 510/B 444–45, 533–34, 538.

106. Derrida, "Cartouches," 210.

107. Clark, "Some Climate Change Ironies," 146. See also Timothy Clark, "Derangements of Scale," in *Telemorphosis: Theory in the Era of Climate Change*, vol. 1, ed. Tom Cohen (Ann Arbor, MI: Open Humanities Press, 2012), 148–66.

108. Derrida, *The Beast and the Sovereign*, 2:280–90. See also Heidegger, *Introduction to Metaphysics*, 159–68.

109. Derrida, *Edmund Husserl's* Origin of Geometry, 83–85; Edmund Husserl, "Foundational Investigations of the Phenomenological Origin of the Spatiality of Nature: The Originary Ark, Earth, Does Not Move," in Maurice Merleau-Ponty, *Husserl at the Limits of Phenomenology*, ed. Leonard Lawlor and Bettina Bergo (Evanston, IL: Northwestern University Press, 2002), 117–31.

110. Husserl, "Foundational Investigations," 122, 123.

111. Derrida, *Edmund Husserl's* Origin of Geometry, 85. See also Derrida, *On Touching—Jean-Luc Nancy*, 357 n. 8.

112. See Timothy Clark, *Poetics of Singularity: The Counter-Culturalist Turn in Heidegger, Derrida and Blanchot and the Later Gadamer* (Edinburgh: Edinburgh University Press, 2005); *Martin Heidegger*, 2nd ed.; David Wood, *The Deconstruction of Time* (Evanston, IL: Northwestern University Press, 2001); *Thinking after Heidegger* (Cambridge: Polity, 2002).

113. Jacques Derrida, "Restitutions of the Truth in Pointing," in *The Truth in Painting*, trans. Geoffrey Bennington and Ian McLeod (Chicago: University of Chicago Press, 1987), 285, 311–12, 345–46, 354.

114. Christopher Johnson, *System and Writing in the Philosophy of Jacques Derrida* (Cambridge: Cambridge University Press, 1993), 24–25; Jacques Derrida, "Force and Signification," in *Writing and Difference*, trans. Alan Bass (Chicago: University of Chicago Press, 1978), n. 23, 303–4.

115. "Restitutions of the Truth in Pointing," 352–56. See Heidegger, "The Origin of the Work of Art," 14–15.

116. Stephen Mulhall, *On Being in the World: Wittgenstein and Heidegger on Seeing Aspects* (London: Routledge, 1990), 170–71. See Haar, *The Song of the Earth*, 14, 60. See also Michael E. Zimmerman, *Heidegger's Confrontation with Modernity: Technology, Politics and Art* (Bloomington: Indiana University Press, 1990); Michael E. Zimmerman, *Contesting Earth's Future: Radical Ecology and Postmodernity*

(Berkeley: University of California Press, 1994); Bruce V. Foltz, *Inhabiting the Earth: Heidegger, Environmental Ethics and the Metaphysics of Nature* (Atlantic Highlands, NJ: Humanities Press, 1995); Charles S. Brown and Ted Toadvine, eds., *Eco-Phenomenology: Back to the Earth Itself* (Albany: State University of New York Press, 2003); Kate Rigby, "Earth, World, Text: On the (Im)possibility of Ecopoiesis," *New Literary History* 35, no. 3 (2004): 427–42; Ladelle McWhorter and Gail Stenstad, eds., *Heidegger and the Earth: Essays in Environmental Philosophy*, 2nd ed. (Toronto: University of Toronto Press, 2009).

117. Gadamer, "Being Spirit God," 190; Irigaray, *The Forgetting of the Air in Martin Heidegger*, 2.

118. "The Origin of the Work of Art," 40. For a good general account of Heidegger's essay see Julian Young, *Heidegger's Philosophy of Art* (Cambridge: Cambridge University Press, 2001).

119. Gadamer, "Being Spirit God," 190.

120. John Sallis, foreword to *The Song of the Earth: Heidegger and the Grounds of the History of Being*, by Michel Haar, trans. Reginald Lilly (Bloomington: Indiana University Press, 1993), xiii.

121. "The Origin of the Work of Art," 4, 11.

122. "The Origin of the Work of Art," 6.

123. Derrida, "Restitutions of the Truth in Pointing," 341–42, 345.

124. "The Origin of the Work of Art," 16.

125. "The Origin of the Work of Art," 42.

126. "The Origin of the Work of Art," 13; Martin Heidegger, "Der Ursprung des Kunstwerkes," in *Holzwege* (Frankfurt am Main: Victor Klostermann, 1976), 18.

127. "The Origin of the Work of Art," 46. See also Heidegger, "Letter on 'Humanism,'" 248–49.

128. "The Origin of the Work of Art," 46.

129. "The Origin of the Work of Art," 14.

130. "The Origin of the Work of Art," 26, 33.

131. "The Origin of the Work of Art," 20, 21; "Der Ursprung des Kunstwerkes," 28.

132. Derrida, "Heidegger's Ear," 187.

133. "The Origin of the Work of Art," 21.

134. "The Origin of the Work of Art," 26, 27.

135. Haar, *The Song of the Earth*, 60, 14.

136. As he observes in his later lecture "The Thing" (1950), "Causes and grounds remain unsuitable for the world's worlding." Martin Heidegger, "The Thing," in *Poetry, Language, Thought*, trans. Albert Hofstadter (New York: Harper & Row, 1975), 180. In other words, the world as a whole cannot be understood from the perspective of what is *in* the world and treated merely as a represented object among others that is given to a subject. At the same time, the jar that he speaks about in this paper, which is filled with wine and accounts for the thing that both gathers and gives, is an "earthen jug out of the earth" that can "stand on the earth" (167). World and the

play of the world are also now constituted by a gathering and unity of "the fourfold": the earth, the sky, divinities and mortals (178–80).

137. "The Origin of the Work of Art," 21, 23.

138. "The Origin of the Work of Art," 21.

139. "The Origin of the Work of Art," 20.

140. "The Origin of the Work of Art," 24.

141. "The Origin of the Work of Art," 24.

142. "The Origin of the Work of Art," 24–25.

143. "The Origin of the Work of Art," 37.

144. "The Origin of the Work of Art," 20.

145. Aristotle, *Metaphysics*, 1018b 33–35.

146. "The Origin of the Work of Art," 54.

147. Aristotle, *Physics*, 209a 31–209b 1. As we recall, Aristotle writes, "For instance, you are now in the world, because you are in the air and the air is in the world; and you are in the air because you are on the earth; and by the same token you are on the earth because you are in this particular place, which contains nothing more than you." In *The Principle of Reason* Heidegger retains, like Aristotle before him, the strange but seemingly self-evident distinction between *in* the world and *on* the earth: he writes of "our stay in this world [*in der Welt*], our sojourn on earth [*über die Erde*]." Heidegger, *The Principle of Reason*, 11; *Der Satz vom Grund* (Frankfurt am Main: Victor Klostermann, 1997), 16.

148. "The Origin of the Work of Art," 39; my emphasis.

149. Martin Heidegger, *Identity and Difference*, trans. Joan Stambaugh (Chicago: University of Chicago Press, 2002), 63.

150. Jacques Derrida and Maurizio Ferraris, "*Istrice 2: Ick bünn all hier*," in *Points . . .: Interviews, 1974–1994*, ed. Elisabeth Weber, trans. Peggy Kamuf (Stanford, CA: Stanford University Press, 1995), 325; "*Istrice 2: Ick bünn all hier*," in *Points de suspension: Entretiens*, ed. Elisabeth Weber (Paris: Galilée, 1992), 335.

151. *Specters of Marx*, 93.

152. See also the account of "geophilosophy" in Gilles Deleuze and Félix Guattari, *What Is Philosophy?* trans. Graham Burchell and Hugh Tomlinson (London: Verso, 1994), 85–113.

153. Paul Ricoeur, *Time and Narrative*, vol. 1, trans. David Pallauer (Chicago: University of Chicago Press, 1984), 103.

154. See also Peter Burke, *The French Historical Revolution: The Annales School 1929–1989* (Stanford, CA: Stanford University Press, 1990).

155. It is worth noting that in quite a different context Derrida asks, in "The 'World' of the Enlightenment to Come," "Is reason (*logos* or *ratio*) first of all a Mediterranean thing?" (119).

156. Fernand Braudel, *The Mediterranean and the Mediterranean World in the Age of Phillip II*, trans. Siân Reynolds, 2 vols. (Berkeley: University of California Press, 1995), 1:17.

157. *The Mediterranean and the Mediterranean World*, 1:21.

158. *The Mediterranean and the Mediterranean World*, 1:20.

159. *The Mediterranean and the Mediterranean World*, 1:21.

160. *The Mediterranean and the Mediterranean World*, 1:23. See also Fernand Braudel, "History and the Social Sciences: The *Longue Durée*," in *On History* (Chicago: University of Chicago Press, 1980), 31.

161. "The Origin of the Work of Art," 14.

162. Ricoeur, *Time and Narrative*, vol. 1, 104–5. See also Braudel, "History and the Social Sciences," 45.

163. Derrida, *The Animal That Therefore I Am*, 24. I have attempted to address the question of Derrida and speeds in *Derrida and Disinterest*, 92–108.

164. "Violence and Metaphysics," 117. See also *The Animal That Therefore I Am*, 105.

165. Clark, "Some Climate Change Ironies," 132. See also Clark, "Derangements of Scale."

166. Tom Cohen, "Anecographics," 32. See also 41–43.

167. Arnaldo Momigliano, "Pagan and Christian Historiography in the Fourth Century," in *Essays in Ancient and Modern Historiography*, foreword Anthony Grafton (Chicago: University of Chicago Press, 2012 [1977]), 107–26.

168. Clark, "Climate and Catastrophe," 165–66.

169. Wood, "Spectres of Derrida," 266. See also Clark, "Some Climate Change Ironies," 134.

170. Hans-Georg Gadamer, *Truth and Method*, translated by W. Glen-Doepel, Joel Weinscheimer and Donald G. Marshall, 2nd ed. (London: Continuum, 2004), 8–11.

171. See Jacques Derrida, "A 'Madness' Must Watch Over Thinking," in *Points . . .: Interviews, 1974–1994*, ed. Elisabeth Weber, trans. Peggy Kamuf (Stanford, CA: Stanford University Press, 1995), 347–49.

172. Sean Gaston, "In the Middle," *Parrhesia* 6 (2009): 62–72. This first attempt to think of "the midst as the uncontained" was later revised by recasting the relation between self and world as "a fragment *of* the cacophony." Sean Gaston, "A Fragment of the Cacophony: Leibniz, Nietzsche and Blanchot," *Inky Needles*, January 6, 2013, http://inkyneedles.com. I'd like to thank Samuel Stolton for the opportunity to publish in this new journal dedicated to "Philosophy, Poetry and Politics."

173. On the fiction of Tlön, see Jorge Luis Borges, "Tlön, Uqbar, Orbis Tertius," in *Labyrinths*, ed. Donald A. Yates and James E. Irby, trans. James E. Irby (London: Penguin, 1981), 27–43.

174. Lévinas, *Existence and Existents*, 52–64.

175. *Existence and Existents*, 21.

176. *Existence and Existents*, 47–48.

177. *Existence and Existents*, 21.

178. *Existence and Existents*, 39, 42–45, 46–50. See Thomas Carl Wall, *Radical Passivity: Lévinas, Blanchot, and Agamben* (Albany: State University of New York Press, 1999).

179. Jean-Luc Nancy, *Hegel: The Restlessness of the Negative*, trans. Jason Smith and Steven Miller (Minneapolis: University of Minnesota Press, 2002), 4–6.

180. Nancy, *The Sense of the World*, 4.

181. *The Sense of the World*, 2–3, 7–8.

182. Jean-Luc Nancy, *Corpus*, trans. Richard Rand (New York: Fordham University Press, 2008), 27, 31, 39–41, 49. See also Nancy, *The Creation of the World or Globalization*, 43–44.

183. *Corpus*, 107, 109. See Ian James, *The Fragmentary Demand: An Introduction to the Philosophy of Jean-Luc Nancy* (Stanford, CA: Stanford University Press, 2006), 65–113.

184. *The Fragmentary Demand*, 219.

185. *Corpus*, 103, 105; *The Sense of the World*, 18.

186. See Christina Lafont, *Heidegger, Language, and World-Disclosure*, trans. Graham Harmon (Cambridge: Cambridge University Press, 2000). Lafont calls this "the world-disclosing function of language" and warns against the idealization of a deterministic language that constitutes the world and the subject in the world. See also Francis Wolff, *Dire le monde* (Paris: Presses Universitaires de France, 2004 [1997]). Wolff argues that "le langage fait du réel *un monde*."

187. Geoffrey Bennington, "The Limits of My Language," in *Not Half No End: Militantly Melancholic Essays in the Memory of Jacques Derrida* (Edinburgh: Edinburgh University Press, 2010), 86–99.

188. Blanchot, *The Infinite Conversation*, 167. He writes, "Le langage qui n'a pas le monde à dire," *L'entretien infini* (Paris: Gallimard, 1969), 250.

189. Ludwig Wittgenstein, *Philosophical Investigations*, trans. G. E. M. Anscombe, 3rd ed. (Oxford: Blackwell, 1967), 34 (1:71). I would like to thank Don Gunner here for first introducing me to Wittgenstein in 1987 at Ormond College, University of Melbourne.

190. *Philosophical Investigations*, 44 (1:96–97), 109 (1:342).

191. *Philosophical Investigations*, 32 (1:67).

# Bibliography

Allison, Henry E. *Kant's Transcendental Idealism: An Interpretation and Defense*. Rev. ed. New Haven, CT: Yale University Press, 2004.

Alweiss, Lilian. *The World Unclaimed: A Challenge to Heidegger's Critique of Husserl*. Athens: Ohio University Press, 2003.

Arendt, Hannah. *The Human Condition*. Chicago: University of Chicago Press, 1999.

———. "'What Remains? The Language Remains': A Conversation with Günter Gaus." In *The Portable Hannah Arendt*. Edited and with an introduction by Peter Baehr, 3–22. London: Penguin, 2000.

Aristotle. *Categories and De Interpretatione*. Edited and translated by J. L. Ackrill. Oxford: Oxford University Press, 1963.

———. *Metaphysics*. Translated by Hugh Tredennick. Cambridge, MA: Harvard University Press, 1975.

———. *The Metaphysics*. Translated and with an introduction by Hugh Lawson-Tancred. London: Penguin, 2004.

———. *On Interpretation*. Translated by H. P. Cooke. Cambridge, MA: Harvard University Press, 2002.

———. *The Physics*. Translated by Philip H. Wicksteed and Francis M. Cornford. 2 vols. London: Heinemann, 1929.

———. *Physics*. Translated by Robin Waterfield. Introduction by David Bostock. Oxford: Oxford University Press, 1996.

Badiou, Alain. *The Logic of Worlds: Being and Event II*. Translated by Alberto Toscano. London: Continuum, 2009.

Barnett, Stuart, ed. *Hegel after Derrida*. London: Routledge, 1998.

Bataille, Georges. "Lettre à X., chargé d'un cours sur Hegel (6 décembre 1937)." In *Oeuvres complètes*. Vol. 5, 563–71. Paris: Gallimard, 1973.

Baugh, Bruce. *French Hegel: From Surrealism to Post-Modernism*. London: Routledge, 2003.

Baumgarten, Alexander Gottlieb. *Metaphysick*. Translated by Georg Friedrich Meier. Edited by Johann August Eberhard. Jena: Dietrich Scheglmann Reprints, 2004 [1783].

Baur, Michael. "From Kant's Highest Good to Hegel's Absolute Knowing." In *A Companion to Hegel*. Edited by Stephen Houlgate and Michael Baur, 452–74. Oxford: Wiley-Blackwell, 2011.

Beck, Lewis White. *Early German Philosophy: Kant and His Predecessors*. Cambridge: Belknap, 1969.

Bennington, Geoffrey. *Frontiers: Kant, Hegel, Wittgenstein*. E-book, 2003.

———. "The Limits of My Language." In *Not Half No End: Militantly Melancholic Essays in the Memory of Jacques Derrida*, 86–99. Edinburgh: Edinburgh University Press, 2010.

Berger, Anne-Emmanuelle, and Marta Segara. *Demenagaries: Thinking (of ) Animals after Derrida*. Amsterdam: Rodopi, 2011.

Bialik, Hayim Nahman, and Yehoshua Hana Ravnitzky. *The Book of Legends—Sefer Ha-Aggadah: Legends from the Talmud and Midrash*. Translated by William G. Braude. New York: Schocken, 1992.

Blake, William. "The Book of Urizen." In *The Complete Poetry and Prose of William Blake*. Edited by David V. Erdman. Commentary by Harold Bloom. Rev. ed., 70–83. New York: Anchor Books, 1988.

Blanchot, Maurice. "The Conquest of Space." In *Maurice Blanchot: Political Writings, 1953–1993*. Translated and with an introduction by Zakir Paul. Foreword by Kevin Hart, 70–72. New York: Fordham University Press, 2010.

———. "The Disappearance of Literature." In *The Book to Come*. Translated by Charlotte Mandell, 195–201. Stanford, CA: Stanford University Press, 2003.

———. *The Infinite Conversation*. Translated by Susan Hanson. Minneapolis: Minnesota University Press, 1993.

———. "La littérature et le droit à la mort." *Critique* 20 (1948): 30–47.

———. "La littérature et le droit à la mort." In *La part du feu*, 305–45. Paris: Gallimard, 1949.

———. *L'entretien infini*. Paris: Gallimard, 1969.

———. "Le règne animal de l'esprit." *Critique* 18 (1947): 387–405.

———. "Literature and the Right to Death." In *The Work of Fire*. Translated by Lydia Davis, 300–344. Stanford, CA: Stanford University Press, 1995.

———. "The 'Sacred' Speech of Hölderlin." In *The Work of Fire*. Translated by Charlotte Mandell, 111–31. Stanford, CA: Stanford University Press, 1995.

———. *The Space of Literature*. Translated by Ann Smock. Lincoln: University of Nebraska Press, 1982.

Borges, Jorge Luis. "Tlön, Uqbar, Orbis Tertius." In *Labyrinths*. Edited by Donald A. Yates and James E. Irby. Translated by James E. Irby, 27–43. London: Penguin, 1981.

Braudel, Fernand. "History and the Social Sciences: The *Longue Durée*." In *On History*, 25–54. Chicago: University of Chicago Press, 1980.

———. *The Mediterranean and the Mediterranean World in the Age of Phillip II*. Translated by Siân Reynolds. 2 vols. Berkeley: University of California Press, 1995.

Bréhier, Émile. *Histoire de la philosophie*. Edited by Lucien Jerphagnon and Pierre-Maxime Schuhl. Paris: Presses Universitaires de France, 2004.

———. *The Nineteenth Century, Period of Systems 1800–1850*. Vol. 6, *The History of Philosophy*. Translated by Wade Baskin. Chicago: University of Chicago Press, 1968.

Brown, Charles S., and Ted Toadvine, eds. *Eco-Phenomenology: Back to the Earth Itself*. Albany: State University of New York Press, 2003.

Bruzina, Ronald. *Edmund Husserl and Eugen Fink: Beginnings and Ends in Phenomenology, 1928–1938*. New Haven, CT: Yale University Press, 2004.

Buchanan, Brett. *Onto-Ethologies: The Animal Environments of Uexküll, Heidegger, Merleau-Ponty*. Albany: State University of New York Press, 2008.

Burke, Peter. *The French Historical Revolution: The Annales School 1929–1989*. Stanford, CA: Stanford University Press, 1990.

Butler, Judith. *Subjects of Desire: Hegelian Reflections in Twentieth-Century France*. 2nd ed. New York: Columbia University Press, 1999.

Calarco, Matthew. *Zoographies: The Question of the Animal from Heidegger to Derrida*. New York: Columbia University Press, 2008.

Casey, Edward S. *The Fate of Place: A Philosophical History*. Berkeley: University of California Press, 1998.

Clark, David L. "Kant's Aliens: The *Anthropology* and Its Others." *New Centennial Review* 1, no. 2 (2001): 201–89.

Clark, Timothy. "Climate and Catastrophe: A Lost Opening?" In *Reading Derrida's Of Grammatology*. Edited by Sean Gaston and Ian Maclachlan, 161–68. London: Continuum, 2011.

———, ed. "Deconstruction, Environmentalism and Climate Change." *Oxford Literary Review* 32, no. 1 (2010).

———, ed. "Deconstruction in the Anthropocene." *Oxford Literary Review* 34, no. 2 (2012).

———. "Derangements of Scale." In *Telemorphosis: Theory in the Era of Climate Change*, vol. 1. Edited by Tom Cohen, 148–66. Ann Arbor, MI: Open Humanities Press, 2012.

———. *Martin Heidegger*. 2nd ed. London: Routledge, 2011.

———. *Poetics of Singularity: The Counter-Culturalist Turn in Heidegger, Derrida and Blanchot and the Later Gadamer*. Edinburgh: Edinburgh University Press, 2005.

———. "Some Climate Change Ironies: Deconstruction, Environmental Politics and the Closure of Ecocriticism." *Oxford Literary Review* 32, no. 1 (2010): 131–49.

Cohen, Tom. "Anecographics: Climate Change and 'Late' Deconstruction." In *Impasses of the Post-Global: Theory in the Era of Climate Change*, vol. 2. Edited by Henry Sussman, 32–57. Ann Arbor, MI: Open Humanities Press, 2012.

——. "The Geomorphic Fold: Anapocalyptics, Changing Climes and 'Late' Deconstruction." *Oxford Literary Review* 32, no. 1 (2010): 71–89.

Critchley, Simon. *Very Little—Almost Nothing: Death*. 2nd ed. London: Routledge, 2004.

Deleuze, Gilles. *Kant's Critical Philosophy: The Doctrine of the Faculties*. Translated by Hugh Tomlinson and Barbara Habberjam. London: Athlone, 1995.

——. *The Logic of Sense*. Edited by Constantin V. Boundas. Translated by Mark Lester and Charles Stivale. New York: Continuum, 2004.

——. *Nietzsche and Philosophy*. Translated by Hugh Tomlinson. London: Continuum, 2006.

Deleuze, Gilles, and Félix Guattari. *What Is Philosophy?* Translated by Graham Burchell and Hugh Tomlinson. London: Verso, 1994.

Derrida, Jacques. *The Animal That Therefore I Am*. Edited by Marie-Louis Mallet. Translated by David Wills. New York: Fordham University Press, 2008.

——. *Aporias: Dying—Awaiting (One Another at) the "Limits of Truth."* Translated by Thomas Dutoit. Stanford, CA: Stanford University Press, 1993.

——. *The Beast and the Sovereign*, vol. 1. Edited by Michel Lisse, Marie-Louise Mallet and Ginette Michaud. Translated by Geoffrey Bennington. Chicago: University of Chicago Press, 2009.

——. *The Beast and the Sovereign*, vol. 2. Edited by Michel Lisse, Marie-Louise Mallet and Ginette Michaud. Translated by Geoffrey Bennington. Chicago: University of Chicago Press, 2011.

——. "Before the Law." In *Acts of Literature*. Edited by Derek Attridge. Translated by Avital Ronell and Christine Roulston, 181–220. London: Routledge, 1992.

——. "Cartouches." In *The Truth in Painting*. Translated by Geoffrey Bennington and Ian McLeod, 183–254. Chicago: University of Chicago Press, 1987.

——. *Chaque fois unique, la fin du monde*. Edited by Pascale-Anne Brault and Michael Naas. Paris: Galilée, 2003.

——. "Cogito and the History of Madness." In *Writing and Difference*. Translated by Alan Bass, 31–63. Chicago: University of Chicago Press, 1978.

——. *De la grammatologie*. Paris: Minuit, 1967.

——. "Différance." In *Margins of Philosophy*. Translated by Alan Bass, 1–28. Chicago: University of Chicago Press, 1982.

——. *Dissemination*. Translated by Barbara Johnson. Chicago: University of Chicago Press, 1981.

——. "The Double Session." In *Dissemination*. Translated by Barbara Johnson, 173–285. Chicago: University of Chicago Press, 1981.

——. *The Ear of the Other*. Edited by Christie McDonald. Translated by Peggy Kamuf. Lincoln: University of Nebraska Press, 1988.

——. "Economimesis." Translated by Richard Klein. *Diacritics* 11 (1981): 3–25.

——. *Edmund Husserl's Origin of Geometry: An Introduction*. Translated by John P. Leavey Jr. Lincoln: University of Nebraska Press, 1989.

——. "The Ends of Man." In *Margins of Philosophy*. Translated by Alan Bass, 109–36. Chicago: University of Chicago Press, 1982.

———. "Envoi." In *Psyche: Inventions of the Other*, vol. 1. Edited by Peggy Kamuf and Elizabeth Rottenberg. Translated by Peter Caws and Mary Ann Caws, 94–128. Stanford, CA: Stanford University Press, 2007.

———. "Envois." In *The Post Card: From Socrates to Freud and Beyond*. Translated by Alan Bass, 1–256. Chicago: University of Chicago Press, 1987.

———. *Eyes of the University: Right to Philosophy 2*. Translated by Jan Plug et al. Stanford, CA: Stanford University Press, 2005.

———. "Faith and Knowledge: The Two Sources of 'Religion' at the Limits of Reason Alone." In *Acts of Religion*. Edited by Gil Anidjar. Translated by Samuel Weber, 40–101. London: Routledge, 2002.

———. "Force and Signification." In *Writing and Difference*. Translated by Alan Bass, 3–30. Chicago: University of Chicago Press, 1978.

———. *Given Time: 1. Counterfeit Money*. Translated by Peggy Kamuf. Chicago: University of Chicago Press, 1992.

———. *Glas*. Translated by John P. Leavey Jr. and Richard Rand. Lincoln: University of Nebraska Press, 1986.

———. *Glas*. Paris: Galilée, 1995 [1974].

———. "Heidegger's Ear: Philopolemology (*Geschlecht IV*)." In *Reading Heidegger: Commemorations*. Edited by John Sallis. Translated by John Leavey Jr., 163–218. Bloomington: Indiana University Press, 1992.

———. "Heidegger's Hand (*Geschlecht II*)." In *Psyche: Inventions of the Other*, vol. 2. Translated by John P. Leavey Jr. and Elizabeth Rottenberg. Edited by Peggy Kamuf and Elizabeth Rottenberg, 27–62. Stanford, CA: Stanford University Press, 2008.

———. *Heidegger: La question de l'Être et l'histoire, séminaire de 1964–65 de Jacques Derrida*. Edited by Thomas Dutoit. Paris: Galilée, 2013.

———. "Khōra." In *On the Name*. Edited by Thomas Dutoit. Translated by Ian McLeod, 89–127. Stanford, CA: Stanford University Press, 1995.

———. "The Law of Genre." In *Parages*. Edited by John P. Leavey Jr. Translated by Avital Ronell, 217–50. Stanford, CA: Stanford University Press, 2011.

———. *Limited Inc*. Edited by Gerald Graff. Translated by Samuel Weber and Alan Bass. Evanston, IL: Northwestern University Press, 1988.

———. "Lyotard et *nous*." In *Chaque fois unique, la fin du monde*. Edited by Pascale-Anne Brault and Michael Naas, 259–89. Paris: Galilée, 2003.

———. "A 'Madness' Must Watch Over Thinking." In *Points . . .: Interviews, 1974–1994*. Edited by Elisabeth Weber. Translated by Peggy Kamuf, 39–65. Stanford, CA: Stanford University Press, 1995.

———. "Mochlos, or the Conflict of the Faculties." In *Eyes of the University: Right to Philosophy 2*. Translated by Richard Rand and Amy Wygant, 83–112. Stanford, CA: Stanford University Press, 2004.

———. "No Apocalypse, Not Now: Full Speed Ahead, Seven Missiles, Seven Missives." In *Psyche: Inventions of the Other*, vol. 1. Edited by Peggy Kamuf and Elizabeth Rottenberg, 387–419. Stanford, CA: Stanford University Press, 2007.

———. "Of an Apocalyptic Tone Recently Adopted in Philosophy." *Oxford Literary Review* 6, no. 2 (1984): 3–37.

———. *Of Grammatology*. Translated by Gayatri Chakravorty Spivak. Baltimore, MD: Johns Hopkins University Press, 1976.

———. *Of Spirit: Heidegger and the Question*. Translated by Geoffrey Bennington and Rachel Bowlby. Chicago: University of Chicago Press, 1989.

———. *On Touching—Jean-Luc Nancy*. Translated by Christine Irizarry. Stanford, CA: Stanford University Press, 2005.

———. "The Pit and the Pyramid: Introduction to Hegel's Semiology." In *Margins of Philosophy*. Translated by Alan Bass, 69–108. Chicago: University of Chicago Press, 1982.

———. "Plato's Pharmacy." In *Dissemination*. Translated by Barbara Johnson, 61–172. Chicago: University of Chicago Press, 1981.

———. *The Problem of Genesis in Husserl's Philosophy*. Translated by Marian Hobson. Chicago: University of Chicago Press, 2003.

———. "Provocation: Forewords." In *Without Alibi*. Translated by Peggy Kamuf, xv–xxv. Stanford, CA: Stanford University Press, 2002.

———. "Punctuations: The Time of a Thesis." In *Eyes of the University: Right to Philosophy 2*. Translated by Kathleen McLaughlin, 113–28. Stanford, CA: Stanford University Press, 2004.

———. "Rams: Uninterrupted Dialogue—Between Two Infinities, the Poem." In *Sovereignties in Question: The Poetics of Paul Celan*. Edited by Thomas Dutoit and Outi Pasanen, 135–69. New York: Fordham University Press, 2005.

———. "The Reason of the Strongest." In *Rogues: Two Essays on Reason*. Translated by Pascale-Anne Brault and Michael Naas, 1–114. Stanford, CA: Stanford University Press, 2005.

———. "Restitutions of the Truth in Pointing." In *The Truth in Painting*. Translated by Geoffrey Bennington and Ian McLeod, 255–382. Chicago: University of Chicago Press, 1987.

———. "Some Statements and Truisms about Neologisms, Newisms, Postisms, Parasitisms, and Other Small Seismisms." In *The States of "Theory": History, Art and Critical Discourse*. Edited by and with an introduction by David Carroll. Translated by Anne Tomiche, 63–94. New York: Columbia University Press, 1990.

———. *Specters of Marx: The State of the Debt, the Work of Mourning, and the New International*. Translated by Peggy Kamuf. London: Routledge, 1994.

———. *Spurs: Nietzsche's Styles/Éperons: Les styles de Nietzsche*. Translated by Barbara Harlow. Introduction by Stefano Agosti. Chicago: University of Chicago Press, 1979.

———. "Structure, Sign and Play in the Discourse of the Human Sciences." In *Writing and Difference*. Translated by Alan Bass, 278–93. Chicago: University of Chicago Press, 1978.

———. "The Theatre of Cruelty and the Closure of Representation." In *Writing and Difference*. Translated by Alan Bass, 232–50. Chicago: University of Chicago Press, 1978.

——. "To Speculate—On 'Freud.'" In *The Post Card: From Socrates to Freud and Beyond*. Translated by Alan Bass, 257–409. Chicago: University of Chicago Press, 1987.

——. *The Truth in Painting*. Translated by Geoffrey Bennington and Ian McLeod. Chicago: University of Chicago Press, 1987.

——. "Tympan." In *Margins of Philosophy*. Translated by Alan Bass, ix–xxi. Chicago: University of Chicago Press, 1982.

——. "Typewriter Ribbon: Limited Ink (2)." In *Without Alibi*. Edited and translated by Peggy Kamuf, 71–160. Stanford, CA: Stanford University Press, 2002.

——. "The University without Condition." In *Without Alibi*. Edited and translated by Peggy Kamuf, 202–37. Stanford, CA: Stanford University Press, 2002.

——. "Violence and Metaphysics: An Essay on the Thought of Emmanuel Lévinas." In *Writing and Difference*. Translated by Alan Bass, 79–153. Chicago: University of Chicago Press, 1978.

——. *Voice and Phenomenon: Introduction to the Problem of the Sign in Husserl's Philosophy*. Translated by Leonard Lawlor. Evanston, IL: Northwestern University Press, 2011.

——. *Who's Afraid of Philosophy: Right to Philosophy 1*. Translated by Jan Plug et al. Stanford, CA: Stanford University Press, 2002.

——. *The Work of Mourning*. Translated by Pascale-Anne Brault and Michael Naas. Chicago: University of Chicago Press, 2001.

——. "The 'World' of the Enlightenment to Come." In *Rogues: Two Essays on Reason*. Translated by Pascale-Anne Brault and Michael Naas, 117–59. Stanford, CA: Stanford University Press, 2005.

Derrida, Jacques, and Maurizio Ferraris. "*Istrice 2: Ick bünn all hier*." In *Points de suspension: Entretiens*. Edited and with an introduction by Elisabeth Weber, 309–36. Paris: Galilée, 1992.

——. "*Istrice 2: Ick bünn all hier*." In *Points . . . .: Interviews, 1974–1994*. Edited by Elisabeth Weber. Translated by Peggy Kamuf, 309–26. Stanford, CA: Stanford University Press, 1995.

Derrida, Jacques, and Dominique Janicaud. "Jacques Derrida." In *Heidegger en France*. 2 vols. Vol. 2, 89–126. Paris: Hachette, 2005.

Derrida, Jacques, and Jean-Luc Marion. "On the Gift: A Discussion between Jacques Derrida and Jean-Luc Marion. Moderated by Richard Kearney." In *God, the Gift, and Postmodernism*. Edited by John D. Caputo and Michael J. Scanlon, 54–78. Bloomington: Indiana University Press, 1999.

Derrida, Jacques, and Elisabeth Roudinesco. *For What Tomorrow . . . Dialogue*. Translated by Jeff Fort. Stanford, CA: Stanford University Press, 2004.

Descartes, René. *Meditations on First Philosophy*. Vol. 1 of *The Philosophical Writings of Descartes*. Translated by John Cottingham, Robert Stoothoff and Dugald Murdoch. 3 vols. Cambridge: Cambridge University Press, 1986.

Dreyfus, Hubert L. *Being-in-the-World: A Commentary on Heidegger's* Being and Time, Division I. Cambridge, MA: MIT Press, 1991.

Duchêne, Joseph. "The Concept of 'World' and the Problem of Rationality in Merleau-Ponty's *Phénoménologie de la perception*." *International Philosophical Quarterly* 17 (1977): 393–413.

Dufrenne, Mikel. *The Phenomenology of Aesthetic Experience*. Translated by Edward S. Casey. Evanston, IL: Northwestern University Press, 1973.

Elden, Stuart. "Eugen Fink and the Question of the World." *Parrhesia* 5 (2008): 48–59.

Ellis, Elisabeth. *Kant's Politics: Provisional Theory for an Uncertain World*. New Haven, CT: Yale University Press, 2005.

Fenves, Peter. *Raising the Tone of Philosophy: Late Essays by Immanuel Kant, Transformative Critique by Jacques Derrida*. Baltimore, MD: Johns Hopkins University Press, 1998.

Fink, Eugen. *Nietzsche's Philosophy*. Translated by Goetz Richter. London: Continuum, 2003.

——. "The Phenomenological Philosophy of Edmund Husserl and Contemporary Criticism." In *The Phenomenology of Husserl: Selected Critical Readings*. Edited and translated by R. O. Elveton, 73–147. Chicago: Quadrangle, 1970.

——. *Spiel als Weltsymbol*. Stuttgart: W. Kohlhammer, 1960.

Fisch, Harold, ed. and trans. *The Holy Scriptures*. Jerusalem: Koren, 1992.

Flay, Joseph C. "Hegel's Inverted World." *Review of Metaphysics* 23, no. 4 (1970): 662–78.

Foessel, Michaël. *Kant et l'équivoque du monde*. Paris: CNRS, 2008.

Føllesdal, Dagfinn. "The *Lebenswelt* in Husserl." In *Science and the Life-World: Essays on Husserl's Crisis of European Sciences*. Edited by David Hyder and Hans-Jörg Rheinberger, 27–45. Stanford, CA: Stanford University Press, 2009.

Foltz, Bruce V. *Inhabiting the Earth: Heidegger, Environmental Ethics and the Metaphysics of Nature*. Atlantic Highlands, NJ: Humanities Press, 1995.

Förster, Eckart. *Kant's Final Synthesis: An essay on the Opus Postumum*. Cambridge, MA: Harvard University Press, 1995.

Forster, Michael N. *Hegel's Idea of a Phenomenology of Spirit*. Chicago: University of Chicago Press, 1998.

Foucault, Michel. *Introduction to Kant's Anthropology*. Edited by Roberto Nigro. Translated by Roberto Nigro and Kate Briggs. Los Angeles: Semiotext(e), 2008.

Fox, Everett, ed. and trans. *The Five Books of Moses*. London: Harvill, 1995.

Friedman, Michael. *Kant and the Exact Sciences*. Cambridge, MA: Harvard University Press, 1992.

Fynsk, Christopher. *Language and Relation . . . That There Is Language*. Stanford, CA: Stanford University Press, 1996.

Gadamer, Hans-Georg. "Being Spirit God." In *Heidegger's Ways*. Translated by John W. Stanley. Introduction by Dennis J. Schmidt, 181–96. Albany: State University of New York Press, 1994.

——. "Hegel's 'Inverted World.'" In *G. W. F. Hegel: Critical Assessments*. Vol. 3, *Hegel's Phenomenology and Logic*. Edited by Robert Stern, 131–47. London: Routledge, 1993.

———. *Truth and Method*. Translated by W. Glen-Doepel, Joel Weinscheimer and Donald G. Marshall. 2nd ed. London, Continuum, 2004.

Ganguly, Debjani, and Fiona Jenkins, eds. "Limits of the Human." *Angelaki* 16, no. 4 (2011).

Gasché, Rodolphe. *Europe, or the Infinite Task: A Study of a Philosophical Concept.* Stanford, CA: Stanford University Press, 2009.

———. *Of Minimal Things: Studies on the Notion of Relation.* Stanford, CA: Stanford University Press, 1999.

Gaston, Sean. *Derrida and Disinterest*. London: Continuum, 2006.

———. "Derrida and the End of the World." *New Literary History* 42, no. 3 (2011): 499–518.

———. "A Fragment of the Cacophony: Leibniz, Nietzsche and Blanchot." *Inky Needles*, January 6, 2013, http://inkyneedles.com.

———. "In the Middle." *Parrhesia* 6 (2009): 62–72.

Guyer, Paul. *Kant and the Claims of Knowledge*. Cambridge: Cambridge University Press, 1987.

Guyer, Paul, and Allen W. Wood. Introduction to *Critique of Pure Reason*, by Immanuel Kant. Translated by Paul Guyer, 1–80. Cambridge: Cambridge University Press, 1998.

Haar, Michel. *The Song of the Earth: Heidegger and the Grounds of the History of Being.* Translated by Reginald Lilly. Bloomington: Indiana University Press, 1993.

Hamacher, Werner. *Pleroma—Reading in Hegel*. Translated by Nicholas Walker and Simon Jarvis. Stanford, CA: Stanford University Press, 1998.

Harries, Karsten. "Descartes and the Labyrinth of the World." *International Journal of Philosophical Studies* 6 (1998): 307–30.

Hart, Kevin. *The Dark Gaze: Maurice Blanchot and the Sacred*. Chicago: University of Chicago Press, 2004.

———. "'Without World': Eschatology in Michel Henry." In *Phenomenology and Eschatology: Not Yet in the Now*. Edited by Neal DeRoo and John Panteleimon Manoussakis, 167–92. Farnham, UK: Ashgate, 2009.

Hegel, G. W. F. *Elements of the Philosophy of Right*. Edited by Allen W. Wood. Translated by H. B. Nisbet. Cambridge: Cambridge University Press, 1991.

———. *The Encyclopaedia Logic, Part 1 of the Encyclopaedia of Philosophical Sciences with the* Zuzsätze. Translated by T. F. Geraets, W. A. Suchting and H. S. Harris. Indianapolis, IN: Hackett, 1991.

———. *La phénoménologie de l'esprit*. Translated by Jean Hyppolite. 2 vols. Paris: Aubier, 1939, 1941.

———. *Lectures on the Philosophy of World History*. Vol. 1, *Manuscript of the Introduction and the Lectures of 1822–3*. Edited and translated by Robert F. Brown and Peter C. Hodgson with William G. Geuss. Oxford: Clarendon Press, 2011.

———. *Phänomenologie des Geistes*. Edited by Johannes Hoffmeister. Hamburg: Felix Meiner, 1952.

——. *Phenomenology of Spirit.* Translated by A. V. Miller. Oxford: Oxford University Press, 1977.

——. *Philosophische Propädeutik.* Vol. 3 of *Sämtliche Werke.* Edited by Hermann Glockner. Stuttgart: Frommans, 1949.

——. *Philosophy of Mind.* Translated by W. Wallace and A. V. Miller. Revised and with an introduction by Michael Inwood. Oxford: Clarendon Press, 2007.

——. *Philosophy of Nature, Part Two of the Encyclopaedia of the Philosophical Sciences* (1830). Translated by A. V. Miller. Foreword by J. N. Findlay. Oxford: Clarendon Press, 1970.

——. *The Science of Logic.* Translated by George di Giovanni. Cambridge: Cambridge University Press, 2010.

Heidegger, Martin. "The Age of the World Picture." In *Off the Beaten Track.* Edited and translated by Julian Young and Kenneth Haynes, 57–72. Cambridge: Cambridge University Press, 2002.

——. *Aristotle's Metaphysics Θ 1–3: On the Essence and Actuality of Force.* Translated by Walter Brogan and Peter Warnek. Bloomington: Indiana University Press, 1995.

——. *The Basic Problems of Phenomenology.* Translated by Albert Hofstader. Rev. ed. Bloomington: Indiana University Press, 1982.

——. *Being and Time.* Translated by John Macquarrie and Edward Robinson. Oxford: Blackwell, 1962.

——. *Being and Time.* Translated by Joan Stambaugh and Dennis J. Schmidt. Albany: State University of New York Press, 2010.

——. *Contributions to Philosophy (From Enowning).* Translated by Parvis Emad and Kenneth Maly. Bloomington: Indiana University Press, 1999.

——. *Der Satz vom Grund.* Frankfurt am Main: Victor Klostermann, 1997.

——. "Der Ursprung des Kunstwerkes." In *Holzwege*, 1–74. Frankfurt am Main: Victor Klostermann, 1976.

——. *Die Grundbegriffe der Metaphysik: Welt—Endlichkeit—Einsamkeit.* Frankfurt am Main: Victor Klostermann, 1983.

——. *The Fundamental Concepts of Metaphysics: World, Finitude, Solitude.* Translated by William McNeill and Nicholas Walker. Bloomington: Indiana University Press, 1995.

——. "Hegel's Concept of Experience." In *Off the Beaten Track.* Edited and translated by Julian Young and Kenneth Haynes, 86–156. Cambridge: Cambridge University Press, 2002.

——. *History of the Concept of Time: Prolegomena.* Translated by Theodore Kisiel. Bloomington: Indiana University Press, 1985.

——. *Hölderlin's Hymn "The Ister."* Translated by William McNeill and Julia Davis. Bloomington: Indiana University Press, 1996.

——. *Identity and Difference.* Translated by Joan Stambaugh. Chicago: University of Chicago Press, 2002.

——. *Introduction to Metaphysics.* Translated by Gregory Fried and Richard Polt. New Haven, CT: Yale University Press, 2000.

——. *Kant and the Problem of Metaphysics.* Translated by Richard Taft. 5th ed. Bloomington: Indiana University Press, 1997.

——. "Kant's Thesis about Being." In *Pathmarks.* Edited by William McNeill. Translated by Ted E. Klein Jr. and William E. Pohl, 337–64. Cambridge: Cambridge University Press, 1998.

——. "Language." In *Poetry, Language, Thought.* Translated by Albert Hofstadter, 187–210. New York: Harper & Row, 1975.

——. "Letter on 'Humanism.'" In *Pathmarks.* Edited by William McNeill. Translated by Frank A. Capuzzi, 239–76. Cambridge: Cambridge University Press, 1998.

——. "On the Essence of Ground." In *Pathmarks.* Edited and translated by William McNeill, 97–135. Cambridge: Cambridge University Press, 1998.

——. "On the Essence of Truth." In *Pathmarks.* Edited by William McNeill. Translated by John Sallis, 136–54. Cambridge: Cambridge University Press, 1998.

——. "The Origin of the Work of Art." In *Off the Beaten Track.* Edited and translated by Julian Young and Kenneth Haynes, 1–56. Cambridge: Cambridge University Press, 2002.

——. *Phenomenological Interpretation of Kant's* Critique of Pure Reason. Translated by Parvis Emad and Kenneth Maly. Bloomington: Indiana University Press, 1997.

——. *The Principle of Reason.* Translated by Reginald Lilly. Bloomington: Indiana University Press, 1996.

——. *Sein und Zeit.* Frankfurt am Main: Victor Klostermann, 1977.

——. "The Thing." In *Poetry, Language, Thought.* Translated by Albert Hofstadter, 165–86. New York: Harper & Row, 1975.

——. "Vom Wesen des Grundes." In *Wegmarken,* 123–76. Frankfurt am Main: Victor Klostermann, 1976.

Heidegger, Martin, and Eugen Fink. *Heraclitus Seminar.* Translated by Charles H. Seibert. Evanston, IL: Northwestern University Press, 1993.

Held, Klaus. "Husserl's Phenomenological Method." In *The New Husserl: A Critical Reader.* Edited by Donn Welton. Translated by Lanei Rodemeyer, 3–31. Bloomington: Indiana University Press, 2003.

——. "Husserl's Phenomenology of the Life-World." In *The New Husserl: A Critical Reader.* Edited by Donn Welton. Translated by Lanei Rodemeyer, 32–64. Bloomington: Indiana University Press, 2003.

Henry, Michel. *I Am the Truth: Toward a Philosophy of Christianity.* Translated by Susan Emanuel. Stanford, CA: Stanford University Press, 2003.

Heraclitus. *Early Greek Philosophy.* Edited and translated by Jonathan Barnes, 100–126. London: Penguin, 1987.

Hill, Leslie. *Blanchot: Extreme Contemporary.* London: Routledge, 1997.

Hill, R. Kevin. *Nietzsche's Critiques: The Kantian Foundations of His Thought.* Oxford: Oxford University Press, 2003.

Hume, David. *Dialogues Concerning Natural Religion and Other Writings*. Edited by Dorothy Coleman. Cambridge: Cambridge University Press, 2007.

———. *A Treatise of Human Nature*. Edited by David Fate Norton and Mary J. Norton. Oxford: Oxford University Press, 2001.

Husserl, Edmund. "Author's Preface to the English Edition." In *Ideas: General Introduction to Pure Phenomenology*. Translated by W. R. Boyce Gibson, 5–25. New York: Collier, 1962 [1931].

———. *Cartesian Meditations: An Introduction to Phenomenology*. Translated by Dorian Cairns. Dordrecht: Kluwer, 1999.

———. *The Crisis of European Sciences and Transcendental Phenomenology: An Introduction to Phenomenological Philosophy*. Translated and with an introduction by David Carr. Evanston, IL: Northwestern University Press, 1970.

———. *Experience and Judgement*. Translated by Ludwig Landgrebe. Evanston, IL: Northwestern University Press, 1973.

———. "Foundational Investigations of the Phenomenological Origin of the Spatiality of Nature: The Originary Ark, Earth, Does Not Move." In *Husserl at the Limits of Phenomenology* by Maurice Merleau-Ponty. Edited and translated by Leonard Lawlor and Bettina Bergo, 117–31. Evanston, IL: Northwestern University Press, 2002.

———. *Ideas Pertaining to a Pure Phenomenology and to a Phenomenological Philosophy: First Book—General Introduction to a Pure Phenomenology*. Translated by F. Kersten. The Hague: Martinus Nijhoff, 1983.

———. *Ideas Pertaining to a Pure Phenomenology and to a Phenomenological Philosophy: Second Book—Studies in the Phenomenology of Constitution*. Translated by R. Rojcewicz and A. Schuwer. Dordrecht: Kluwer, 1989.

———. *Ideen zu einerreinen Phänomenologie und phänomenolischen Philosophie: Erstes Buch*. Edited by Walter Biemel. The Hague: Martinus Nijhoff, 1950.

———. *The Origin of Geometry*. In *The Crisis of European Sciences and Transcendental Phenomenology: An Introduction to Phenomenological Philosophy*. Translated and with an introduction by David Carr, 353–78. Evanston, IL: Northwestern University Press, 1970.

———. "Phenomenology." In *Deconstruction in Context: Literature and Philosophy*. Edited by Mark C. Taylor, 121–40. Chicago: University of Chicago Press, 1986.

———. *The Phenomenology of Internal Time Consciousness*. Edited by Martin Heidegger. Translated by James S. Churchill. Introduction by Calvin O. Schrag. The Hague: Martinus Nijhoff, 1964.

Hyppolite, Jean. *Genesis and Structure of Hegel's* Phenomenology of Spirit. Translated by Samuel Cherniak and John Heckman. Evanston, IL: Northwestern University Press, 1974.

Inwood, Michael. Introduction to *Philosophy of Mind*, by G. W. F. Hegel. Translated by W. Wallace and A. V. Miller. Revised by Michael Inwood, ix–xxvii. Oxford: Clarendon Press, 2007.

Irigaray, Luce. *The Forgetting of the Air in Martin Heidegger*. Translated by Mary Beth Mader. Austin: University of Texas Press, 1999.

James, Ian. *The Fragmentary Demand: An Introduction to the Philosophy of Jean-Luc Nancy*. Stanford, CA: Stanford University Press, 2006.

———. *The New French Philosophy*. Cambridge: Polity, 2012.

Janaway, Christopher. *Self and World in Schopenhauer's Philosophy*. Oxford: Oxford University Press, 1999.

Johnson, Christopher. *System and Writing in the Philosophy of Jacques Derrida*. Cambridge: Cambridge University Press, 1993.

Kant, Immanuel. *An Answer to the Question: What Is Enlightenment?* In *Practical Philosophy*. Edited and translated by Mary J. Gregor. Introduction by Allen Wood, 11–22. Cambridge: Cambridge University Press, 1999.

———. *Anthropology from a Pragmatic Point of View*. Edited and translated by Robert B. Louden. Introduction by Manfred Kuehn. Cambridge: Cambridge University Press, 2006.

———. *Correspondence*. Edited and translated by Arnluf Zweig. Cambridge: Cambridge University Press, 1999.

———. *Critique of Practical Reason*. In *Practical Philosophy*. Edited and translated by Mary J. Gregor. Introduction by Allen Wood, 133–272. Cambridge: Cambridge University Press, 1999.

———. *Critique of Pure Reason*. Translated by Paul Guyer. Cambridge: Cambridge University Press, 1998.

———. *Critique of the Power of Judgement*. Edited by Paul Guyer. Translated by Paul Guyer and Eric Matthews. Cambridge: Cambridge University Press, 2000.

———. *Groundwork of the Metaphysics of Morals*. In *Practical Philosophy*. Edited and translated by Mary J. Gregor. Introduction by Allen Wood, 37–108. Cambridge: Cambridge University Press, 1999.

———. *Kritik der reinen Vernunft*. Edited by Jens Timmermann. Hamburg: Felix Meiner, 1998.

———. *Lectures on Metaphysics*. Edited and translated by K. Americks and S. Naragon. Cambridge: Cambridge University Press, 1997.

———. *Metaphysical Foundations of the Natural Sciences*. In *Theoretical Philosophy after 1781*. Edited by Henry Allison and Peter Heath. Translated by Michael Friedman, 171–270. Cambridge: Cambridge University Press, 2002.

———. *Natural Science*. Edited by Eric Watkins. Cambridge: Cambridge University Press, 2012.

———. *Of the Different Races of Human Beings*. In *Anthropology, History and Education*. Edited by Günter Zöller and Robert B. Louden. Translated by Holly Wilson and Günter Zöller, 82–97. Cambridge: Cambridge University Press, 2007.

———. "On a Recently Prominent Tone of Superiority in Philosophy." In *Theoretical Philosophy after 1781*. Edited and translated by Henry Allison, 425–46. Cambridge: Cambridge University Press, 2002.

———. *On the Form and Principle of the Sensible and Intelligible World*. In *Theoretical Philosophy 1755–1770*. Edited and translated by David Walford and Ralf Meerbote, 373–416. Cambridge: Cambridge University Press, 1992.

———. *Opus Postumum*. Edited and with an introduction by Eckart Förster. Translated by Eckart Förster and Michael Rosen. Cambridge: Cambridge University Press, 1993.

———. *Prolegomena to Any Future Metaphysics That Will Be Able to Come Forward as Science*. In *Theoretical Philosophy after 1781*. Edited by Henry Allison and Peter Heath. Translated by Gary Hatfield, 29–170. Cambridge: Cambridge University Press, 2002.

———. *Religion within the Boundaries of Mere Reason*. In *Religion and Rational Theology*. Edited by Allen W. Wood. Translated by George di Giovanni, 39–216. Cambridge: Cambridge University Press, 1996.

———. *Toward Perpetual Peace*. In *Practical Philosophy*. Edited and translated by Mary J. Gregor. Introduction by Allen Wood, 311–52. Cambridge: Cambridge University Press, 1999.

Kates, Joshua. *Essential History: Jacques Derrida and the Development of Deconstruction*. Evanston, IL: Northwestern University Press, 2005.

Keller, Pierre. *Husserl and Heidegger on Human Experience*. Cambridge: Cambridge University Press, 1999.

Kleingeld, Pauline. *Kant and Cosmopolitanism: The Philosophical Ideal of World Citizenship*. Cambridge: Cambridge University Press, 2012.

Kocklemans, Joseph. *The World in Science and Philosophy*. Milwaukee, WI: Bruce Publishing Company, 1969.

Kofman, Sarah. "Nietzsche et l'obscurité d'Héraclite." In *Séductions: De Sartre à Héraclite*, 87–138. Paris: Galilée, 1990.

Kojève, Alexandre. *Introduction à la lecture de Hegel: Leçons sur la* Phénoménologie de l'esprit *professes de 1933 à 1939 à l'École des Hautes Études réunies et publiées par Raymond Queneau*. Paris: Gallimard, 1968 [1947].

———. *Introduction to the Reading of Hegel: Lectures on the* Phenomenology of Spirit. Edited by Raymond Queneau and Alan Bloom. Translated by James H. Nichols. Ithaca, NY: Cornell University Press, 1991 [1969].

Krell, David Farrell. *Derrida and Our Animal Others: Derrida's Final Seminar*, The Beast and the Sovereign. Bloomington: Indiana University Press, 2013.

Lacoste, Jean-Yves. *Experience and the Absolute: Disputed Questions on the Humanity of Man*. Translated by Mark Raftery-Skehan. New York: Fordham University Press, 2004.

Lacoue-Labarthe, Philippe. *Heidegger, Art and Politics: The Fiction of the Political*. Translated by Chris Turner. Oxford: Blackwell, 1990.

Laertius, Diogenes. *Lives of Eminent Philosophers*. Translated by R. D. Hicks. 2 vols. Cambridge, MA: Harvard University Press, 1980.

Lafont, Christina. *Heidegger, Language, and World-Disclosure*. Translated by Graham Harmon. Cambridge: Cambridge University Press, 2000.

Lawlor, Leonard. *Derrida and Husserl: The Basic Problem of Phenomenology*. Bloomington: Indiana University Press, 2002.

———. *There Is Not Sufficient: An Essay on Animality and Human Nature in Derrida*. New York: Columbia University Press, 2007.

Leibniz, G. W. *Discourse on Metaphysics*. In *Philosophical Texts*. Translated by Richard Francks and R. S. Woolhouse. Introduction by R. S. Woolhouse, 53–93. Oxford: Oxford University Press, 1998.

———. *Monadology*. In *Philosophical Texts*. Translated by Richard Francks and R. S. Woolhouse. Introduction by R. S. Woolhouse, 267–84. Oxford: Oxford University Press, 1998.

———. *Principles of Nature and Grace, Based on Reason*. In *Philosophical Texts*. Translated by Richard Francks and R. S. Woolhouse. Introduction by R. S. Woolhouse, 258–66. Oxford: Oxford University Press, 1998.

———. *Specimen Dynamicum: An Essay in Dynamics*. In *Philosophical Texts*. Translated by Richard Francks and R. S. Woolhouse. Introduction by R. S. Woolhouse, 153–79. Oxford: Oxford University Press, 1998.

Lévinas, Emmanuel. *De l'existence à l'existant*. Paris: J. Vrin, 1986 [1947].

———. *Discovering Existence with Husserl*. Translated by Richard A. Cohen and Michael B. Smith. Evanston, IL: Northwestern University Press, 1998.

———. *Existence and Existents*. Translated by A. Lingis. Dordrecht: Kluwer, 1988.

———. "Heidegger, Gagarin and Us." In *Difficult Freedom: Essays on Judaism*. Translated by Seán Hand, 231–34. Baltimore, MD: Johns Hopkins University Press, 1990.

———. "On Maurice Blanchot." In *Proper Names*. Translated by Michael B. Smith, 125–70. Stanford, CA: Stanford University Press, 2000.

———. *Time and the Other*. Translated by Richard A. Cohen. Pittsburgh, PA: Duquesne University Press, 1987.

———. *Totality and Infinity: An Essay on Exteriority*. Translated by Alphonso Lingis. Pittsburgh, PA: Duquesne University Press, 1969.

Lingis, Alphonso. "The World as a Whole." *Research in Phenomenology* 25 (1995): 142–59.

McWhorter, Ladelle, and Gail Stenstad, eds. *Heidegger and the Earth: Essays in Environmental Philosophy*. 2nd ed. Toronto: University of Toronto Press, 2009.

Malpas, Jeff. *Heidegger's Topology: Being, Place, World*. Cambridge, MA: MIT Press, 2006.

Marrati, Paola. *Genesis and Trace: Derrida Reading Husserl and Heidegger*. Translated by Simon Sparks. Stanford, CA: Stanford University Press, 2005.

Marx, Karl. *The Marx-Engels Reader*. Edited by Robert C. Tucker. New York: W. W. Norton, 1978.

McNeill, William. "Life beyond the Organism: Animal Being in Heidegger's Freiburg Lectures, 1929–1930." In *Animal Others: On Ethics, Ontology, and Animal Life*. Edited by H. Peter Steeves. Foreword by Tom Regan, 197–248. Albany: State University of New York Press, 1999.

———. *Writings of the Young Marx on Philosophy and Society*. Edited and translated by Lloyd D. Easton and Kurt H. Guddat. New York: Anchor, 1967.

Merleau-Ponty, Maurice. *Phenomenology of Perception*. Translated by Colin Smith. London and New York: Routledge, 2002.

———. *The Visible and the Invisible*. Edited by Claude Lefort. Translated by Alphonso Lingis. Evanston, IL: Northwestern University Press, 1968.

Miller, J. Hillis. "'Don't Count Me In': Derrida's Refraining." In *For Derrida*, 174–90. New York: Fordham University Press, 2009.

Moland, Lydia L. *Hegel on Political Identity: Patriotism, Nationalism and Cosmopolitanism*. Evanston, IL: Northwestern University Press, 2011.

Momigliano, Arnaldo. "Pagan and Christian Historiography in the Fourth Century." In *Essays in Ancient and Modern Historiography*. Foreword by Anthony Grafton, 107–26. Chicago: University of Chicago Press, 2012 [1977].

Mulhall, Stephen. *On Being in the World: Wittgenstein and Heidegger on Seeing Aspects*. London: Routledge, 1990.

Naas, Michael. *Miracle and Machine: Jacques Derrida and the Two Sources of Religion, Science, and the Media*. New York: Fordham University Press, 2012.

Nancy, Jean-Luc. *Corpus*. Translated by Richard Rand. New York: Fordham University Press, 2008.

———. *The Creation of the World or Globalization*. Translated by François Raffoul and David Pettigrew. Albany: State University of New York Press, 2007.

———. *Hegel: The Restlessness of the Negative*. Translated by Jason Smith and Steven Miller. Minneapolis: University of Minnesota Press, 2002.

———. *The Sense of the World*. Translated by Jeffrey S. Librett. Minneapolis: University of Minnesota Press, 1993.

Nietzsche, Friedrich. *Beyond Good and Evil*. Edited by Rolf-Peter Horstmann and Judith Norman. Cambridge: Cambridge University Press, 2002.

———. *The Birth of Tragedy and Other Writings*. Edited by Raymond Geuss and Ronald Speirs. Cambridge: Cambridge University Press, 1999.

———. *Ecce Homo*. In *Basic Writings of Nietzsche*. Edited and translated by Walter Kaufmann, 657–791. New York: Modern Library, 1968.

———. *The Gay Science*. Edited by Bernard Williams. Translated by Josefine Nauckhoff and Adrian Del Caro. Cambridge: Cambridge University Press, 2001.

———. *On the Genealogy of Morality*. Edited by Keith Ansell-Pearson. Translated by Carol Diethe. Cambridge: Cambridge University Press, 2007.

———. *The Pre-Platonic Philosophers*. Edited and translated by Greg Whitlock. Champaign: University of Illinois Press, 2000.

———. *Twilight of the Idols*. In *The Anti-Christ, Ecce Homo, Twilight of the Idols, and Other Writings*. Edited by Aaron Ridley. Translated by Judith Norman, 153–230. Cambridge: Cambridge University Press, 2005.

———. *Writings from the Late Notebooks*. Edited by Rüdiger Bittner. Translated by Kate Sturge. Cambridge: Cambridge University Press, 2003.

O'Connor, Patrick. *Derrida: Profanations*. London: Continuum, 2010.

Otto, Peter. *Multiplying Worlds: Romanticism, Modernity and the Emergence of Virtual Reality*. Oxford: Oxford University Press, 2011.

Overgaard, Søren. *Husserl and Heidegger on Being in the World*. Dordrecht: Kluwer, 2004.

Pinkard, Terry. *German Philosophy 1760–1860: The Legacy of Idealism*. Cambridge: Cambridge University Press, 2002.

——. *Hegel: A Biography*. Cambridge: Cambridge University Press, 2000.

——. *Hegel's Phenomenology: The Sociality of Reason*. Cambridge: Cambridge University Press, 1994.

Plato, *Gorgias*. Translated by Robin Waterfield. Oxford: Oxford University Press, 1994.

——. *Lysis, Symposium, Gorgias*. Translated by W. R. M. Lamb. Cambridge, MA: Harvard University Press, 1925.

——. *The Republic*. Translated by G. M. A. Grube and C. D. C. Reeve. Indianapolis, IN: Hackett, 1992.

——. *Timaeus*. In *Timaeus, Critias, Cleitophon, Menexenus, Epistles*. Translated by R. G. Bury. Cambridge, MA: Harvard University Press, 1925.

Plotinus, *The Enneads*. Edited by John Dillon. Translated by Stephen Mackenna. London: Penguin, 1991.

Polt, Richard. *The Emergency of Being: On Heidegger's Contributions to Philosophy*. Ithaca, NY: Cornell University Press, 2006.

Ricoeur, Paul. *Husserl: An Analysis of His Phenomenology*. Translated by Edward G. Ballard and Lester E. Embree. Introduction by David Carr. Evanston, IL: Northwestern University Press, 2007.

——. *Time and Narrative*, vol. 1. Translated by David Pallauer. Chicago: University of Chicago Press, 1984.

——. *Time and Narrative*, vol. 3. Translated by Kathleen Blamey and David Pallauer. Chicago: University of Chicago Press, 1988.

——. "World of the Text, World of the Reader." In *A Ricoeur Reader: Reflection and the Imagination*. Edited by Mario J. Valdes, 491–98. London: Harvester Wheatsheaf, 1991.

——. "Writing as a Problem for Literary Criticism and Philosophical Hermeneutics." In *A Ricoeur Reader: Reflection and the Imagination*. Edited by Mario J. Valdes, 320–37. London: Harvester Wheatsheaf, 1991.

Rigby, Kate. "Earth, World, Text: On the (Im)possibility of Ecopoiesis." *New Literary History* 35, no. 3 (2004): 427–42.

Romano, Claude. *Event and World*. Translated by Shane Mackinlay. New York: Fordham University Press, 2009.

Roth, Michael S. *Knowing and History: Appropriations of Hegel in Twentieth-Century France*. Ithaca, NY: Cornell University Press, 1988.

Sallis, John. *Chorology: On Beginnings in Plato's Timaeus*. Bloomington: Indiana University Press, 1999.

——. Foreword to *The Song of the Earth: Heidegger and the Grounds of the History of Being*, by Michel Haar. Translated by Reginald Lilly, xi–xiii. Bloomington: Indiana University Press, 1993.

Sartre, Jean-Paul. *What Is Literature?* Translated by Bernard Frechtman. London: Routledge, 2001.

Schelling, F. W. J. *The Grounding of Positive Philosophy: The Berlin Lectures*. Translated and with an introduction by Bruce Matthews. Albany: State University of New York Press, 2007.

Schiller, Friedrich. *Philosophical Writings*. Translated by Caroline Bland. Edited by T. J. Reed. In *Immanuel Kant: Critical Assessments*. Edited by Ruth F. Chadwick. 4 vols. Vol. 1, 7. London: Routledge, 1992.

Schopenhauer, Arthur. *The World as Will and Representation*, vol. 1. Translated and edited by Judith Norman, Alistair Welchman and Christopher Janaway. Cambridge: Cambridge University Press, 2010.

——. *The World as Will and Representation*, vol. 2. Translated by E. F. Payne. New York: Dover, 1966.

Schulte Nordholt, Anne-Lise. *Maurice Blanchot: L'écriture comme expérience du dehors*. Genève: Droz, 1995.

Shapiro, Gary. "Notes on the Animal Kingdom of Spirit." In *The Phenomenology of Spirit Reader: Critical and Interpretative Essays*. Edited by Jon Stewart, 225–42. Albany: State University of New York Press, 1998.

Speight, Allen. *Hegel, Literature and the Problem of Agency*. Cambridge: Cambridge University Press, 2001.

Steffen, Will, Paul J. Crutzen and John R. McNeill. "The Anthropocene: Are Humans Now Overwhelming the Great Forces of Nature?" *Ambio* 38 (2007): 614–21.

Steiner, Gary. *Anthropocentrism and Its Discontents: The Moral Status of Animals in the History of Western Philosophy*. Pittsburgh, PA: Pittsburgh University Press, 2005.

Stengers, Isabelle. *Cosmopolitics II*. Translated by Robert Bononno. Minneapolis: Minnesota University Press, 2011.

Stewart, Jon. *The Unity of Hegel's Phenomenology of Spirit*. Evanston, IL: Northwestern University Press, 2000.

Strawson, P. F. *The Bounds of Sense: An Essay on Kant's Critique of Pure Reason*. London: Routledge, 1975 [1966].

Terada, Rei. *Looking Away: Phenomenality and Dissatisfaction, Kant to Adorno*. Cambridge, MA: Harvard University Press, 2009.

Turnbull, Neil. "The Ontological Consequences of Copernicus: Global Being in the Planetary World." *Theory, Culture & Society* 23 (2006): 125–39.

von Uexküll, Jakob. *A Foray into the World of Animals and Humans, with a Theory of Meaning*. Translated by Joseph D. O'Neil. Minneapolis: Minnesota University Press, 2010.

Vaihinger, Hans. *The Philosophy of "As If": A System of the Theoretical, Practical and Religious Fictions of Mankind*. Translated by Charles Kay Ogden. London: Routledge, 2000 [1911].

Wall, Thomas Carl. *Radical Passivity: Lévinas, Blanchot, and Agamben*. Albany: State University of New York Press, 1999.

Warminski, Andrzej. *Readings in Interpretation: Hölderlin, Hegel, Heidegger*. Minneapolis: University of Minnesota Press, 1987.

Welton, Donn. *The Other Husserl: The Other Horizons of Transcendental Phenomenology*. Bloomington: Indiana State University Press, 2000.

Wittgenstein, Ludwig. *Philosophical Investigations*. Translated by G. E. M. Anscombe. 3rd ed. Oxford: Blackwell, 1967.

Wolff, Christian. *Theologia Naturalis: Methodo Scientifica Pertractata*. Verona: Dionisio Ramnanzini, 1738.

Wolff, Francis. *Dire le monde*. Paris: Presses Universitaires de France, 2004 [1997].

Wood, David. *The Deconstruction of Time*. Evanston, IL: Northwestern University Press, 2001.

———. "On Being Haunted by the Future." *Research in Phenomenology* 36, no. 1 (2006): 274–98.

———. "Spectres of Derrida: On the Way to Econstruction." In *Ecospirit: Religions and Philosophies for the Earth*. Edited by Laurel Kearns and Catherine Keller, 264–90. New York: Fordham University Press, 2007.

———. *Thinking after Heidegger*. Cambridge: Polity, 2002.

Wordsworth, William. *The Prelude: The Four Texts (1798, 1799, 1805, 1850)*. Edited by Jonathan Wordsworth. London: Penguin, 1995.

Young, Julian. *Heidegger's Philosophy of Art*. Cambridge: Cambridge University Press, 2001.

Zahavi, Dan. *Husserl's Phenomenology*. Stanford, CA: Stanford University Press, 2003.

Zimmerman, Michael E. *Contesting Earth's Future: Radical Ecology and Postmodernity*. Berkeley: University of California Press, 1994.

———. *Heidegger's Confrontation with Modernity: Technology, Politics and Art*. Bloomington: Indiana University Press, 1990.

# Index

233

236    Index

118, 120, 121, 128, 127, 149, 153, 155, 156, 161; and abyss, 85, 127, 128
grounding. *See* Heidegger
Gunner, Don, 211n189

Haar, Michel, 156
Hamacher, Werner, 40
Hart, Kevin, 200n200
Hegel, G. W. F., ix, xi, xii, xiii, xiv, 2, 29–46, 47, 53, 55, 56, 57, 61, 88, 96, 97, 99, 100, 102, 103, 116–17, 135–47, 156, 158, 160, 161, 163, 174n11; actuality and world, xii, 29–38, 41, 42, 46, 56–57, 136, 139; consciousness, self-consciousness and world 29–35, 46, 136, 138, 141, 142; and Kant, 29, 33, 34, 35; objective world as idea, 29, 36–38, 41; plants, animals and humans 39–41, 140; world as spirit, xii, 2, 29, 36, 42, 57, 61, 102, 136, 139, 141, 160; world-history, xii, 44–6. *See also* Hegel, works
Hegel, works: *Elements of the Philosophy of Right*, 42; *Encyclopaedia Logic*, 38, 40; *Encyclopaedia of Philosophical Sciences*, 38, 46, 88; *Phenomenology of Spirit*, xii, xiii, 29–36, 40, 42, 43, 44, 46, 102, 135–45, 155; *Philosophy of Mind*, xii, 38, 40–3; *Philosophy of Nature*, xii, 38–40; *Science of Logic*, xii, 29, 36–8, 102
Heidegger, Martin, ix, x, xi, 2, 18, 24, 25, 39, 43, 44, 49, 52, 61, 62, 64, 65, 67–98, 99, 100, 103, 104, 106, 108, 113, 116, 122, 123, 124, 125, 127, 128–32, 146, 152, 160, 161, 162; animal (*see* animals and world); anxiety and world, xi, 73, 77–79, 80, 106; apophantic logos, 77–78, 80, 86, 95, 130; and Aristotle, 87–88; as-structure, 78, 86, 90, 92–97; "as such," 73, 90, 94, 95–97, 129; being-

in-the-world, xii, xiii, 2, 61, 67–79, 86, 98, 120, 125, 129, 130, 131, 149, 153, 154, 160, 162; comparative world, xiii, 69, 79, 80, 83, 85–98, 99, 100, 123, 126, 127, 130, 131, 143, 153, 155, 160; and Descartes, 71, 72, 78; earth and world, 97, 153–57, 197n132, 208–9n136, 209n147; grounding and world, 82–85, 97, 127; and Hegel, 175n36; historical world, xiii, 79–85, 86, 98, 130, 153; and Husserl, 68, 69, 70, 74, 78, 84, 88, 90, 98; and Kant, 24, 72, 76, 81–82; the play of the world, 93, 125; poverty in world, 85, 89, 91–96, 129; spiritual world, 97, 128, 155; stone, animal, man, 87–96, 126, 127, 128–33, 143, 155, 156; world as phenomenon, 2, 69–79, 80, 81, 82, 98; world-forming, 83, 85, 89, 91–96, 129; having a world, 70, 80, 83, 91–94, 130; worldhood of the world, 73, 74, 77, 154; worldless, 70, 71, 72, 85, 89, 91–96, 129, 156, 194n140. *See also* Heidegger, works
Heidegger, works: *Being and Time*, xii, 67–79, 80, 81, 84, 85, 86, 96, 86, 88, 92, 106, 128, 153, 155, 186n129, 197–98n140, 200n200; *History of the Concept of Time*, 79; *Identity and Difference*, 157; *Introduction to Metaphysics*, 97, 128, 155; "Language," 185–86n102; *Kant and the Problem of Metaphysics*, 77, 191n282; "Letter on 'Humanism,'" 95–6; "On the Essence of Ground," xiii, 68–69, 79–85, 114, 155; *Phenomenological Interpretation of Kant's* Critique of Pure Reason, 81; *The Fundamental Concepts of Metaphysics*, xiii, 69, 80, 85–96, 128, 129, 143, 155, 190n259; "The Origin of the Work of Art," 97–98,

153–57; *The Principle of Reason*, 127,
209n147; "The Thing," 208–9n136
Held, Klaus, 61
Heraclitus, 81, 95, 125–26
Hill, Leslie, 137
historical world. *See* Heidegger
Hobbes, Thomas, 62
Hölderlin, Friedrich, 18, 146
humans and world, 3, 14, 23, 39–40,
56–57, 68, 80, 82, 83, 87–96, 112,
113, 125–33, 138, 139, 143, 150,
151–60; post-human, 151, 152, 158,
160
Hume, David, 4, 63, 64, 167n22
Husserl, Edmund, ix, x, 2, 24, 28, 39,
40, 44, 47–65, 68, 88, 89, 90, 96,
97, 98, 99, 100–4, 106, 108–11, 112,
115, 116, 117, 123, 124, 125, 127,
129–30, 132, 133, 153, 155, 160,
161, 178n16, 181n135; body and
world, xii, 53–54, 55, 57, 59, 61,
64; consciousness and world, 48–52,
53, 54, 58, 60, 101, 103, 124, 125,
137; and Descartes, 47, 50–2, 55, 57,
58, 59, 62, 63; and Heidegger, 65;
horizon, 51, 56, 61, 64–65, 103, 107,
115, 122, 124, 153; and Hume, 63,
64; ideality and world, 58, 59, 60–65;
and Kant, 24, 63, 64, 65; life-world,
xii, 2, 47, 52, 57–65, 117, 124, 153,
160; phenomenological world, xii,
48–52, 53, 61, 103, 107, 160, 162–
63; soul, spirit and world, xii, 54,
57, 59, 61, 64, 102; spatio-temporal
world, 48, 49, 52, 53, 54, 55, 57, 62,
100, 101; spiritual world, xii, 52, 53–
57, 63, 64, 88, 153, 160; suspension
of "natural attitude" toward world,
xii, 47–52, 53–57, 57–65, 99, 100,
101, 107, 109, 111, 124
Husserl, works: *Cartesian Meditations*,
52, 57–60, 109–11; "Foundational
Investigations," 153; *Ideas 1*, xii,

47–52, 53, 101, 103, 153; *Ideas 2*, xii,
40, 53–57, 59, 64, 65, 88, 153; *The
Crisis of European Sciences*, 57, 58,
60–65, 117; *The Origin of Geometry*,
24, 54
Hyppolite, Jean, xiii, 29, 100, 135–42,
145

immersion, xiv, 44–45, 52, 60, 68, 74,
76, 78, 80, 84, 85, 86, 89, 90, 93–94,
98, 163, 164
in and outside the world: and Blanchot,
148, 149, 150; and Derrida, 100–
104, 108, 110, 125; and Fink, 100,
108, 127; and Kant, 12–14, 17, 19,
26; and Hegel, 102, 103, 138; and
Heidegger, 71; and Husserl, 50, 58,
100, 103, 108
intelligible world and sensible world,
62, 72, 87, 107, 118, 122, 128, 163.
*See also* Kant
in the world, x, 161; and Blanchot,
150; and Derrida, 109–10, 125,
127; and Fink, 127; and Kant, 23,
61; and Hegel, 34, 38, 41, 45, 142;
and Husserl, 50, 52, 54, 58, 61; and
Heidegger, 67, 70, 75, 79, 80, 96,
156, 208n136
Inwood, Michael, 40
Irigaray, Luce, 154, 197n132

James, Ian, 163
Johnson, Christopher, 153

Kant, Immanuel, ix, x, xi, xii, 1–28,
29, 33, 34, 35, 37, 38, 43, 46, 47,
48, 52, 61, 62, 63, 64, 65, 72, 76,
81–82, 86, 87, 89, 95, 96, 111–23,
132, 135, 149, 152, 154, 170n131,
171n143, 171n155; "as if" there is a
world, xi, 16–18, 28, 33, 52, 95, 106,
111–23, 133, 149, 160; categorical
world, xi, 18–28, 29, 34, 36, 37, 41,

things and world, 67–68, 70, 72, 76,
81–82, 90, 94, 142–45, 154, 157,
208–9n136
time, xi, xiii, 7, 11, 13, 37, 48, 49, 55,
57, 76, 77, 79, 89, 90, 100, 123, 125,
128, 159
Torah, 99, 104
totality, 10, 11, 13, 17, 19, 22, 26,
73–75, 77, 80, 81, 82, 94, 105, 107,
112, 115, 148, 152, 154, 159
touching and world, 53, 55, 70, 103,
109–10, 122, 197–98n140; and
untouchable, 103, 110, 122
transcendence, xiv, 52, 68, 74, 80–85,
86, 93, 98, 108, 142, 154, 163, 164

Uexküll, Jakob von, 190n243
unconditionality of the uncontained.
*See* containment and world
unconditioned, xiii, 10, 12–14, 16, 19,
38, 82, 112, 113, 118–23, 152. *See
also* Derrida; Kant
universe, xi, 120, 122

vantage point of the world, x, xi, xii,
xiv, 161, 162; and Blanchot, 148,
150; and Derrida, 100, 103, 104,
105, 106, 108, 112, 115, 117, 119,
120; and Kant, 10, 13, 14, 20, 23–24,
28; and Hegel, 31, 32, 34, 38, 44;
and Heidegger, 69, 73, 77, 80, 90,
96, 98, 154, 156; and Husserl, 47, 52,
56, 58, 60, 64; and Nietzsche, 126
virtual world, 65, 106, 114, 132, 137,
147, 150

Warminski, Andrzej, 137
wider perspective of the world. *See*
vantage point of the world
Wittgenstein, Ludwig, 163–64
Wolff, Christian, 3, 9
Wolff, Francis, 211n186

Wood, David, 160
world: as always already there, x, 16,
29, 34, 49, 58, 74, 124, 163; as
concept, x, xi, 15, 26, 27, 29, 37,
40, 41, 44, 69, 80, 82, 84, 85–86,
104, 112, 114, 117, 135, 143, 158;
definition of, 2–3, 160; as idea,
xi, xii, 9–18, 19, 21, 25, 26, 27,
28, 29, 30, 36–38, 40, 41, 43, 44,
45, 61, 62, 82, 111, 114, 125, 148,
149; as *haolam*, x, 99; as *kósmos*, x,
3–4, 18, 19, 81, 82, 99, 126, 163;
as my world, x, 56, 164; natural
descriptors of, 120; not starting
with, 6–8, 29–30, 43–4, 67, 69,
135–36; self-evident uses of, xi, 22–
24, 28, 31, 45, 49, 50, 58, 62, 63,
65, 67, 68, 69, 74, 95, 98, 100, 116,
136; as word, 9, 69, 80–82, 85–86;
the world and a world, x, 27, 34, 42,
55, 56, 61, 63, 70, 124, 140, 147
world and earth, 1–3, 22–23, 25, 28,
41, 97, 112, 114, 116, 119, 120,
121, 135, 151–61, 162, 163. *See also*
earth; Derrida; geo-logocentrism;
Heidegger
world as a whole, x, xi, xii, xiv, 161;
and Blanchot, 148, 150; and Derrida,
100, 103–6, 108, 112, 115, 119, 120,
129, 130, 132; and Kant, 5, 9, 10,
11, 12–13, 15, 16, 18–20, 22–28; and
Hegel, 31, 33, 38, 41, 45, 46, 142;
and Heidegger, 69–70, 72, 73, 74,
75, 77–79, 80, 81, 86, 89, 90, 92, 96,
97, 129, 130, 149, 154; and Husserl,
48, 49, 50, 51, 52, 56, 58, 60, 61,
64, 65
world as idea. *See* Kant
world as ordered whole, xi, 3–4, 126,
163
world as phenomenon. *See* Heidegger
world as spirit. *See* Hegel

# About the Author

**Sean Gaston** is Reader in English at Brunel University, London. He studied at the University of Melbourne. His publications include *Derrida and Disinterest* (2005); *The Impossible Mourning of Jacques Derrida* (2006); *Starting With Derrida* (2007); *Derrida, Literature and War—Absence and the Chance of Meeting* (2009); *Reading Derrida's Of Grammatology* (2011).